THE DEVELOPMENT OF PLATO'S ETHICS

Nos auteurs classiques sont riches de toutes
les interprétations qu'ils permettent. Leur
précision est d'autant plus admirable qu'elle
ne se prétend pas exclusive.

ANDRÉ GIDE, *Les Faux-Monnayeurs*

THE
DEVELOPMENT OF
PLATO'S ETHICS

BY

JOHN GOULD

Student of Christ Church, Oxford
Formerly Research Fellow of Jesus College,
Cambridge

NEW YORK / RUSSELL & RUSSELL

FIRST PUBLISHED IN 1955
REISSUED, 1972, BY RUSSELL & RUSSELL
A DIVISION OF ATHENEUM PUBLISHERS, INC.
WITH THE PERMISSION OF CAMBRIDGE UNIVERSITY PRESS
L. C. CATALOG CARD NO: 70-180609
ISBN: 0-8462-1642-6
PRINTED IN THE UNITED STATES OF AMERICA

PREFACE

THE book that follows contains no systematic account of Plato's ethics in all its aspects; it is a piece of research, not a text-book. It is also a first piece of research. It was begun in 1950 and submitted in 1952 as a Fellowship dissertation to my Cambridge college: since then, I have rewritten the first two chapters and made a number of alterations and additions to the remainder of the book.

In writing this essay, I have incurred numerous obligations of gratitude: to the University of Cambridge, the Electors to the Charles Oldham Classical Scholarship, and to the Master and Fellows of Jesus College, Cambridge, for making it possible; to Professor W. K. C. Guthrie, for allowing me to use some unpublished work of Professor Cornford; and to Mr D. J. Allan, for reading my manuscript and making several valuable suggestions, and, indeed, for prompting me to seek publication. My debt to Mr J. E. Raven, my research supervisor at Cambridge, is very great: his kindness and encouragement gave me the determination to finish what I had rather doubtfully begun, and his restraining hand kept me from many errors more serious than those that now remain. Lastly, I should like to thank Mr G. E. L. Owen and Mr G. S. Kirk who have helped me in correcting the proofs; the staff of the University Press for coping skilfully with a somewhat untidy manuscript; and the many friends, professional scholars and otherwise, who have so often helped me and listened with patience to my recitals.

That the finished work might profit from complete revision and greater coherence I am only too well aware, but even now I cannot claim that if I were the reviser, it would be much different from what it is. For its faults are mine.

J. G.

CHRIST CHURCH, OXFORD
August 1954

CONTENTS

CONTENTS

INTRODUCTION

IN reading the dialogues of Plato, we look back on a world whose differences from our own we may find it difficult to realize. It seems worth while pointing out that a contemporary reader who turns to this book after reading (say) Professor Stevenson's *Ethics and Language* is likely to find himself in a very different atmosphere, strange but not, I think, irrelevant to him. Even within the works of one age, we are accustomed to finding different answers suggested to the peculiar problems of ethics. But what we must here remember above all, is that even the identity of the questions which have seemed important at different times, itself undergoes changes. This difference of approach to moral philosophy has been well set out by Mr Stuart Hampshire in a recent article; [1] he rightly suggests that the typical question of recent moral philosophy is: 'What do we mean by, and how (if at all) do we establish the truth of, sentences used to express moral judgments about our own or other people's actions?' Now this is not at all the sort of question which we find Plato asking in the dialogues: Plato, like Aristotle, is concerned with the problems of the moral '*agent*', not the moral '*judge* or critic', to quote Mr Hampshire again. The roots of this difference of outlook on what we loosely call 'ethics' may perhaps be put psychologically: Plato, it will appear, is not subject to any basic doubt about the reliability of moral decisions, nor even, to put the matter more largely, about the existence of any valid and arguable 'aim' in human life. His own most urgent efforts were directed towards the discovery of a viable method of *attaining* (in practice) an aim which, for him, is in some sense 'given'. Thus the question, if I may formulate it in general terms, which I have chosen as the guiding issue in this essay is: 'How is a man to achieve his true (moral) stature?' I cannot and do not claim that all that Plato has to say of ethical problems can be adequately considered under this head, but I am convinced that it remains his central concern, and

[1] 'Fallacies in Moral Philosophy', in *Mind*, n.s. LVII (1949), pp. 466 ff.

other matters must make their appearance only on the side-lines of the present inquiry. The chapters that follow turn on Plato's various and differing answers to the question I have just set out.

It is curious, but true, that Plato has been little studied for what he has to say about the problems of action. In our total picture of Plato, which in some areas is minutely detailed, comparatively little light is thrown on the ethical preoccupations which he inherited from Socrates. A dialogue such as the *Republic* has for years been the happy hunting-ground of historians of metaphysics, epistemology and political theory. But it must be obvious that it offers just as much illumination to the man who seeks to discover what happened, in Plato's middle and last years, to the ethical ideas and ideals which occupied Socrates' mind so much. In this book, it is just such a focal-point that I have tried to give to our interest in Plato. To take another concrete example, critical attention among Platonists has recently been absorbed with the dialectical method of the 'late period' dialogues, to such an extent that the *Laws*, which has nothing to say of this matter, might, for all the attention it has received, almost have disappeared from the Platonic corpus. This is a good example of the way in which the general acceptance of some theory, say of Plato's development, can affect the degree to which different parts of his writings seem to his readers significant, and viewed from this angle, the present attempt to put forward an account of Plato's ethical development implies a different canon of significance.

In the first section of this book, I have tried to reconstruct the answer which Socrates gave to the question I have described as central to the inquiry. Much of the first chapter turns of necessity on the meaning of certain Greek words, and here I have been unable to translate many of the quotations which I use as evidence. But the main trend of the argument will, I hope, be clear: Socrates, starting from a parallel that has often been drawn in the history of ethics, between the moral agent and the artist or craftsman, arrived, I believe, at the hope that the moral agent might learn to direct his actions in accordance with the same assured and acceptable procedures which the artist adopts to produce his concrete works; that is, in general terms, that he might achieve some 'technique' of moral decision-making and behaviour, not so much in the sense of a set of rules, as of an intense personal conviction, evinced in his day-to-day actions. The second chapter is taken up with an attempt to delimit the area of applicability which Socrates supposed this analogy to have, and the remaining chapters of Part I with filling in as much of the general picture of Socrates' approach to moral philosophy as now seems possible. Following upon this, I have switched my attention to the other end of the Platonic time-scale, to a consideration of the *Laws*, which presents Plato's own convictions in their final form. The difference in atmosphere will readily appear: here Plato abandons the personal and particular ideal of Socrates and seems to regard the individual as merely one unit in a moral phalanx which has to be disposed as effectively as possible in the battle between good and evil. The *Laws* displays, in great detail, a joint pursuit of the good, steering the individual as near as possible towards his goal by an inter-locking system of teaching, conscious, and unconscious (i.e. pro-paganda), and enactment. The craftsman ideal has not altogether vanished, but where Socrates envisaged the moral 'technician' operating upon unruly material in himself, Plato's expert moral agent has his own welfare only as a side issue in his life; his primary task is to direct the shaping of society *en masse* within the dimen-sions of the moral dilemma.

Having seen the gap wide open between Socrates and Plato, our final task is to examine the genesis of the split, and the third and longest section of the present essay contains a survey of the no-man's-land between. The trend from the *Meno*, with its first hints of a new world to come, to the *Politicus* and *Philebus*, which leave the *Laws* hardly more than round the corner, is, I suggest, a progressive coming to terms with the possible. The fifty or more years which separate the Plato of the *Laws* from Socrates con-demned and dead, involved, we must remember, the collapse of that Athenian society and civilization which Plato had known in his youth; the world he was born into broke up, and the tensions of social crack-up and decay are too obviously reflected in his dialogues to need comment. Socrates could conceive of a man achieving his own moral aim unaided (if unoppressed) by society, but this was possible for him only because social support, to some degree at least, could be taken for granted. For Plato at the end of his life, no such assumption could stand the test of even the most cursory inspection of the world as it now was: a coherent society, capable of buoying up its members by the density of its moral tradition, was lost way back in the past, and Plato's deep realization of this led him to the belief that it was only by the remoulding of a rational and self-sufficient social frame, that any but the most morally tenacious of men could arrive at a positive moral stature. I have tried to plot the stages on this way to acceptance of reality as they appear in the dialogues of Plato's middle and last years. They can be seen in the new conception of 'true conviction' in the *Meno*, in the first (and perhaps the greatest) attempt to construct an entire new moral fabric in the *Republic*, in the *Timaeus* with its emphasis on impossibility, through the *Politicus* to the moment of acceptance, with its discordant undertone of irrational revolt, that we find in the *Philebus*. This progress is brought out by such incidental comment as seemed necessary in order to make possible an understanding, rather than a criticism, however reasonable or justified, of Plato's changing views.

Two related problems have been obvious to me all the way. Involved in any attempt at exposition is a drive towards definitive statement; but the latter is beyond our grasp. Before all other difficulties lies the fact that the language I must use to express my interpretation, inevitably embodies distinctions and gradations of sense that are foreign to the world I am trying to understand. An example is at hand in my first chapter: as I have mentioned, the purpose of this chapter is to rediscover the meaning of Socrates' dictum that 'Virtue (ἀρετή) is knowledge (ἐπιστήμη)'. Now the word 'knowledge', in current English, most commonly denotes awareness of facts; I cannot believe that this was what the Greek word ἐπιστήμη meant for Socrates. I have used here Professor Ryle's careful distinction between 'knowing *how*' and 'knowing *that*'; but this distinction or dichotomy is already at least inherent in the meaning of 'know', whereas an examination of the evidence shows us that the two, to us different, meanings were at one in the Greek word. Thus in attempting to redress the balance of interpretation, I am forced into a reconstruction of Socrates' ideas which still, I am well aware, contains an ineradicable element of distortion. Dilemmas such as this constantly recur, and I would ask the reader to bear them in mind while he reads.

But this is a general difficulty which must beset all who try to establish a picture of the past with the only tools they possess, the tools of current language. My second problem is more intimately connected with the subject of this essay. In such a work as this, some sort of apparent definitiveness was unavoidable; yet finality, definitiveness of exposition, were among the last things at which Plato himself ever aimed: indeed they were among the first which he set himself to avoid. His commentators have always baulked at this truth; they have denied it, quarrelled with it, proceeded silently as if it were untrue, but it remains a stone to trip them within sight of their goal. Even in the early period of Plato's work, where there is at least a superficial atmosphere of coherence and veiled finality from dialogue to dialogue, I have been aware all along that the seeds of different and later ideas, together with caveats and half-withdrawals, are there to be observed. In the end, I think, we must recognize that the attempts, of which this book is one, to reconstruct Plato's philosophical outlook along some roughly systematic lines run counter to the whole tendency of the writer they set out to 'reconstruct'. However much he may seek to avoid the charge, the historian of thought is bound to value the definitive, which he can clearly formulate, above the tentative indication, the no more than suggested reaction; and Plato is not there to help him, but to offer a reminder only of the way, the other way, he himself has gone. As Professor Ryle said in one of his 1953 Tarner lectures:[1] 'Plato was...a very unreliable Platonist. He was too much of a philosopher to think that anything he had said was the last word. It was left to his disciples to identify his footmarks with his destination.' Which leaves the historian, quite as much as the true believer, looking by virtue of his office for destinations. The reader must for himself translate the concrete world of sign-posted terminal stations back into the sometimes ambiguous traces which are all that Plato has left us.

[1] Published as *Dilemmas* by the Cambridge University Press (1954), p. 14.

PART I

THE PERSONAL IDEAL

To have made an advance on Socrates without
having understood what he understood is at any
rate not 'Socratic'.
S. A. KIERKEGAARD, *Unscientific Postscript*

CHAPTER I

THE SOCRATIC THEORY OF KNOWLEDGE AND MORALITY

ABOUT the relations between the Protean figure known as the 'historical' Socrates and Plato, there is likely to be no final agreement in the present state of the evidence, and I do not propose to raise the matter here.[1] But the main point at issue in this debate has always been the relative contribution of the two men to the development of the metaphysical theories which we find in Plato's dialogues. On questions of ethics there is somewhat more agreement. It is almost universally accepted, for example, that Socrates was the author of certain ethical propositions which appear, or are referred to, in the writings of both Plato and Aristotle; among them, the propositions that virtue (ἀρετή) is knowledge (ἐπιστήμη), that evil actions are involuntary and the result of ignorance (ἀμαθία), and (though there is less certainty on this point)[2] that the various moral virtues, justice, courage, self-control and the rest are merely *aspects* of ἀρετή, which is in all essentials one. But agreement extends beyond the mere attribution of these theories to Socrates. There is, in this country at least, an accepted interpretation of them, so widely held that by now its premises are scarcely ever questioned. It is this theory that I wish to consider in the present chapter: I shall suggest that it involves a misunderstanding of the original meaning of ἐπιστήμη, a misunderstanding which has generated a number of

[1] The most convenient discussions, and the sanest, are probably those of Ross and Field: Ross, edition of Aristotle's *Metaphysics*, pp. xxxiii–xlv and Field, *Plato and his contemporaries*, pp. 202 ff. A more radical view of Socrates' comparative unimportance is held by O. Gigon in his *Sokrates*. But the question is in any case irrelevant to the subsequent discussion. I am concerned, not with problems of authorship, but with the original intention of a number of passages whose unity of conception is not likely to be denied. This problem would remain, whatever solution of the 'Socratic question' might be offered.

[2] See below, pp. 65 f.

problems about Socrates' ethical beliefs which could not have occurred to their author. Although we have the impression that in discussing these Socratic ethical propositions we are talking about the concepts of ἀρετή and ἐπιστήμη as Socrates used them, most of our discussions seem rather to be bounded by preconceptions about what are taken to be their English 'equivalents', the words virtue and knowledge. The only way out of this difficulty is to examine in some detail the functioning of these words in their Greek context in the hope of gaining a more accurate picture of what these propositions were intended to mean by Socrates and Plato.

My first task, however, is to give an account of the 'official theory', as we might term it, of what is meant by saying that ἀρετή is a matter of ἐπιστήμη. Moral virtue, Socrates is supposed to have claimed, is to be achieved only by an understanding of the moral truths of the universe, that is by an intellectual insight into the nature of right and wrong. It is presumed that he believed that knowledge of moral facts [1] involves morally correct behaviour and conversely, that wrongdoing is caused by intellectual ignorance of the same moral facts. According to this view, the situation of the moral man behaving morally is for Socrates somewhat the same as the explanation we often put forward of a chess-player playing an intelligent game of chess: he is able to act as he does because, in his mind, he knows the 'rules of the game', because he possesses the theoretical equipment which is required for correct practice. Thus ἐπιστήμη denotes the successful conclusion of a process of ethical theorizing, necessarily prior to morally acceptable behaviour: the sense of ἐπιστήμη is cognitive or, to adopt Professor Ryle's terminology, some form of knowing *that*.[2] This, I take it, is what underlies such statements as A. E. Taylor's:

---

[1] There is an instructive ambiguity about the nature of the 'moral facts' which the accepted theory takes to be the object of ἐπιστήμη: if 'right' and 'wrong' are taken as applying to individual actions, not only would this involve a peculiar sort of mental feat, but it would run counter to the whole of Book I of the *Republic* (see Joseph, *Essays*, p. 6). If on the other hand the moral facts are those of the nature of Right and Wrong, this would seem to involve a metaphysical theory of the object which few would attribute to Socrates.

[2] Ryle, *Concept of Mind*, ch. II.

'virtue, moral excellence, is identical with knowledge...vice, bad moral conduct is therefore in all cases ignorance, intellectual error';[1] or M. Léon Robin's: 'ainsi la nature de la vertu...apparaît comme essentiellement intellectuelle: l'intelligence est la condition dernière de la moralité'.[2] These are no doubt extreme statements of the accepted theory and I do not wish to suggest that the majority of scholars would necessarily formulate their views in quite the same manner. But even in the interpretations of more guarded critics, the same fallacy, it seems to me, is to be found. Cornford's exposition, for example, though closer to a common-sense view of what moral behaviour is actually like, involves a fundamentally similar approach. Socrates, he writes, 'declared that human perfection lies in the knowledge of good and evil....I shall not know that this or that is good or right until I can see it directly for myself....Knowledge of values, in fact, is a matter of direct insight, *like seeing that the sky is blue, the grass green.*'[3] In spite of the use of such semi-metaphorical words as 'insight', it is clear that Cornford, like Taylor and Robin, believed that ἐπιστήμη implies a theoretical knowledge of moral 'facts' (or 'rules' or 'imperatives'): even for him, ἐπιστήμη is the 'bit of theory' which precedes the 'bit of practice'.

Such is the current interpretation of what is perhaps the central thesis of Socratic ethics. It is of distinguished parentage. Aristotle in a passage of the *Eudemian Ethics*[4] describes Socrates' theory as follows: 'the elder Socrates held it to be the aim [of ethics] to know what virtue (ἀρετή) is....He believed that all the moral virtues were forms of knowledge; in such a way that when one knew what justice was, it followed that one would be just.... And yet where moral virtue is concerned, the most important

---

[1] Taylor, *Socrates*, p. 141. Cf. p. 143.
[2] Robin, *Platon*, p. 258. See also Richard Robinson, *Plato's Earlier Dialectic* (2nd ed.), pp. 14f.
[3] Cornford, *Before and after Socrates*, pp. 45f. (my italics). Cf. *C.A.H.* vol. VI, pp. 305f. and for his latest view, *Principium Sapientiae*, pp. 46f., especially 'Socrates had been convinced that all men...cannot be just until they know what Justice is.'
[4] *Eth. Eud.* 1216b 2ff. The essence of Aristotle's interpretation (and of his criticism) lies in the phrase: οὐ γὰρ εἰδέναι βουλόμεθα τί ἐστιν ἀνδρεία, ἀλλ' εἶναι ἀνδρεῖοι. Cf. *Eth Eud.* 1230a 6ff., 1246b 33ff.; *Eth. Nic.* 1147b 9ff.

thing is not to know what it is, but how it arises: we do not wish to know what courage is: we wish to be courageous.' It is obvious that Aristotle's conception of what Socrates meant is substantially the same as that of modern commentators: he departs from them only in offering a criticism. As to this latter, what he is saying in effect is this: Socrates was wrong in supposing that if a man achieved an understanding of what justice involves, he would necessarily become just in behaviour, since the whole problem of choice intervenes between knowledge and action. On the interpretation which we have been considering, this is clearly a pertinent objection and the embarrassment of it has been acknowledged in one way or another by most modern critics. But there is no need here to consider the various answers which they have made to Aristotle, since the main purpose of this chapter is to put forward an alternative interpretation of Socrates' meaning, in the light of which Aristotle's objection becomes irrelevant.

Before doing this, I should like to add something to what I have already said about the roots of the intellectualist theory. The question, I believe, goes somewhat deeper than the effects of a misleading terminology. Professor Ryle has well pointed out how confused are our ideas about the relationship between knowing *how* and knowing *that*.[1] We have the idea that, in general, 'the capacity to attain knowledge of truths is the defining property of a mind' and therefore that to act rationally is 'to have one's non-theoretical propensities controlled by one's apprehension of truths about the conduct of life'. We are thus led to believe that in order to explain what we mean by describing someone as behaving 'intelligently', we must point to some prior condition of the intellect, such as the careful application of rules or the observance of theoretical maxims: 'he knew', we might say, '*what* he was doing'. In this way we can see that there is an almost universal tendency to assimilate cases of knowing *how* to cases of knowing *that*. Nor is this merely a confusion of our own era. As Professor Onians has pointed out,[2] cognition and conation are often hardly

---

[1] Ryle, *op. cit.* pp. 27ff. The whole book might be read with profit by those who are concerned to understand this difficult phase in the history of Greek ethical ideas.   [2] R. B. Onians, *The Origins of European Thought*, pp. 13–22.

distinguishable in the vocabulary of the *Iliad* and *Odyssey*; but in this instance the assimilation seems to be the other way about. As we shall see, the basic meaning of several Greek words for the concept of knowledge seems to be that of knowing *how*. In any case, although I am by no means sure that the distinction between the two modes of knowing was as clear to Socrates and Plato as the following pages may inevitably suggest, I am convinced that the Socratic proposition that we are now discussing is far better understood in the light of earlier usage, going back to Homer and beyond, than in the misleading light of a later attachment to intellectual or contemplative theories of the mind, which stem in the main from the subsequent work of Plato and Aristotle.

Briefly what I wish to suggest is this. In putting forward the thesis that ἀρετή is only to be attained by ἐπιστήμη, Socrates was *not* asserting that ἀρετή necessarily results from a personal apprehension of the nature of good and evil (still less, of Good and Evil), but that for the achievement of ἀρετή what is required is a form of moral *ability*, comparable in some respects to the creative or artistic ability of potters, shoemakers and the like; that the ἐπιστήμη which Socrates envisaged was a form of knowing *how*, knowing, that is, *how to be moral*. In order to give substance to this suggestion, I shall examine the usage of ἐπιστήμη and its cognates in Greek literature both before Plato and in the dialogues themselves, as well as in the works of some of his near-contemporaries.[1] The rest of Part I of this work will consider some of the other ethical propositions of the early dialogues and their relationship to this central thesis.

The word ἐπιστήμη is comparatively late in appearing in Greek literature,[2] but the verb from which it is derived, ἐπίσταμαι, is

[1] I am much indebted in the following pages to the invaluable work already done in this field by Bruno Snell in his two books, *Die Ausdrücke für den Begriff des Wissens in der vorplatonischen Philosophie* (1924), and *Die Entdeckung des Geistes* (1948), especially ch. VIII. (References to *Die Entdeckung des Geistes* are to the English edition, referred to as *Discovery*; see Bibliography, p. 229). Professor René Schaerer's study, Ἐπιστήμη et τέχνη: *Étude sur les notions de connaissance et d'art d'Homère à Platon*, despite its title, is not of much assistance in this inquiry: M. Schaerer is more concerned with the externals of these concepts than with their nature as states of mind.

[2] Its first appearance is (presumably) at Bacchylides, x, 38 (Snell).

already found in the *Iliad*. The etymology of ἐπίσταμαι is perhaps still obscure,[1] but its usage in the *Iliad* is unambiguous: it denotes, not awareness of the facts of a case, but always the ability to carry out some action. Scamander, speaking to his brother Simois in *Iliad* XXI, boasts that he will bury the body of Achilles so deep in sand that the Achaeans will not be able to collect his bones:

κὰδ δέ μιν αὐτὸν
εἰλύσω ψαμάθοισιν ἅλις χέραδος περιχεύας
μυρίον, οὐδέ οἱ ὀστέ' ἐπιστήσονται 'Αχαιοὶ
ἀλλέξαι.[2]

The precise shade of meaning varies somewhat: in this case it is not far removed from the idea of a merely physical ability (a scholiast on the passage paraphrases it by δυνήσονται); on other occasions it is nearer to an acquired capability, a mark of intelligence, as in the phrase ἐπιστάμενοι πολεμίζειν,[3] or in the description of Harmonides, ὃς χερσὶν ἐπίστατο δαίδαλα πάντα τεύχειν.[4] The use of ἐπίσταμαι with the infinitive to denote capability is, of course, a well-known Greek construction, usually recorded in lexicons as the primary meaning.[5] But it is essential to remember it as the basic significance of the word: we must not suppose that because it comes later to denote 'knowing *that*', the earlier meaning altogether disappears. So pervasive is the denotation 'knowing *how*' in the *Iliad* that on two occasions no 'explanatory' infinitive occurs: the sense is clear, merely because there is only one possible significance. The phrases are ἐπιστάμενος ἄκοντι[6] (where μάχεσθαι or πολεμίζειν must be supplied) and the odd conjunction ἐπισταμένοισι πόδεσσι[7] (of dancers' feet). Similarly we may compare the usage of ἐπισταμένως, always of the *manner* in which something is done.[8] Finally, for what it is worth, the scholiasts and

---

[1] See Boisacq, *Dictionnaire Etym. de la Langue Grecque*, and Ebeling, *Lexicon Homericum*, s.v. ἐπίσταμαι.

[2] *Il.* XXI, 318 ff.   [3] *Il.* II, 611, etc.   [4] *Il.* V, 60.

[5] See Liddell-Scott-Jones, s.v. ἐπίσταμαι.

[6] *Il.* XV, 282.

[7] *Il.* XVIII, 599. An instructive use of ἐπίσταμαι is to be found in Archilochus' phrase (fr. 1, Diehl): καὶ Μουσέων ἐρατὸν δῶρον ἐπιστάμενος.

[8] E.g. *Il.* VII, 317. Cf. *Od.* XI, 368; XII, 307; *Hymn to Hermes*, 390; Hesiod, *Theogony*, 87.

lexicographers are unanimous in paraphrasing Homer's use of ἐπίσταμαι in the *Iliad* by the word δύναμαι.[1] They were aware, as we sometimes are not, of the changes in meaning which are so frequent in the history of Greek between Homer and their own day.[2] From the fourth century onwards ἐπίσταμαι was almost exclusively used in the sense 'knowing *that*', but these writers had enough historical awareness to know that this was not its original meaning. Erotian, commenting on the meaning of ἐπίστασθαι in a passage of the Hippocratic treatise περὶ ἄρθρων ἐμβολῆς,[3] gives as his note: ἐπίστανται· δύνανται, ὡς καὶ Ὅμηρος, and quotes *Iliad* XIV, 92.[4] In much the same vein, a scholiast on *Iliad* XVI, 142 ends with the remark (which aptly summarizes the transition in meaning): τῇ ἐπιστήμῃ δὲ προσάπτει τὴν δύναμιν.[5]

In the *Odyssey* the word is rarer, but most of the instances, like those in the *Iliad*, are instances of knowing *how*. When Odysseus, in Book XXI, wields his bow with skill, he is compared to an accomplished musician, ἀνὴρ φόρμιγγος ἐπιστάμενος καὶ ἀοιδῆς.[6] It is true that in the *Odyssey* we find the first example of ἐπίσταμαι in the sense 'know *that*':[7] yet Bruno Snell is clearly right in general when he says that for Homer 'ἐπίσταμαι is still completely expressed by its original meaning, denoting a practical activity, and it remains wholly in the sphere of capability (Sphäre des Könnens)'.[8] A fragment from the Pseudo-Homerica completes the picture: the famous quotation from the *Margites*, πολλὰ ἠπίστατο ἔργα, κακῶς δ' ἠπίστατο πάντα.[9] In spite of Socrates' commentary on this in the second *Alcibiades* (closely akin to his 'commentary' on a fragment of Simonides in the *Protagoras*), this surely means 'was a jack of all trades and a master of none'.

In the lyric poets ἐπίσταμαι, understandably enough, is even

---

[1] See Hesychius, s.v. ἐπίσταμαι; Lehrs, *De Aristarchi studiis Homericis*, p. 147 and the scholia on *Il.* XVI, 142; XXI, 320, etc. (*Scholia Graeca in Homeri Iliadem*, ed. Dindorf-Maass, vol. II, pp. 100, 222; vol. VI, p. 168).
[2] Lehrs, *op. cit.* pp. 35 ff. [3] [Hippocrates], *De Artic.* 37.
[4] *Erotiani vocum hippocraticarum collectio* (Nachmanson), p. 39.
[5] *Scholia in Iliadem* (Dindorf-Maass), vol. IV, p. 117.
[6] *Od.* XXI, 406. Cf. IX, 49; XIII, 207, 313; *Hymn to Hermes*, 479.
[7] *Od.* IV, 730. [8] Snell, *Ausdrücke*, p. 82.
[9] *Margites*, fr. 3 (Allen), quoted by [Plato], *Alcibiades II*, 147B. Cf. fr. 2.

rarer. Before Pindar it seems to be used only once, by Sappho, in the meaning 'know *how*'.[1] But Herodotus provides us with more material. He has over a hundred instances of the word, some fifteen of which have this meaning.[2] In view of Plato's later equation of ἐπιστήμη with τέχνη, an interesting example is the phrase τεχνάζειν ἐπιστάμενος.[3] Most of the instances in Herodotus refer to acquired abilities, to cases of intelligent practice, as in the common phrase νέειν ἐπιστάμενος. There is another usage of the word in Herodotus, equally interesting, although it denotes knowing *that*: there are a number of examples of ἐπίσταμαι in the meaning 'to be convinced', where any translation that might imply objectivity is impossible, since the conviction is mistaken. In one case ἐπίσταμαι is modified by the addition of δόξῃ,[4] but in the majority of instances only an examination of the context reveals that the translation 'to know' is incorrect. Thus when in Book v Herodotus says of Dorieus, the younger brother of Cleomenes, εὖ ἠπίστατο κατ' ἀνδραγαθίην αὐτὸς σχήσων τὴν βασιληίην[5] it is only after reading the following sentence, in which it becomes clear that he did *not* in fact become king, that we can be sure whether ἠπίστατο denotes an awareness of the (objective) facts or merely a subjective feeling, which we should have to translate by certainty or conviction. As we shall see, one of the major problems which seems to arise over Plato's use of ἐπιστήμη is precisely the question of subjectivity. Not only should we remember the precedent which Herodotus affords, but also that there is no sense in which ἐπιστήμη, *qua* ability, could be other than subjective. Moral ability cannot solve the problem, if it is a problem, of moral objectivity. With the subjective examples from Herodotus, Snell compares a fragment of Heraclitus[6] and says of it: 'here too the decisive element in the meaning of the

---

[1] Sappho, Γ 6 (App.) (Lobel). Cf. Pindar, *Pyth.* VIII, 6f.; *Olymp.* VI, 25f. etc.

[2] Herodotus, I, 95, 1; II, 16, 1; III, 15, 2; 130, 2; IV, 174; VI, 44, 3; VII, 29, 3; 135, 2; VIII, 89, 1, 2; 129, 2, etc.

[3] III, 130, 2.   [4] VIII, 132, 3.

[5] V, 42, 1. Cf. III, 67, 1; 139, 3; VI, 139, 4; VII, 218, 3; VIII, 10, 2, etc. (fourteen instances in all).

[6] Heraclitus, fr. 57 (DK). Cf. fr. 19.

word is subjective certainty, the certainty of having hold of a truth, not any objective authority which the feeling possesses.'[1] This too, as we shall see, is among the connotations of ἐπιστήμη in many passages of Plato's early dialogues.

The examples from Homer and Herodotus give us ample evidence for the use of ἐπίσταμαι to denote 'knowing *how*'. To appreciate Plato's meaning, we have primarily to rid ourselves of the notion that 'knowledge', in Greek, invariably implies the possession of factual information, even if these facts are supposed to be facts of a peculiar order, queer facts such as the 'rules' of swimming or the 'principles' of correct conduct. A second troublesome idea which we must abandon is the supposition that ἐπιστήμη, in Plato's writings, bases its claim to acknowledged supremacy in the sphere of ethics (and human behaviour in general) on being in direct touch with objective truths or objective values. The passages which we have so far considered provide a substantial counter-balance to these temptations.

The dramatists bear out what we have seen in Homer and Herodotus, but they raise a further point which it may be worth considering. We tend even now to understand the whole pantheon of Greek virtues in terms of intellectual transactions, in accordance with our general assumption that behaviour is to be explained and valued by reference to prior mental states. We translate σωφροσύνη, for example, by the words 'prudence', 'discretion', 'self-control' or even, if we follow the authority of Liddell and Scott, by the phrase 'soundness of mind', thus implying that to discover whether a man was indeed σώφρων, we should have to 'inspect' his intellectual situation.[2] This habit is grossly misleading. I have deliberately chosen σωφροσύνη as my example because it is in many ways a test case, being the most difficult of the Greek 'cardinal' virtues to understand in our terms. We shall never come nearer to understanding, it seems to me, while we retain this reliance on mental states as the key. The traditional connection of σωφροσύνη is with behaviour, not with mental outlook: Hermes, when in Aeschylus' *Prometheus* he taunts Prometheus with the

[1] Snell, *op. cit.* p. 83.
[2] See, as an example, A. E. Taylor, *Plato: the Man and his Work*, pp. 47 f.

words: καὶ μὴν σύ γ' οὔπω σωφρονεῖν ἐπίστασαι,[1] refers not to Prometheus' state of mind, not even to his *Weltanschauung*, but to his behaviour in cursing the gods and threatening revenge upon them. It is even perhaps worth pointing out that this is merely what we might expect from a consideration of the essential features of Greek religion, at least in its Olympian or Apolline aspect. It is, I think, obvious that Greek religion is primarily concerned not with dogma, but with ritual and cult observance, and that in any attempt to throw the stress elsewhere we thereby distort the picture.[2] Thus σωφρονεῖν ἐπίστασθαι does not imply an intellectual acceptance of 'correct' religious beliefs, so much as a proper respect *in behaviour* for the superior physical power of the gods. Dike is not the representative of a divine thought-police, but the controller (by force) of human behaviour in accordance with Zeus' wishes.[3] Whatever may be the right solution of the textual and grammatical problems of *Agamemnon* 167–83, the context of the chorus, indeed of the play as a whole, makes it clear that φρονεῖν and σωφρονεῖν in that passage refer to conduct, to the circumspection in action required of men faced with the violence and power of the gods, βιαίως σέλμα σεμνὸν ἡμένων, just as conversely the word ὕβρις, implying the denial of all that σωφροσύνη involves, denotes the violent unthinking actions of pride and self-assertion.[4] Finally, to obtain a proper perspective for our understanding of Greek ethical ideas, we should remember the fact that the word ἀρετή means first 'superiority', especially in fighting, secondly any form of efficient and intelligent *practice*, and that only in the philosophers is its meaning sometimes restricted to '*moral* virtue'. If we were more accustomed to consider the important question of levels of abstraction in Greek, we should find that ἀρετή tended at all times towards the concrete: at its most concrete, it can even mean 'feats' (i.e. concrete examples of efficient action)[5] and it is always nearer to this sense than to the

---

[1] Aeschylus, *Prometheus*, 982. Cf. Soph. *O.T.* 589; Euripides, fr. 805; [Epicharmus], fr. 286 (Kaibel); Thucydides, III, 44, 1; Plato, *Meno*, 90D 1.
[2] See Snell, *Discovery*, pp. 25 ff.; cf. p. 128.
[3] See, for example, *Pap. Oxyr.* 2256, fr. 9 (*a*).
[4] E.g. *Od.* XVII, 487; Hesiod, *Works and Days*, 217; Aesch. *Eum.* 533.
[5] See Pindar, *Pythians* I, 41; Theocritus, XVII, 137, with Gow's note.

English idea of 'virtue'.[1] Even for Socrates and Plato, to achieve ἀρετή is not to arrive at a valid ethical theory, but to attain valid moral behaviour. Its variation in sense is bounded simply by the changing valuation of various aspects of action implicit in the development of the Greek world.[2]

The purpose of this prolonged interjection was to set the idea of ἐπιστήμη against its proper background of ethical values. The dramatists, who gave us our starting-point, supply more testimony for the 'knowing *how*' sense of ἐπίσταμαι. Nor is it the case that the connotations of the word tend, even now, to become decisively more 'theoretical' or 'intellectual'. In saying of the house of Atreus, πένεσθαι δ' οὐκ ἐπίσταται δόμος,[3] Clytaemnestra employs a turn of phrase which in fact tends backwards towards the usage of the *Iliad*. We can indeed observe a transitional use in the *Eumenides*:[4]

> ἐγὼ διδαχθεὶς ἐν κακοῖς ἐπίσταμαι
> πολλοὺς καθαρμούς, καὶ λέγειν ὅπου δίκη
> σιγᾶν θ' ὁμοίως,

where ὅπου δίκη seems to imply that ἐπίσταμαι means 'know *when*' as much as 'know *how*'. Yet even here practice, not theory, is in question, not 'das Wissen um ein factum', but 'die Kenntnis, die eine Tätigkeit ermöglicht'.[5]

It is, of course, theoretically possible that, although ἐπίσταμαι (especially with the infinitive) means in origin, and continues to mean at least until Plato, 'knowing *how*', the noun ἐπιστήμη might solely be used in the sense 'knowledge of facts'. But consideration of the actual usage of the word proves this possibility to be false. From its very first appearance onwards there is evidence that ἐπιστήμη, too, frequently denotes ability: μυρίαι δ' ἀνδρῶν ἐπιστᾶμαι πέλονται, writes Bacchylides[6] and in listing some of them reveals the close connection of the word with

---

[1] Cf. Plato, *Apol.* 18A 5f., *Prot.* 322d 7; Jaeger, *Theology of the Early Greek Philosophers*, p. 82 and *Paideia*, vol. I, pp. 5, 418 n. 10. See also pp. 44 n. 1, III n. 1, below.　　　　　[2] See Snell, *Discovery*, pp. 158ff.

[3] *Agamemnon*, 962. Cf. 1066, etc.　　　[4] *Eumenides*, 276ff.

[5] Snell, *Ausdrücke*, p. 83.　　　　　[6] Bacchylides, x, 38ff. (Snell).

knowing *how*. Skill in poetry, in divination, in athletics or in the pursuit of wealth are for him typical ἐπιστῆμαι. ἐπιστήμη here, as M. Schaerer points out,[1] 'semble être…l'exact synonyme de τέχνη'. Headlam, in a note on this passage quoted in Jebb's commentary,[2] remarked on a parallel with some lines of Solon,[3] where equally there is no doubting the practical stress: in this latter poem the poet is described as ἱμερτῆς σοφίης μέτρον ἐπιστάμενος. Similarly in Thucydides, ἐπιστήμη denotes intelligent ability, in particular tactical ability, or the ability to wield a weapon with skill, as distinct from mere strength or physical courage.[4] In a passage of Sophocles,[5] it is extended to mean innate wisdom in the conduct of life (*Lebensweisheit*—Snell): more specifically, archery is referred to as both an ἐπιστήμη and a τέχνη,[6] just as in a fragment of Euripides' *Meleager*, weaving and skill at arms are called ἐπιστῆμαι.[7] The author of the Hippocratic treatise περὶ ἀρχαίης ἰητρικῆς, in rejecting theoretical speculations as a basis for medicine and in offering in their place a *practical* and *empirical* approach, terms the latter indiscriminately τέχνη and ἐπιστήμη. ἐπιστήμη, as denoting practical experience and ability, is frequently set against ὑποθέσεις or theoretical (and unverifiable) assumptions.[8] In a significant phrase he writes that in medicine πάντες (εἴσιν) ἐπιστήμονες διὰ τὴν χρῆσίν τε καὶ ἀνάγκην ('experts because they cannot avoid practising it').[9] Other indicative examples can be found in the works of Plato's near contemporaries, Democritus, Xenophon and Isocrates.[10] One passage of

---

[1] Schaerer, *op. cit.* p. 5. He compares Bacchylides, XI, 33 and XIII, 49 (Snell); and comments: 'l'idée d'abondance ou de variété s'ajoute fréquemment à celle d'art' (p. 5 n. 1).

[2] Jebb, edition of Bacchylides, pp. 319, 479f.

[3] Solon, fr. 1 (Diehl), ll. 43 ff.

[4] Thucydides, I, 49, 3; 121, 4; VI, 68, 2, etc. Cf. the equation of τέχνη and ἐπιστήμη at II, 87, 4 and the phrase τῆς τε φωνῆς τῇ ἐπιστήμῃ (the ability to speak a dialect) at VII, 63, 3.

[5] Sophocles, *Antigone*, 721.　　　　[6] *Philoctetes*, 1057; *Ajax*, 1121.

[7] Euripides, fr. 522 (Nauck²).

[8] See W. H. S. Jones, *Philosophy and Medicine in Ancient Greece*, p. 41.

[9] [Hippocrates], *Ancient Medicine*, ch. 4. Cf. ch. 1: ἄπειροί τε καὶ ἀνεπιστήμονες, where I would reject Festugière's interpretation (*A.M.*, pp. 29 ff.).

[10] E.g. Democritus, frs. 173, 181; Xenophon, *Mem.* II, 1, 20; *Oec.* I, i; II, xii; xv, iff.; Isocrates, *Panath.* 238D.

Isocrates in particular has a phrase which recalls both the use of ἐπίστασθαι in Homer and the equation of ἐπιστήμη and τέχνη in Plato and elsewhere: τῶν περὶ τὰς τέχνας καὶ τὰς ἐπιστήμας καὶ τὰς δυνάμεις διαφερόντων.[1]

To summarize this investigation into the meaning of ἐπιστήμη, I return once again to the excellent commentary of Bruno Snell.[2] ἐπίσταμαι and ἐπιστήμη, like σοφία and unlike γιγνώσκειν and συνιέναι, have as their primary meaning 'efficiency in practice', practical intelligence; sometimes denoting a restricted technique (ability in some specified field), sometimes a generally intelligent approach to living. The foundations of their meaning, as with those of σοφία and ἀρετή, were laid before the Ionian interest in cosmological theory and in the outside world had produced a reaction, among philosophers, away from the moral interests of earlier writers such as Hesiod, interests which might have provided the basis for constructive ethical speculation, however crudely expressed. The Ionians, philosophers and others, tend to use as the normal expressions for 'knowledge' words like γνῶσις, σύνεσις, εἴδησις and ἱστορίη, which, deriving from perception and observation, imply an apprehension of some external object. Such is not the case with ἐπιστήμη: if Boisacq is right in paraphrasing ἐπίσταμαι by the phrase 'se placer dans l'attitude requise pour', it is likely that from the beginning ἐπιστήμη involved practical capability. If there is any problem in the meaning of the word as Plato uses it, it is not that which the intellectualist hypothesis inevitably raises, the problem of choice, but the question of subjectivity. As we saw from Herodotus, subjectivity and ἐπιστήμη were early connected in the meaning 'certainty' or 'conviction'. Since ἐπιστήμη does not imply contemplation of an object, but understanding, in the sense of an ability to act, it remains a purely subjective 'faith'. It retains this characteristic, or so I believe, in Plato's early dialogues, and it was perhaps this problem which suggested a metaphysical solution to Plato.

Our inquiry so far has been merely a preamble, an attempt to provide a background against which to set the views of Socrates,

---

[1] Isocrates, *loc. cit.*   [2] Snell, *Ausdrücke*, pp. 86 f.

as they seem to be expressed in Plato's early dialogues.[1] We have yet to see how far Plato's own usage is in accordance with that of his predecessors, or whether in fact there is not a contrast rather than a development of their precedent. Let us now examine the evidence.

The most striking statement of the 'virtue as knowledge' theory occurs in the *Protagoras*.[2] Socrates and Protagoras have been discussing the unity of the 'virtues'. Protagoras has been brought to admit that all except courage are at least very similar, but about courage he is adamant in believing it to be something quite different from the rest. At this point Socrates changes his ground and says:

There is another thing, Protagoras, that I should like you to reveal to me about your views. What is your attitude to knowledge (ἐπιστήμη)? Is it the same as that of the majority of men, or do you think differently? Most people view knowledge as being something without force, without the power to lead or direct men. Indeed their conception of it is quite otherwise: they believe that knowledge is often present in a man without its being knowledge that directs his behaviour, but rather other forces, sometimes the desire to assert oneself, sometimes attraction towards pleasure or revulsion from pain, occasionally love, more frequently fear. They seem to view knowledge precisely as they would a slave, believing it dragged about by every other force. Is something like this your view too, or do you believe it to be a thing worth possessing, capable of directing a man, so that if one recognizes good things and bad for what they are (γιγνώσκῃ τἀγαθὰ καὶ τὰ κακά), such knowledge cannot be subverted by anything else, nor can one act otherwise than as one's knowledge (ἐπιστήμη) dictates? Do you believe in fact that understanding (φρόνησις) is sufficient to support a man at the crisis?

The view which is here explicitly contrasted with that of οἱ πολλοὶ ἄνθρωποι is generally believed to be Socrates' own and there seems no reason to quarrel with the attribution. It asserts

[1] I.e. those dialogues which are generally held to have been written before the *Meno* (see Ross, *Plato's Theory of Ideas*, pp. 2 ff.). Only about the *Cratylus* am I doubtful: it seems quite probable that this work was actually written at about the time of the *Theaetetus*.

[2] *Prot.* 352 A 8 ff.

that ἐπιστήμη is *the* governing principle in the man who possesses it, which cannot be rendered ineffective by any other factor in his make-up. It is here set against a series of typical emotions or drives which in the popular view overmaster it on many occasions, treating it as everyone treats a slave, dragging it about this way and that.[1] Two things are worth noticing: one, that ἐπιστήμη is said to recognize (γιγνώσκειν) good and bad; the second that ἐπιστήμη and φρόνησις are used indiscriminately to denote the 'knowledge' which is to direct human actions. The first is equivocal: it seems to imply that ἐπιστήμη has the connotations of knowing *that*; yet clearly we could say of an intelligent practitioner in any field that he recognized the object of his activity for what it was: all still depends on whether we regard this as an *explanation* of his activity and its excellence. In the present example we need to know more before we can pass judgment on this all-important question.[2] The second is not much more helpful: both ἐπιστήμη and φρόνησις have a traditional connection with practice, but no very firm conclusion can be drawn from this meagre fact.

What we cannot discover, from the account in the *Protagoras*, is precisely what mode of knowing is denoted by ἐπιστήμη. Some clearer indications are to be found in other passages. One point emerges directly from a consideration of the evidence: it is that ἐπιστήμη is concerned with practical activities, with use and behaviour. In the *Euthydemus*, during the discussion with Cleinias, philosophy is defined as the attainment of knowledge (κτῆσις ἐπιστήμης) and Socrates pursues the question further by asking: 'What form of knowledge (ἐπιστήμη) will be the right one for us to try to achieve? Surely simply that which benefits us?'[3] Certainly, answers Cleinias, and a little later this hint is filled out by the description of ἐπιστήμη as being that 'in which making and the ability to use what one makes are combined in one'.[4] A corollary of this view is stated in the *Cratylus*, during an attempt to determine who is the right person to decide upon the correctness

---

[1] Cf. Aristotle, *Eth. Nic.* 1147b 15ff. οὐ γὰρ τῆς κυρίως ἐπιστήμης εἶναι δοκούσης παρούσης γίνεται τὸ πάθος, οὐδ' αὐτὴ περιέλκεται διὰ τὸ πάθος.
[2] See below, p. 30.
[3] *Euthyd.* 288D 9ff.   [4] 289B 4ff.

of names. The inventor of names, it has been agreed, is the legislator, but bearing in mind the closely parallel situation of the
τεχνικός, he will clearly need to consult the opinions of whoever
is to *use* his products, since only the latter can have real knowledge
of them: 'which man is going to know whether the right shape
for a shuttle is embodied in this or that piece of wood? The car-
penter who has made it, or the weaver, who will use it?' 'The man
who is going to use it, I imagine, Socrates.'[1] ἐπιστήμη, it appears
from this case, is knowing *how*, not knowing *that*: it is expressed
in practice, and conversely the true ἐπιστήμων is he who knows
how to use whatever is in question.

We are still, however, very far from attaining an adequate
notion of what ἐπιστήμη is to the man who possesses it: all we
have so far done is to delimit its sphere. An important passage of
the *Gorgias* may take us some way towards such a notion. It is to
be linked with a number of other pronouncements by Plato and
though it has caused some rather aggrieved discussion, it throws
much light on the task of the philosopher as Plato conceived it.
At the climax of his verbal duel with Polus in the *Gorgias*,
Socrates protests against Polus' continual attempts to prove him
wrong by producing witnesses against him, as one might in a
court of law (ῥητορικῶς). He claims that his own approach is
radically different: 'For my part', he says, 'whatever the subject
of our discussion, I do not think that I shall have achieved anything worth talking of, unless I can produce *you* as my witness,
though you may be my only one, willing to accept my views.'[2]
The implication of this seems to be that the business of a philosopher is simply to produce conviction in those with whom he
talks, and this suggestion is strikingly corroborated by a sentence
somewhat later in the same dialogue: 'In fact', Socrates claims,
'when you and I agree, we shall finally possess the truth.'[3] These
passages raise a number of important points which merit some

---

[1] *Crat.* 390B 1 ff. Cf. *Rep.* X, 601D 4ff.   [2] *Gorg.* 472B 6ff.

[3] 487E 1 ff. (τῷ ὄντι οὖν ἡ ἐμὴ καὶ ἡ σὴ ὁμολογία τέλος ἤδη ἕξει τῆς ἀληθείας).
Compare further *Rep.* I, 340A 1 ff.; 348A 7 ff.; also II, 357A 4 ff., on the importance of genuine conviction. On the related concept of ὁμολογία as a moral
and political 'contract' (*Crito*, 50 ff. etc.), see G. Bornkamm in *Hermes*, 71
(1936), pp. 377 ff.

discussion. Mr Richard Robinson, commenting on these and other passages in a similar vein in the *Gorgias*, writes as follows:

By addressing itself always to this person here and now, elenchus takes on particularity and accidentalness, which are defects. In this respect it is inferior to the impersonal and universal and rational march of a science axiomatized according to Aristotle's prescription. Plato might urge, however, that elenchus is the means by which the irrational and accidental individual is brought to the appreciation of universal science, brought out of his individual arbitrariness into the common world of reason.[1]

Professor Dorothy Tarrant seems to echo Mr Robinson's view in saying: 'Plato's thought, in its farthest reach, still carries the quality and limitations of a Socratic λόγος as being the outcome and expression of a human ὁμολογία.'[2] These criticisms involve a basic misunderstanding of Plato's intention. Mr Robinson (and, I suspect, Professor Tarrant) is concerned with what he terms Plato's 'earlier dialectic', and his approach is epistemological. But it should be abundantly clear that the ἐπιστήμη of the early dialogues is the end-point not of any theory of truth, but of a search for a valid basis for moral actions. Whether as knowing *how* or as knowing *that*, ἐπιστήμη is ethical 'knowledge' (certainty or conviction): its certainty is expressed in action, which is personal and individual.[3] There can be no 'axiomatization' in ethics and Mr Robinson's quarrel with Plato on this point is baseless. The aim of dialogues like the *Gorgias*, *Euthydemus*, *Laches* or *Protagoras* is to clarify the meaning of Socrates' well-known propositions, which offered an analysis of the springs (actual or possible) of moral decisions and behaviour. Mr Robinson sees the idea of ἐπιστήμη as a proffered solution to some problem of epistemology, but it emerges quite clearly from these dialogues that it is put forward as an answer to the question: upon what can one base moral decisions? Certainty in action is what is here in view and

---

[1] R. Robinson, *Plato's Earlier Dialectic*, p. 16. See also pp. 15 ff., 26. The other passages of the *Gorgias* referred to are at 474A 5 ff.; 475E 7 ff.

[2] *Classical Quarterly*, vol. XLII (1948), p. 28.

[3] On the essential particularity of the individual, especially as moral subject, see M. B. Foster, *Political Philosophies of Plato and Hegel*, pp. 58 f.

Socrates pointed to the analogy of creative 'certainty', evinced by craftsmen in all fields.[1] If one *knows how*, then action ceases to present a problem. But, as Plato was aware, knowing *how* has not the objective status of knowing *that*, where this implies awareness of existing facts. There is only one way in which a man's claim to know how to act can be accepted or rejected, and that is by inspection of the observable actions of such a man and these actions themselves can only be accepted or rejected. There seems no question in these early dialogues of looking for an objective justification for moral behaviour: the assumption appears to be that moral behaviour (the phrase is now heavily 'loaded') justifies itself, and that the problem is how to achieve it. Whether or not this is accepted, there can be no doubt that ἐπιστήμη is to be evinced *in* action: it is not some separable state of mind. The agreement (ὁμολογία) which Socrates hopes to reach with Polus is to be tested by reference to *action*. Thus when Callicles bursts in upon the conversation in the *Gorgias* with his violent expression of astonishment at Socrates' argument, he says: 'If you are serious and what you say happens to be true, there is only one conclusion. The whole life of mankind is standing on its head; we are all of us, it seems, doing the reverse of what we should (πάντα τὰ ἐναντία πράττομεν, ὡς ἔοικεν, ἢ ἃ δεῖ).'[2] The truth of Socrates' assertions is to be expressed in action. The point is made again later, in such remarks as: 'And if you find that now I agree with you and later do not act as I agreed was right (μὴ ταὐτὰ πράττοντα ἅπερ ὡμολόγησα), you are welcome to think me a fool.'[3] This implicit connection between agreement and action is repeatedly stressed in the *Gorgias*: it may explain in part the violence of the argument.[4]

There is nothing so far to suggest that ἐπιστήμη is in any way to be understood either as contemplation of moral truth or as 'the

[1] The ambiguity of the Greek word ποιεῖν, which means both 'to make' and 'to do', must have played a part in suggesting this analogy to Socrates.
[2] *Gorg.* 481 C 1 ff.   [3] *Gorg.* 488 A 6ff. Cf. 500 C 1 ff.
[4] Cf. A.-J. Festugière, *Contemplation et vie contemplative selon Platon*, p. 66: 'La fin est de pratiquer la vertu, de se conduire en homme.' Also (p. 68): 'Si le maître [Socrates] tendait à une doctrine morale, c'est en vue de la pratique.' Cf. Robin, *Platon*, p. 254; Stenzel-Allan, *Plato's Method of Dialectic*, p. xxvi.

appreciation of universal science'. It represents rather a moral assurance, perhaps without objective justification, but sufficient to make action follow. Its existence is to be ascertained by inspection of the actions themselves, not by some feat of mental surgery, designed to discover whether 'knowledge' is really 'present'. From the standpoint of external justification, ἐπιστήμη, as we might expect, may be paralleled by the English phrase 'morally certain', defined by the *Oxford English Dictionary* as 'so sure that one is morally justified in acting upon the conviction'.[1] The 'particularity and accidentalness' of which Mr Robinson complains are inseparable from the function of ἐπιστήμη, *qua* moral certainty (knowing *how* to act). If we insist on disregarding Plato's own statements and considering ἐπιστήμη from the point of view of epistemology, then we cannot help but generate for ourselves problems which have little relevance to Plato's actual meaning. An excellent commentary on Plato's conception of certainty (and its claim to be 'truth') may be found in a passage of Kierkegaard's *Journals*: 'What is truth but to live for an idea? Ultimately everything must rest upon a postulate; but the moment it is no longer outside (a man), and he lives in it, then and only then does it cease to be a postulate for him.'[2] Considered from the point of view of an outside observer, this represents the essence of Socratic ἐπιστήμη: from within, it is the conviction of knowing how to act.

If we understand the starting-point of Plato's ethics in this way —and his main concern throughout his life was, as I believe, ethical—we have a clue to the solution of several other Platonic puzzles, which cause Mr Robinson, among others, some anxiety. Viewing 'particularity' with suspicion as he does, he is forced into a long and, in the result, wholly negative inquiry[3] into the reasons why Plato adopted the dialogue form for his philosophical writings; why too he so often expresses mistrust of the written word, a mistrust which, though coming to the fore in the *Phaedrus* (274 D f.) and in *Letters* II and VII, is already to be found in the *Protagoras* and other early dialogues.[4] 'Why', Mr Robinson asks, 'was Plato so

---

[1] *O.E.D.* s.v. 'certain'.   [2] Kierkegaard, *Journals*, p. 16.
[3] Robinson, *op. cit.* pp. 77 ff.
[4] *Prot.* 329 A 2 ff.; 347 E 1 ff.; *Hipp. Min.* 365 C 8 f.

convinced of a proposition which to us is something like a paradox?' The question may seem far enough removed from the
problem of ἐπιστήμη, but an answer to it throws much light even
on that vexed subject.

Mr Robinson is right in regarding these remarks as constituting
a philosophical problem. In the past they have been more often
treated as demanding a historical or literary explanation and many
scholars have pointed to the verse mimes of Sophron and Xenar-
chus, to the Σωκρατικοὶ λόγοι of Aeschines of Sphettus, Xenophon
and others, or to the dramatic and satirical talents of Plato himself
as an explanation for his choice of literary form. But Plato's own
pronouncements go beyond this. Dialogue, or better conversation (the word savours less of a literary 'form'), is said to be the
only method both of expressing philosophical argument and even
of doing philosophy. His expressed mistrust is of συγγράμματα
and of τέχναι, which we should probably translate by 'definitive
statements' or 'text-books'.[1] If we may interpret him, his
meaning, I think, is this: a written statement of philosophical views
is a thing controlled solely by the author's intentions and the
assumptions of his age and milieu. The essential difference between
this and the spoken word is that the latter is placed in context by
all those taking part: it takes account of all their assumptions and
their private convictions: it is moulded and directed by them. The
meaning of a written sentence may or may not impinge on my
own outlook: it may, that is, *mean* something to *me*, as an individual, or it may not. The writer has little or no control over that,
nor can he prevent me from believing that I have understood him
when in fact I have not. But in conversation the situation is quite
different: its development is not implicit in the intentions of one
man, but pursues its course as it is directed this way or that by the
demands of all present and involved. Socrates, on the other hand,
as the centre of the conversation, can discover whether his remarks

[1] See, for example, *Letter* VII 341 B ff., and compare the ῥητορικαὶ τέχναι of
writers like Gorgias and Thrasymachus. Wittgenstein wrote, in the preface to
the *Tractatus* (p. 27): 'This book will perhaps only be understood by those who
have themselves already thought the thoughts which are expressed in it—or
similar thoughts. It is therefore not a text-book.' Wittgenstein's 'Lehrbuch'
is Plato's σύγγραμμα.

are rightly aimed and expressed, and he can probe their acceptance by his friends to see whether they have been correctly understood and genuinely accepted. Philosophy is the achievement of certainty, and certainty, as Socrates meant it, is the inward agreement of one with another's views, only to be achieved in 'ad hominem' conversation, only to be expressed in action. Hence the dialogue form; for, as we might expect from Plato's known views on the inadequacy of the written word, his own works are not *statements* of his fundamental beliefs, but rather illustrations of the philosophic method in action on typical subjects. To say this is not to commit the psychological fallacy of supposing that the dialogues contain no hint of Plato's most serious convictions: such an assertion, I believe, misinterprets the meaning of such passages as *Letter* VII 341 C.[1] What Plato is there denying is that there is any universal and finally definitive account of thoughts and ideas whose very nature addresses them to the individual, in different forms as the situation of the individual varies. Hence also the mistrust of writing, which is addressed to all men indiscriminately and may be read by all men, always in the same terms, and is incapable of answering the individual's private difficulties and queries. But philosophy as the 'ad hominem' attempt to achieve moral conviction has already been rejected by Mr Robinson as a falling away from the ideal of universality; from his point of view, the choice of conversation as *the* philosophical medium can only seem a 'paradox'; from Plato's, it is the inevitable conclusion of his philosophical assumptions.[2] We can even see that one of the objections most commonly felt by readers of Plato's works is precisely what Plato himself might have led us to expect. Often, we feel, the difficulties expressed and the agreements reached are

[1] See, for example, Burnet, *Greek Philosophy: Thales to Plato*, pp. 178, 214; edition of the *Phaedo*, pp. xlv–xlvi; Taylor, *Plato*, p. 10.

[2] On the significance of the dialogue form in Plato, see D. Grene, *Man in his Pride*, p. 139: 'It is the peculiar value of the dialogues that they constitute the artistic recreation of the moments of illumination—in conversation, in chance happenings, and, as it were, in particular intellectual silhouettes. They are not philosophy, as philosophy has since been understood, but the artistic correlative of the experience that makes philosophy.' See also, F. Solmsen *Plato's Theology*, p. 77; Stenzel, *Platon der Erzieher*, p. 1.

not those which recommend themselves to us, so that our faith in the conclusions of such arguments is vitiated. Yet this is no more than Plato, as we have seen, was himself aware of, and in part contributes to his mistrust of the definitive, which he felt to be more often illusory than real.

To return to our main subject, ἐπιστήμη now appears as an inward and decisively personal moral conviction (analogous perhaps, though we must beware of being misled by the connotations of the word, to the Christian 'faith').[1] It is personal, as knowing *how* inevitably is; inward, because it is not the subsuming of the individual into a universal and objective principle. But at this point Plato introduces a 'caveat', which we should do well to note. ἐπιστήμη, though its certainty is personal, is not and cannot ever be the product of the sort of 'persuasion' practised by Gorgias and the rhetoricians. This is one of the principal assertions of the *Gorgias*. True ἐπιστήμη is reached by teaching (διδασκαλική) : 'nor indeed can the orator teach the juries and other crowds which he addresses anything of what is just or unjust: he can only produce conviction (πίστις).'[2] The reason for this assertion we shall consider at length elsewhere: briefly it is this. The subject of morals is too great, the aims and circumstances of the orator too narrow, for him to produce anything more valid than πίστις. The contrast between πίστις and ἐπιστήμη is drawn at length in the *Gorgias* (and, of course, elsewhere in the dialogues outside the scope of this chapter). The terms of the opposition fill out our total picture of the nature of ἐπιστήμη.

ἐπιστήμη, unlike πίστις, is irrefutable and cannot be deceived into thinking itself refuted by rhetoric. Though ἐπιστήμη is conviction, it is conviction based on a genuine presence of intelligent ability. πίστις, on the other hand, is easily shaken by the appearance of knowledge in the orator, who may in the face of mere πίστις make a genuine expert appear wrong: he cannot do this

---

[1] Cf. the remark of Stenzel: 'Knowledge and faith, then, are to be seen indissolubly united in his [Plato's] individuality: they are opposites which supplement each other, and which he tried to combine in his conception of reason, νόησις' (Stenzel, *Plato's Method of Dialectic*, p. 13).

[2] οὐδ' ἄρα διδασκαλικὸς ὁ ῥήτωρ ἐστὶν δικαστηρίων τε καὶ τῶν ἄλλων ὄχλων δικαίων τε πέρι καὶ ἀδίκων, ἀλλὰ πιστικὸς μόνον (*Gorg.* 455 A 2 ff.).

if he is confronted by ἐπιστήμη. Socrates obtains Gorgias' admission that this is so in the following exchange:

Soc. You said just now that even about health the orator will be more convincing (πιθανώτερος) than the doctor.

Gor. Yes, so long as he is speaking to the mob.

Soc. But surely 'to the mob' amounts to saying 'to those who know nothing about the matter'? Presumably the orator won't be more convincing than the doctor before an audience of experts.

Gor. True.[1]

The reason for this is given later: 'what is true is never proved false'.[2] And if it be objected that ἐπιστήμη is not necessarily 'what is true', we may note that Socrates' reply to Polus' attempted ἔλεγχος is 'my dear Polus, you're trying to scare me; you're not proving me wrong, just as a moment ago you were summoning witnesses': we are back at 'particularity'.

The difference between πίστις and ἐπιστήμη (or μάθησις) is elsewhere expressed as being that between what is capable of being true or false and what is not so capable. πίστις can be both: ἐπιστήμη, it is agreed, cannot.[3] There can only be true ἐπιστήμη and consequently it is not the same as πίστις.

About its intrinsic character there is little more to be found in these early dialogues. We do, however, learn that it is concerned with values, in the practical sense of an ability to make value judgments about courses of action: 'Must not the doctor know (γιγνώσκειν)', says Socrates in the *Charmides*, 'when his treatment is valuable and when it is not?'[4] We see that ἐπιστήμη is somehow concerned with assessing the value of our various actions, not in the sense that a doctor, by virtue of his specific knowledge, can assess the medical value of different methods of treatment, but in a more important sense, the total inherent value of an action, considered from all points of view. In much the same way, a definition of ἀμαθία is given in the *Protagoras* in the following terms: 'Then you mean something like this by ignorance: having a false view (δόξαν), or being deceived about matters (πράγματα) of great importance?'[5] Here it is worth inserting a comment: this

---

[1] *Gorg.* 459A 1ff. [2] 473B 10f. [3] 454D 6f.
[4] *Charm.* 164B 7f. [5] *Prot.* 358C 4ff.

formula in the *Protagoras* is at first glance a clear statement of the 'intellectualist' theory of ἐπιστήμη, yet we should notice that δόξα is very often in Plato close in meaning to the use of δοκεῖν in the sense 'seem good', 'decide', and that πρᾶγμα is similarly derived from a verb (πράττειν) which is firmly set in the sphere of action, not theory. Even here, there is nothing which can outweigh what we infer from so many other passages, that ἐπιστήμη is intended by Plato to mean 'knowing *how*', not awareness of the (moral) facts of a situation, or of the world.[1] The value of ἐπιστήμη to Socrates lay in the fact that it implied the ability to live intelligently; it was distinguished from the more specific τέχναι not by any difference of 'subject-matter', but by an over-all greater significance in its field of expression: it is the only knowledge which is essential to happiness, because it represents, through its ability to balance good and evil, the capacity for *living* intelligently: 'Living knowledgeably (ἐπιστημόνως, i.e. knowing *that*, as the context indicates) is not what makes for happiness and genuine success (εὖ πράττειν τε καὶ εὐδαιμονεῖν), not even if one's life is based upon the knowledge that one knows all the other branches of knowledge: only one thing creates happiness, a life based on the sole knowledge that has to do with good and evil.'[2]

Because of this, and because of its inner certainty, ἐπιστήμη is universally trusted. In the *Lysis*, the fact that Lysis is not allowed to do exactly as he likes, though his parents certainly wish him to be happy, is traced back by Socrates to its true cause, Lysis' lack of knowledge. At present he is still unable to act with knowledge (intelligently): 'but when the day comes that your father thinks that you behave more sensibly than he (βέλτιον αὐτοῦ φρονεῖν), then he will give both himself and all he owns into your care'. The general conclusion is drawn later: 'This is how it is, my dear Lysis (I said); all those matters in which we behave sensibly (ἃ ἂν φρόνιμοι γενώμεθα) people will entrust to us, whether they are Greeks or barbarians, men or women, and in those matters we

---

[1] For a fuller discussion of the problem of apparent statements of the intellectualist theory in Plato himself, see below pp. 29f.

[2] *Charm.* 174B 12ff. For the interpretation of this difficult and almost untranslatable passage, see T. G. Tuckey, *Plato's 'Charmides'*, pp. 77f.

can do whatever we like.'[1] As I have indicated in translating, the knowledge that Lysis must wait upon for the attainment of full freedom is clearly enough the capacity to behave 'sensibly' (φρονίμως) and we may remember the earlier connection of φρονεῖν with action. Plato is still closer to his tradition than we, at our remove, can sometimes realize.

ἐπιστήμη, for Socrates, is ultimate; it depends on nothing superior for its value. Why he believed this to be so, we learn from an interesting passage of the Euthydemus. Socrates and Cleinias are providing a demonstration of constructive argument to set against the displays of eristic virtuosity given by the two sophists of the dialogue, Euthydemus and Dionysodorus. The subject of their discussion is happiness, which they are led to allow only to wisdom (σοφία, i.e. skill in matters of common life): 'Wisdom, then, everywhere gives men happiness. For wisdom can never fail to achieve its object; it must always succeed and always act correctly (ὀρθῶς πράττειν). Or it would no longer be wisdom.'[2] This last sentence raises a point which must sooner or later be considered in any discussion of Socratic ethics: are propositions such as 'virtue is knowledge', 'knowledge is the unfailing key to happiness' and the rest merely analytic? The argument of this section of the Euthydemus may be systematized as follows: wisdom never acts in error—absence of error entails happiness—therefore wisdom entails happiness. To decide whether this was in fact true or not, we might be tempted to investigate cases of σοφία and examine them to see whether σοφία ever did act in error. But a moment's reflection would show that this would in fact be quite irrelevant, since if σοφία were detected in error, 'it would no longer be wisdom'. The proposition is not, therefore, verifiable by any process of empirical investigation and appears to be merely a tautology. Yet the word 'merely' seems to beg the question: after a reading of the early dialogues, it cannot be doubted that Socrates' propositions are analytical, but to say this is not necessarily to damage his ethical theory. Mr D. J. Allan has remarked (concerning Thrasymachus' extremism in Book I of the Republic) that 'this is a good example of the danger which attends any attempt

[1] Lysis, 209C 5–210D 8.   [2] Euthyd. 280A 6ff.

to reverse the meaning of ethical terms. Ethics is like science in being an attempt to find order and system amid apparently unrelated facts; it is unlike science in having for its material the judgments and opinions of common men. It must take this material as it is, and may not alter it for the sake of a neat generalization.'[1] This judgment applies equally to the ethical theories which Plato inherited from Socrates, but it maintains an Aristotelian view of the subject which, in all probability, would not have commended itself either to Socrates or to Plato. As the passage from the *Protagoras* which I have already quoted clearly indicates, they refused to accept the 'popular' interpretation of moral situations. The ethical theories of both are intended to be more normative than descriptive, and the consequence of their refusal to adopt 'the judgments and opinions of common men' is that they are forced, on occasion, to do violence to the normally accepted significance of certain words, which in turn results in their being misunderstood by those who, like Mr Robinson, continue naturally enough to use these words in their normal sense. The proposition 'virtue is knowledge' is a disguised recommendation, a 'persuasive definition' (to adopt a phrase of Professor Stevenson);[2] like the other ethical propositions of Plato's dialogues, it is an attempted redefinition of ethical terminology, necessarily analytic. Provided, however, that we realize this, to say so is not to raise an objection to Plato's moral outlook: his redefinitions do us the service of making us reflect that the dimensions of our ethical thought are contingent, not necessary, and by setting before us a new description of moral situations, they represent, from the point of view of Socrates, more than half the battle, since the ἀμαθία against which he was fighting was not mental vacuity, but 'a false view of matters of great importance'.

Recognition of the fact that Plato is bound by the rejection of 'popular' ethics leads us to another point of importance which is made in the early dialogues. The man who possesses ἐπιστήμη is on a different moral plane from the rest of humanity. Without ἐπιστήμη, the majority of mankind dwells in a sort of twilight

[1] Plato, *Rep.* I (ed. D. J. Allan), pp. 29f.
[2] Charles L. Stevenson, *Ethics and Language*, ch. IX, especially pp. 224ff.

world of morals where real good and evil are unknown. Socrates in the *Crito*, waiting in prison for his execution, wishes that this were not so: 'If only, Crito, the majority of men *were* capable of doing the worst of evils, so that they might also be capable of the greatest of goods. Then things might be well. As they are, they can do neither; they cannot give a man understanding; they cannot rob him of it (οὔτε φρόνιμον οὔτε ἄφρονα δυνατοὶ ποιῆσαι); they merely do to us whatever occurs to them.'[1] Perhaps a remark of weariness, but there are indications that Plato at least was troubled by the ambivalence of 'knowing *how*'. Real evil, as much as real good, is beyond most men, for if ἀρετή is ἐπιστήμη, then it is not the norm, not the natural uncultivated possession of every man. Already, though any man may have the ability to gain it, ἐπιστήμη is outside the actual grasp of the majority of mankind. Yet to assert that ἀρετή results from the successful influence of environment and upbringing, as Protagoras seems to have done, was more than Socrates could admit. It would be to reduce ἀρετή, so the *Laches* seems to indicate, to the level of animal courage, an instinctive and irrational reaction to crises that demand more than instinct.[2]

The discussion of courage in the *Laches* raises, in a more acute form, a problem which we have touched upon before. Nicias suggests, developing Socrates' own view, that courage is not to be separated from σοφία. By σοφία, Nicias intends a comparison with practical aptitudes (τέχναι); but a comparison, not an identification. Courage is *like* knowing how to play the flute or the harp, but it is only like these: its sphere of action is different. It is defined as 'knowing what one must fear and what one may venture' (τὴν τῶν δεινῶν καὶ θαρραλέων ἐπιστήμην).[3] At this point we seem to pass abruptly from a description of knowing *how* to one of knowing *that* and it is noticeable that in the following discussion the word γιγνώσκειν appears several times. Yet Nicias insists that courage is only different from the recognized τέχναι in that it goes beyond them in scope. A doctor can know what is

---

[1] *Crito*, 44D 6ff.   [2] *Laches*, 196c ff.

[3] *Laches*, 194E 11f. The discussion of courage occupies virtually the whole of the *Laches*, but the suggestion that courage is ἐπιστήμη is introduced at 194c 6ff.

to be feared, *from a medical viewpoint,* but whether health is worth venturing upon at all is beyond his awareness, as a doctor. One general point must here be made: the distinction which I have used throughout this chapter is not, at least in the form in which I have adopted it, a distinction of Plato's own. It has been used largely as a tool of investigation, a heuristic method employed to fit together the pieces of the Platonic jig-saw puzzle into a new picture. We can hardly be surprised if it does not fit exactly. But the essential is this: whatever *description* Plato may offer of the workings of ἐπιστήμη, it is the *explanation* of its value that he adopts which alone can decide for us whether what he has in mind is knowing *how* or *that*. The question which we must ask is this: if and when it comes to the point, does Plato suggest that ἐπιστήμη is to be thought of as evinced *in* action, as a manner of acting, or as a prior state of mind upon which action follows? Is 'knowing' a manner of behaving or of thinking? From what we have seen so far and from what will emerge later, I believe that Plato would answer, however little in our terms: a manner of behaving.

CHAPTER II

MORALITY AS A TECHNIQUE

IN the previous chapter, I suggested that our traditional interpretation of Socrates' equation of ἀρετή with ἐπιστήμη rested upon a misunderstanding; particularly of the meaning of the latter word. This misunderstanding was merely a single instance of our mental habit of explaining intelligent practice in terms of theoretical (that is, intellectual) competence, a habit which almost unconsciously we carry back into our attempt to understand a world even so remote as Plato's. Plato himself, we saw, was clearly the inheritor of his tradition, and none the less so because, in dialogues which we have yet to examine, he took what was perhaps the decisive step in dissociating practical from intellectual ability, and by the time of the *Republic* at least was already troubled by the consequences of his own dissociation.[1]

One of the most significant indications of the meaning of ἐπιστήμη as Plato inherited it, was the traditional equivalence of that word with τέχνη. It was upon this equivalence, already built into the fabric of linguistic usage, that Socrates constructed his theory of moral ability, in suggesting that the practical competence of the professional craftsman was the ideal at which men in general should aim when faced with the moral problems of daily life.[2] But we find, already in the early dialogues, certain doubts expressed about the limits within which this analogy could be applied.[3] These doubts, and their solution, are to be the subject of

---

[1] See below, pp. 187f.

[2] Echoes of Socrates' theory are to be found in later philosophers who have been influenced by Plato: see, for example, Chrysippus, fr. 178 (Arnim, *Stoicorum Veterum Fragmenta*, vol. III, p. 43, especially l. 20); Plotinus, *Enn.* I, 6, 9.

[3] It is misleading to suggest, as Richard Robinson (*Plato's Earlier Dialectic*, p. 206) does, that Socrates *assumes* an analogy between moral virtue and technical skill. In so far as it is not embedded in the Greek language, Socrates *creates* the analogy.

the present chapter. Let me first give a general indication of their nature.[1]

The certainty of a craftsman is limited by several factors. There is firstly the limitation of object: his task is restricted by the need merely to achieve competence in the production of some specific *thing* (ἔργον). Moreover this limitation is not simply a restriction upon his efficacy; it affects the whole field of his interest. It is true, though obvious, that the builder cannot produce a shoe, or the sculptor a house. But in addition the whole horizon of a craftsman is bounded by the limits of his professional occupation; it is not his *business* to be capable of directing what should be done with the product of his skill. His is a professional competence both in the sense that it is specific, that is restricted by the concrete creative purpose to which his skill is geared, and in the further sense that the question of how his product should be used falls within the sphere of some further skill, which is in turn limited by the same factors as his own. But there is another, more important respect in which his technical ability, in so far as it can be restricted to his status as a professional, has a clearly marked horizon, beyond which he cannot, merely as a craftsman, be called to account. To take a concrete example: the skill of an expert in forgery who is employed by a bank to keep a check on attempts to misappropriate its funds, will in all probability make him capable of succeeding in the very attempt which he is employed to prevent, and it cannot strictly be regarded as a diminution of his *professional* ability if he should be tempted to use his skill in this way. Here, we shall see, lies the essential ambiguity or ambivalence of a professional ability.

The realization of these limitations is one which must follow readily enough upon a consideration of the notion of technical skill, and we are entitled to believe, in the light of passages to which we shall soon turn, that either Socrates or Plato was aware

[1] A thesis similar to that which I suggest in the following pages has, I discover, been put forward by two previous scholars: J. Hirschberger (*Die Phronesis in der Philosophie Platons vor dem Staate*, 1932) and J. Moreau (*La Construction de l'Idéalisme Platonicien*, 1939). I keep to my own statement merely because I believe my standpoint to be sufficiently different.

of them. At all events, in the early dialogues we encounter a successful attempt to rescue the idea of moral ἐπιστήμη or τέχνη from embroilment in these difficulties. Professor Moreau aptly summarizes this attempt: 'L'effort principal des dialogues socratiques consiste, après avoir établi la technicité de la vertu, l'avoir rangée parmi les compétences, à dégager sa spécificité radicale à l'égard de toutes les techniques, pour aboutir précisément à la notion d'un savoir pratique.'[1] He further specifies the difference between the desired moral τέχνη and the limited τέχναι of normal professional life: 'La moralité réalise dans l'activité totale ce que réalise chaque technique dans son champ d'action particulier; c'est l'idée de totalité qui absout la puissance de son ambiguité, de son caractère matériel, et l'égale au Bien en la soumettant définitivement à l'unité.'[2] To this effort towards defining the limits within which the τέχνη analogy is applicable we must now turn.

The first step must be to see what positive qualities in the idea of technical ability led Socrates to create the analogy. As immediately strikes one on reading the dialogues of Plato, the word τέχνη is of frequent occurrence, particularly in the early works.[3] The vast majority of these instances indicate that the word, as used by Plato, conveys approval, as it does in the phrase 'properly made' (τεχνικῶς εἰργασμένα).[4] This remains true, even though on at least one occasion[5] the word implies contempt and has all the connotations which βαναυσία, a term of disdain, so frequently has in Plato's writings. To get an idea of the tone of voice with which Plato uses the word, we may look at a passage where it conveys approval without being connected with ἀρετή and moral capability. In the *Laches*, Socrates is invited to join in a discussion which turns on the merits of learning to fight in armour from a

---

[1] Moreau, *Construction*, p. 57 n. 1. Cf. p. 85: 'C'est seulement parce que la compétence technique est la forme la plus notoire de la science, qu'il se contente, pour un premier aperçu, d'en rapprocher la moralité; la distinction des espèces de la compétence viendra ensuite.'   [2] Moreau, p. 200.

[3] Ast's list, which is far from complete, gives thirty-seven examples.

[4] *Charm.* 173 C 1. Cf. *Laws*, XI, 921 B 4f. and Solmsen, *Plato's Theology*, pp. 144, 148 n. 38.

[5] *Prot.* 312 B 3; cf. 318 E 1ff., *Symp.* 203 A 4ff. Another case of τέχνη as a term of disdain, though in a different sense, occurs at *Ep.* VII, 341 B 4; cf. Taylor in *Mind*, n.s., XXI (1912), p. 348.

professional teacher. He suggests that, in a matter of this sort, we need the advice of an expert: 'Surely we should first simply ask this question: Is one of us an expert (τεχνικός) on the subject we are discussing? If one of us is, we should forget the rest and be persuaded by him, even though he is only one; if not, we should look for someone else who is.'[1] τεχνικός in this passage clearly enough denotes what we would call an 'expert', the sort of man in any particular field whose opinion one would trust unreservedly. Such a man is likely to go about his tasks in a rational and dependable manner: his products will be 'properly made'.

Like ἐπιστήμη, τέχνη is not the possession of the majority of men: 'Is it the business of any man to decide what things are pleasant, and good, what are pleasant, but evil; or do we need an expert?' 'An expert', replies Callicles.[2] There are not many people that one will consult with confidence, but only a few specialized and rarely encountered individuals.

The confidence that we feel in the face of τέχνη derives as much as anything from a feeling that it is dependable, or rather rational and predictable. Unlike the statues of Daedalus, we feel we know what it will do next; we feel that it should behave consistently. In the *Ion*, for example, Plato draws a distinction on these grounds between τέχνη and poetical inspiration.[3] At one point τέχνη is equated once again with ἐπιστήμη, and in a manner which reminds us of the conclusion of the *Symposium*, it is argued that if poetry were founded solely on technical ability, there ought to be found no arbitrary divisions of poetical talent, either in creation or interpretation: 'It should be clear to anyone that it is not by some technical skill or knowledge that you are able to interpret Homer: if it was by means of technical skill, you would be able to interpret all the other poets as well. For it is all within the scope of poetry.'[4]

These characteristics—rational procedure, comparative rarity and dependability—are all attributes of technical ability in general. Socrates hoped that they would attach also to the moral ability which he established as his ideal. There is another significant

---

[1] *Laches*, 184E 11ff. Cf. *Crito*, 48A 5ff.   [2] *Gorg.* 500A 4ff.
[3] *Ion, passim*; but especially 533D 1ff., E 6, 536C 1ff., 542B 4.
[4] *Ion*, 532C 5ff. Compare *Symp.* 223C 6ff.; Xenophon, *Mem.* III, 4, 6.

attribute which, as Plato insists, should be assigned to τέχνη or ἀρετή within the terms of this analogy. It figures prominently in the *Gorgias*, where, as elsewhere,[1] moral decisions are said to require the application of a technique. It is there stressed very heavily that an essential element in the nature of technical competence is a serious concern for the welfare of the material upon which it works. The pretensions of rhetoric to be a matter of craftsmanship are at stake in this discussion, and in denying these pretensions Plato draws an elaborate distinction between technical ability, properly so called, and a mere knack (ἐμπειρία), which as the Greek word implies is the result simply of crude trial and error. 'I would assert that rhetoric is not a technique, but merely a knack, because it has no rational procedure whereby it employs its arguments, whatever their nature. And I cannot give the name of craft (τέχνη) to something, whatever it is, which is irrational.'[2] The attack on rhetoric in the *Gorgias* is a passage as violent as any in Plato's writings and is carried on in an atmosphere of extreme moral indignation. We reach the new emphasis on concern for the well-being of the subject-matter of a craft with the division of occupations (πραγματεῖαι) into two categories: κολακεῖαι, those whose aim is merely to arouse pleasure, irrespective of the result, harmful or beneficial; and τεχνικαί, 'which have some forethought for what is best where the soul is concerned'.[3] Consequently Plato confines the status of a technical ability to the work of a genuine philosopher, 'one who whispers with three or four kids in a corner', as Callicles contemptuously calls him.[4] The philosopher is one who both needs a technique as the basis of his moral judgments and, having realized the need, has acquired this technique. For it is agreed that it is not sufficient for a man not to want to do wrong;[5] if it were, there would be no wrongdoers. For justice something more is demanded, and this something is the moral competence which Socrates had heralded.[6]

---

[1] For example, *Crat.* 388 E 4f., *Alcibiades I*, 133 D 12 ff.; compare Xenophon, *Mem.* IV, 2, 2.

[2] *Gorg.* 465 A 2 ff. (the text of this passage is in dispute); cf. 463 A 6 ff., 504 D 5 ff.

[3] *Gorg.* 501 B 4f.   [4] *Gorg.* 485 D 7f.

[5] The question of βούλησις will be discussed in the next chapter.

[6] *Gorg.* 509 D 7 ff.

Earlier in this same dialogue, Socrates had given a general indication of the limits within which the analogy between justice and technical skill might be expected to work. Experts in various crafts, men who have learnt their trade, acquire the characteristics of that trade. 'A builder is one who has learnt the art of building, surely?'[1] This Gorgias agrees to be so, and in the cases of music and medicine also. Socrates then suggests that the analogy covers justice as well, so far as it goes:

Soc. So then it will be the same in the other fields, the man who has learnt a matter will become such as his skill (ἐπιστήμη) makes him in each case?

Gorg. Certainly.

Soc. According to this principle then, the man who has learnt justice (τὰ δίκαια) will be just?

Gorg. I entirely agree.[2]

We may find fault with Gorgias' delighted acceptance of this suggestion on logical grounds, but for our present purpose, what we must notice is that the significant element in this discussion is the phrase: 'a man becomes such as his skill makes him'. The possibility that there are differences between various types of technical ability as important as their common characteristics here appears for the first time, even though nothing is made of the possibility in the *Gorgias*.

So far then we have been dealing with the positive qualities which a skill confers on its possessor; we have not yet been brought up against the limitations from which Plato is at pains to extricate his ideal of a moral competence. We now turn to a group of three dialogues which we have not so far noticed in detail: they are the *Charmides*, *Hippias Minor* and the first book of the *Republic*. They are not frequently discussed in connection with one another, but they have at least one thing in common: they may all be termed Plato's 'problem plays'. All three have been the subject of many attempts to determine their real significance.[3]

---

[1] *Gorg.* 460 B 1 ff.   [2] 460 B 4 ff.

[3] In discussing *Republic* I at this point, I am not committing myself to the view, which is not mine, that it is an independent dialogue of Plato's youth: it is considered here purely for the sake of convenience.

The *Charmides*[1] has been interpreted in a puzzling variety of ways. Professor Taylor believed 'that serious examination of the implications of the current conceptions of *sophrosyne* conducts us straight to the two famous Socratic "paradoxes" of the unity of virtue and its identity with knowledge of good',[2] while Constantin Ritter saw in it the first attempt to disengage the intention of an action from its consequences: 'By carefully considering some of the conclusions of the *Charmides* we arrive at the result that we are not to judge the external consequence of an action as moral, but rather the will alone.'[3] These ideas are indeed contained in the dialogue, but the true aim of the work has been indicated by Professor Cornford: 'What Plato now undertakes is a subtle and searching investigation... with a view to explaining what the dark saying "Virtue is Knowledge" meant and what it did *not* mean. He has in view the significance of this central doctrine of Socrates and of the Socratic method of examination.'[4]

The subject of the discussion in the *Charmides* is σωφροσύνη, and after Charmides himself, the young centre of attraction at the gymnasium where the conversation takes place, has made several attempts at definition, a suggestion is put forward and clearly attributed to Critias,[5] another of the conversationalists. The suggestion is that σωφροσύνη is the same as 'minding one's own business': it is amended to 'doing good',[6] and finally to 'knowing oneself'.[7] This latter step is taken because it has been pointed out that without some such awareness of his own actions and their consequences, a doctor, for example, may do good (and hence, under the current definition, act with σωφροσύνη) without in-

---

[1] The late Mr T. G. Tuckey's book *Plato's 'Charmides'* appeared after this chapter was first written. On reading it, I did not feel any necessity to change my general interpretation, though in a more detailed account I would have made use of his valuable arguments. I have added references to his book where this seemed useful.

[2] A. E. Taylor, *Plato: the Man and his Work*, p. 57.

[3] C. Ritter, *The Essence of Plato's Philosophy*, p. 45.

[4] In a course of lectures on the *Charmides* delivered at Cambridge. Cf. Tuckey, *op. cit.* p. 17.

[5] *Charm.* 161 B 8f., 162 B 10f. and Critias' intervention on behalf of the theory; also Tuckey, *op. cit.* p. 20.

[6] *Charm.* 163 E 10.   [7] *Charm.* 164 D 4.

tending to do so. The amended definition is in accordance with the advice of Delphi: 'Know thyself', and this in effect means σωφρόνει, says Critias: [1] it is a piece of advice rather than the greeting for which it is usually taken. Two questions are now raised and continue to be the subject of attention throughout the rest of the dialogue: What is the object of such knowledge? and What is its use?

Socrates' first objection turns on the fact that if this form of ἐπιστήμη is assumed to be akin to other forms, it is unique in having no ἔργον (concrete product). Critias replies to this that Socrates is on the wrong track: 'the nature of this knowledge is not the same as that of other forms'.[2] There is, we now see, a limit to the validity of the analogy between σωφροσύνη and productive techniques. This warning should not be taken to mean, as Professor Taylor understands it, that the distinction here is between theoretical and practical forms of knowledge;[3] σωφροσύνη is far from having 'no further end than the perfecting of itself'. It is the first hint, the first of many, that we are at last brought up against the inherent limitations of a specific professional skill, and therefore of the analogy between moral skill and such techniques. The first distinction indicates that moral skill has no tangible product, such as the production of buildings or health. Has it then some object of attention external to itself, as numbers are in the case of arithmetic? No, Critias replies; here again we have come upon a distinguishing mark of σωφροσύνη: 'your inquiry has brought you up against the very thing which marks off self-control from every other skill (ἐπιστήμη)'.[4] Socrates accordingly points out that there is no other mental activity which is self-regarding. Yet its apparent uniqueness is not allowed to rule out this theory of the nature of σωφροσύνη: 'It will certainly be strange if it exists after all, but we should not yet insist that it does *not* exist. We must still pursue the inquiry into whether it does.'[5] This remark is characteristic of the *Charmides*. Throughout the dialogue apparently conclusive disproofs of the theory that σωφροσύνη is a

---

[1] Compare Plutarch, *De E apud Delphos*, 392A 4ff.
[2] *Charm.* 165E 3f.   [3] Taylor, *Plato*, p. 53.
[4] *Charm.* 166B 7f.   [5] *Charm.* 169A 3f.

form of skilled mental activity are set aside: this in itself should make it clear that the main purpose of the work is to mark off those respects in which the τέχνη analogy cannot be literally applied to the field of moral decisions. For, behind all these conclusive disproofs, lies the premise that σωφροσύνη is analogous, *exactly and in all respects*, to other techniques.

It is now agreed that two things, so far, mark off σωφροσύνη as a form of skilled ability from other skills: the facts that it possesses no concrete product (ἔργον) and acknowledges no external field of objects. It is next pointed out that σωφροσύνη, as self-knowledge, is, alone among mental activities, a relation to itself. That is to say, it is both relative and correlative; as knowledge, it both knows and is known. 'It possesses, then, its own function towards itself':[1] to admit the possibility of this would need, Socrates asserts, a greater than himself, but this objection too is shelved and we pass to a discussion of the *usefulness* of σωφροσύνη, as we have defined it. Once again the argument turns on the assumption that σωφροσύνη *is* on all fours with other varieties of technical ability. On this assumption it proves to be useless. First, since it does not acknowledge a specific field of external objects on which to exercise its function, it will recognize the *state* of knowledge, but the *facts known* will lie outside its range. Thus to make any use of its power of recognizing knowledge and ignorance, σωφροσύνη must be combined with some other professional competence, in the normal sense. Only *qua* expert (in the normal sense, i.e. doctor, builder, etc.) can I know ἅ οἶδα; *qua* σώφρων I know merely ὅτι οἶδα.[2] 'Well then, unless a man has the additional advantage of skill in the field of health or justice; if, that is, he can only recognize the *state* of knowledge (since that is where his skill lies, in detecting knowledge and realizing that *something* is known), this is all he *will* recognize, both in his own case and in that of others. ...With an ability such as this, how can he know what it is that he detects?'[3] (i.e. what is the subject-matter of the state of knowing that he recognizes).

---

[1] *Charm.* 169A 3 f.
[2] Tuckey has well pointed out the fallacies of this argument (pp. 54 ff.).
[3] *Charm.* 170B 6 ff.

The mere σώφρων, therefore, is quite unable to detect the pretensions to specialist knowledge of would-be doctors, for example. 'Well, Critias', asks Socrates, 'what benefit could accrue to us from "self-control" such as this?'[1] It could indeed have no use for us on these terms. It is agreed by all present that σωφροσύνη could only be valuable to us, defined as it now is, if we assumed the possibility of a super-expert in every sort of technical competence, who might then direct a Wellsian utopia of departmentalized efficiency: however, 'no such ability has anywhere appeared'. Within the restricted sphere of some one technique this situation might occur, but the narrow scope of such an ability makes it impossible for us to conceive of σωφροσύνη as something on these lines.

As a super-expertise, there seemed some value in σωφροσύνη. But Socrates now inquires whether, even so, it would do us any good.[2] He suggests we might endow our hypothetical expert with complete knowledge of happenings past, present and future, and make him efficient indeed, without being any the happier. The reason for this conclusion is that σωφροσύνη will still be subject to the limitations of the notion of technical skill, being merely an aggregate of such skills. Happiness, which is beyond the competence of individual techniques (in the normal sense), will still be beyond that of σωφροσύνη, *qua* technique. There is only one form of knowledge that can secure us happiness, as we saw in the last chapter: 'that which has to do with good and evil'.[3] All the various skills can operate *efficiently*, within their restricted spheres, without this knowledge; but with its disappearance disappears also their overall value and usefulness, as guides towards happiness in general life.

This picture, revealed only for a moment, of a unique skill in matters of good and evil, vanishes almost at once, though it is, as all commentators have seen,[4] the real end of Socrates' search.

---

[1] *Charm.* 171 D 1 ff.
[2] Plato's super-skill and his reception of it reminds us of Heraclitus' πολυμαθίη and his well-known comment on it: DK 22 B 40; cf. also the following fragment.
[3] *Charm.* 174 C 2 f.
[4] Except perhaps Professor Grube, *Plato's Thought*, pp. 218 f.

Though we are told no more of it here, it is clear now in what respects it must be sought outside the orbit of techniques, as they are usually understood.

This conclusion is now masked by Plato in pointing out almost disingenuously that this 'knowledge of good and evil' does not correspond to σωφροσύνη as we have defined it: the latter is still without value. Our search, says Socrates, must have been somehow misdirected, since the conclusion that σωφροσύνη is useless is manifestly absurd.[1] We are now in a position to assess the purpose of the *Charmides*. As Professor Cornford has remarked of Plato's method in this dialogue, 'he [Plato] is putting into Socrates' mouth his own study of Socrates' central doctrine'.[2] The result of this study is apparently negative, as so often in these early dialogues, but by comparing it with the conclusion of another such dialogue we may be aided in arriving at the conclusion that Plato intends to mask. In the *Laches*, the investigation of the nature of courage is abandoned when courage has been equated with that knowledge of good and evil which is moral virtue as a whole. Courage has lost its status as merely a part of moral virtue; the inquiry is therefore agreed to have gone astray. It is, of course, universally recognized that we should conclude from this apparent setback in the *Laches* that the point at which we have in fact gone astray lies in assuming that courage *is* only a part of virtue: the conclusion of the discussion conflicts with this premise: we must therefore abandon one or the other.

In the *Charmides*, as we have seen, the conclusion stands that σωφροσύνη, if we regard it as some specific form of technical skill and apply the analogy quite literally, will be entirely useless. It should, I think, be abundantly clear that the implication we should discover in this is that the analogy between techniques and morality cannot be applied to the letter, at least in the respects which we have seen discussed in the *Charmides*. Only by regarding the technique of morality as standing to some degree outside the bounds set for the professional arts and crafts can it retain its value.[3]

---

[1] *Charm.* 175 A 9 ff.   [2] In a Cambridge lecture.

[3] On the opposition between 'les Valeurs' and the idea of a technique, see Goldschmidt, *Les Dialogues de Platon*, pp. 101 f. Cf. also pp. 59, 66 n. 4, 67 *ad init.*

In the second of our group of three dialogues, Plato turns his critical attention to the limitation of ambiguity or ambivalence which besets the notion of a technique. The *Hippias Minor* is by no means so complex or intricate a work as the *Charmides*, but in some ways it has proved as puzzling. Professor Taylor comments: 'On reflection we see that the key to Plato's meaning is really supplied by one clause in the proposition which emerges as the conclusion of the matter: "the man who does wrong on purpose, if there is such a person, is the good man". The insinuation plainly is that there is really no such person as "the man who does wrong on purpose" and the paradox does not arise simply because there is no such person.'[1] This we may readily accept, since it contains a point which, as we shall see in the next chapter, Plato frequently makes. But we should be mistaken in thinking that this is all that the *Hippias Minor* implies. There is more in the dialogue than a rather laboured joke.

Socrates questions Hippias on the merits of the characters of Achilles and Odysseus, and Hippias replies that Achilles is the finer character, being straightforward and upright, where Odysseus is wily and resourceful.[2] Yet it is the latter, as Socrates points out, who relies on knowledge for his ability to deceive: only knowledge could give a would-be deceiver the certainty of achieving his purpose. This is clearly true, for example, in the case of arithmetic: we cannot be sure of giving the wrong answer to a sum, without knowing what the right one is.[3] Socrates declares this to be the case with all techniques.[4] But Hippias naturally resents the application of this dictum to the case of Achilles and Odysseus: 'But, Socrates, how can men who willingly do wrong, willingly plot against others and commit injustices be better than those who do these things unwittingly?'[5] Socrates, however, points to the

---

[1] Taylor, *Plato*, p. 37.

[2] A point worth remarking on is that Hippias is himself the exponent of technical virtuosity (*Hipp. Min.* 368 B–E) and that Socrates attacks him on a question of *value*: 'Is Achilles *better than* Odysseus?' See Moreau, *Construction*, p. 102. Note also that Odysseus is said to possess φρόνησις (365 E 4 ff.); this is certainly not Socratic φρόνησις. Cf. 368 E 5.

[3] *Hipp. Min.* 366 E 3 ff.   [4] *Hipp. Min.* 368 A 8 ff.

[5] *Hipp. Min.* 371 E 9 ff.

case of running; a good runner is one who runs slowly only when he wishes to do so, not involuntarily, because he can run no faster. Similarly with parts of the body, tools 'and everything else that has to do with techniques and skills; in each case, the better is that which behaves wrongly, or unsuitably, or fails in its aim, only of set purpose; the worse is one which does these things because it cannot do otherwise'.[1] If we apply our rule to justice, then, which is 'a capacity (δύναμις)...or a skill or both',[2] it will be the part of the just man to do wrong on purpose, since this is the characteristic of capacities and skills. We must conclude that the good man is 'one who goes astray on purpose, who acts shamefully and unjustly on purpose...if such a man exists'.[3]

Neither Socrates nor Hippias can accept this conclusion; but neither can they suggest a way out. The Socratic irony has triumphed. Yet, as usual, we are shown when Socrates is being ironical; it is then up to us to look beyond the irony and inquire *why* it has triumphed. Repeatedly Socrates indicates that it is the 'argument' (λόγος) that is forcing him into these uncomfortable positions: 'I hold the previous arguments responsible for our present situation.'[4] Somewhere, perhaps, we have made a mistake. Professor Taylor, as we saw, suggested that this consisted merely in assuming that there can be such a person as a voluntary wrongdoer. In Plato's own view, this is, of course, true, and the assumption that it is untrue lies behind part of the present perplexity. But as in the case of the *Charmides*, something more is being brought out. The argument of the *Hippias Minor*, which Socrates 'holds responsible' for the unsatisfactory conclusion, is only cogent if we assume that morality as a technique is open to the same charge of ambivalence as technical skill in general.[5] This ambivalence of professional competence consists in its ability to be used for good *or* bad purposes: 'The same man then is best capable of giving the right *or* the wrong answer in matters of calculation. And this man is whoever is good at these matters, the

---

[1] *Hipp. Min.* 375 B 8 ff.   [2] *Hipp. Min.* 375 D 8 f.
[3] *Hipp. Min.* 376 B 4 ff.
[4] *Hipp. Min.* 372 E 3 f.; cf. 375 D 5, 376 B 8 ff.
[5] See Moreau, *Construction*, p. 107.

expert arithmetician.'[1] Clearly it would make nonsense of Socrates' conception of a technique of morality, if we were to suppose it capable of this sort of ambivalence; yet if ἀρετή is to act only towards what is right (as it must), we must abandon, in using the technique analogy, yet another connotation of the notion of skill. There can be no occasions where the moral 'technician' will wish to break the canons of his craft, as there might conceivably be in the case of other experts.[2]

From the *Charmides* and *Hippias Minor*, we have found that Plato saw two principal errors in pressing too far home the analogy between morality and the idea of a technique. Morality is not to be tied to the specific objective that distinguishes most skills from one another, nor is it to be allowed to remain subject to the destructive ambivalence which is another of the hall-marks of a technique. These two points are made once again in the first book of the *Republic*. The *Republic* is concerned with justice: it is not therefore surprising that the subjects we have seen discussed in the *Charmides* and *Hippias Minor* recur in the introductory part of the conversation.

After the departure of Cephalus, the idea brought forward for discussion arises out of a quotation from Simonides, 'that it is just in all cases to repay what one owes'.[3] This is equated with doing harm to one's enemies and good to one's friends. Yet the person most competent to do this, as having the necessary ability, will not be the just man, but various experts; the doctor, the ship's captain and the like. In war (an 'untechnical' matter, it is implied) the just man, *qua* just, will perhaps be useful, but in peace he is useful only as the incorruptible guardian of idle money; once it is to be put to some use, we need an expert in some department of commerce to make effective use of it. 'And in any other field, (mere) justice is useless when anything has to be put into use,

---

[1] *Hipp. Min.* 367 C 2 ff. We should note that this passage indicates another way in which ἀρετή may easily be equated with τέχνη—the use of ἀγαθός to mean 'good at', and indeed the usage of ἀρετή itself. Cf. Pindar, *Pyth.* I, 41; Plato, *Apol.* 18 A 5 f.; *Protagoras* 318 C 3 ff., 322 D 7; *Alc.* I, 133 B 7 ff., *Lach.* 194 D 1 ff., *Laws*, I, 637 D 3 ff.

[2] Compare Aristotle, *Eth. Nic.* 1129 a 11 ff., where the same point is made.

[3] *Rep.* I, 331 E 3 f.

and only useful when whatever is in question lies in disuse.'[1]
Then again, the expert at preservation will always be the one most
able to inflict damage; the policeman may always make a good
thief. Thus the just man, being good at keeping money safe,
will also be good at 'converting' it.

These arguments in *Republic* I seem not to have been given any
real measure of attention; they have been dismissed as fallacious,
even as merely frivolous. For our present purpose, however, we
are concerned not so much with their cogency as with Plato's
reasons for putting them forward, which were surely serious
enough, in spite of the slighting references of scholars. Cornford,
for example, opens his summary of the next section with the
remark: 'The argument now becomes more serious.'[2] Mr D. J.
Allan, in his edition of the first book, has more to say. On Plato's
first point, he comments: 'From these consequences Polemarchus
could have escaped, broadly speaking, in either of two ways: he
could have stated firmly that it [justice] was in no sense a kind of
knowledge focused on a special object, i.e. he could have refused
to admit the analogy of the arts: or, allowing it to be comparable
to an art, he could have said that it exercised a regulative function
in respect to the other arts, and therefore had no special province
of its own.'[3] Mr Allan suggests that Plato chooses the second form
of escape from his difficulties, but from our discussion of the
Charmides it has become clear, I think, that Plato in fact chose the
first. As to the second of the two arguments in *Republic* I,
Mr Allan, like other commentators, is silent, believing it to be
fallacious, which we may admit. Yet bearing in mind the *Hippias
Minor* here, we may agree that Plato's *intention* in using it was to
make clear that the technique of morality cannot be allowed to
fall foul of the limitation of ambivalence.

From these three dialogues, the fact seems to emerge with some
clarity that Plato has himself subjected the notion of a possible
technique of morality to a severe examination, giving particular

---

[1] *Rep.* I, 333 D 10f.
[2] Cornford, translation of the *Republic* of Plato, p. 11. Adam's note and
appendix, in his edition of the dialogue, is similarly disdainful.
[3] D. J. Allan, *op. cit.* p. 23.

attention to those limitations which were sketched in at the beginning of this chapter. He has, as the outcome of this examination, set the limits within which the analogy of a technical certainty may validly (or usefully) be applied to the solution of problems which the moral decisions of daily life may raise. On the positive side of the analogy is the ability which it conveys of stressing the need for a rational, dependable and predictable technique for coping with these problems, as against the normal irrational and haphazard approach.[1] Where he is not so sure of the value of Socrates' analogy is in the vexed matter of restricted scope and ambiguity of application which is characteristic of the very idea of a technique as it is commonly understood. No technique of morality can afford to allow the establishment of these limits.[2]

[1] It is worth noticing that the necessity for a serious concern with the real welfare of the subject (see above, p. 35) is also stressed at *Republic* I, 342 A ff.; cf. 346 E 3 ff.

[2] M. B. Foster, in his book *The Political Philosophies of Plato and Hegel* (pp. 21 ff.), also argues that Plato abandoned the strict analogy of a technique in the *Republic*, but for different reasons. The analogy requires a firm distinction between the craftsman and the matter on which he works. The craftsman can never work on himself. Yet the Guardians in the *Republic* do just this; they are, that is, themselves part of the threefold division of classes which it is their duty, as political craftsmen, to enforce. This suggested abandonment would also remain merely implicit. See further, *op. cit.* pp. 31 f. and App. A and B (pp. 36 ff.).

CHAPTER III

PURPOSE AND IMPULSE

Celui qui n'agit pas comme il pense, pense imparfaitement. GUYAU

IN this chapter we shall be concerned chiefly with some remarks in Plato's works concerning the verbs βούλεσθαι and δύνασθαι and their respective nouns.[1] These remarks reveal the existence, in Plato's philosophy, of a theory of what Professor Cornford calls 'the true self',[2] and shed light on the Socratic paradox 'no one does wrong on purpose' (οὐδεὶς ἑκὼν ἁμαρτάνει). In general, it may be said that here, as elsewhere, Plato's verbal usage strains the natural (or better, inherited) meaning of words, and is intended, since he scrupulously avoids the formation of 'technical terms', to throw light upon his ideas by the creation of new, yet not rigidly 'technical', meanings.

Towards the beginning of the *Lysis* there is a simple discussion, which may serve as our introduction to this subject.[3] Socrates asks Lysis whether his parents love him dearly, and, when he replies that they do, and also wish him to be happy, inquires further whether they allow him to do what he wants.[4] Not at all, says Lysis; they most certainly deny him many of his wishes. And yet, as it transpires, things which his parents will not allow Lysis to do, they will permit some servant, and even pay him, to do them. More extraordinary still, they place him under the supervision of a slave in his everyday life, and at home his mother punishes him if he tries to have his way with her weaving. Lysis

---

[1] The use of the noun βούλησις in the exact meaning to be discussed in the present chapter is Professor Cornford's rather than Plato's, though it is used in a somewhat similar sense at *Gorg.* 467 A ff., *Charm.* 167 E—as against ἐπιθυμία— etc. (Cf. Aristotle, *Eth. Nic.* III, 4 ff.) A reflection of its use in this meaning is perhaps to be found in the Academic Ὅροι: Βούλησις ἔφεσις μετὰ λόγου ὀρθοῦ· ὄρεξις εὔλογος· ὄρεξις μετὰ λόγου κατὰ φύσιν (413 C 8 f.).

[2] *Cambridge Ancient History*, vol. VI, p. 306.   [3] *Lys.* 207 D 1 ff.

[4] ὧν ἐπιθυμοῖ: *Lys.* 207 E 2, but in E 6 this has become ἃ βούλει: nothing can be argued from the language of this passage.

suggests that he is not yet old enough to be allowed these privileges: however, as Socrates points out, in some things this is evidently not the case. If he wishes to read or write, no one stands in his way. Perhaps the reason is that about these things Lysis has some knowledge. This explanation Socrates accepts and amplifies, as we have already seen.[1]

Apart from what has been said of this passage elsewhere, we find in it also the germ of those ideas which we are now to discuss. It is assumed, at the beginning of the *Lysis*, that, for happiness, one requires the ability to do as one wishes, and the paradox is that Lysis' parents, while presumably wishing him to be happy, do not allow him this freedom. But is such a licence, in fact, essential to happiness? Elsewhere Plato insists, even in the earliest dialogues,[2] that the object of one's desire is what is really good and that, consequently, only a man who knows what is really good can interpret, and therefore attain, his fundamental purpose.

In the first *Alcibiades*, the former point is made in its simplest and most obvious form. '"Which would you prefer to have, good things or bad?" "Good things." "And presumably the greatest goods at that, and of these you would least allow yourself to be robbed?" "Of course."'[3] There is nothing untoward here: the object of a man's desire is what is good (for him), good being interpreted without any moral connotations, since these are not required for this stage of the argument.[4] The terminology is slightly different in the *Euthydemus*, where the point is made again: '"Success (εὖ πράττειν), then, is what we all want? Or is that one of those absurd questions which I was fighting shy of just now? I suppose it is rather pointless even to ask such questions. For who does not want success?" "No one", said Cleinias.'[5] The proposition is still not in doubt and might be accepted by anyone. All that has so far been suggested is that every man is bent on his real happiness: it is also implied, as we shall see later on, that a man may be in error as to where his real happiness lies.

[1] Pp. 26f. above.   [2] E.g. *Alcibiades I.*
[3] *Alc. I*, 115 c 9 ff.
[4] It is worth noticing that the ἐπιστήμη ἡ περὶ τὸ ἀγαθόν τε καὶ κακόν of *Charm.* 174 c is not understood by Critias as having a moral sense.
[5] *Euthyd.* 278 E 3 ff.

But at present, the thesis may be taken to mean that each man is aiming at what he supposes to be best for him. This essential notion of a guiding belief as to where one's interest lies is introduced towards the end of the *Protagoras*. No one, says Socrates, willingly aims at what he believes to be bad:[1] indeed such a proceeding is contrary to human nature, 'to be willing to aim at what one feels is bad, instead of what is good'.[2] Moreover, in the event of an enforced choice between two evils, no one will choose the greater, while the opposite choice is open to him.

The end of every action is our real happiness, and we act, not at random, but because in each instance we feel it better to act in one way rather than another. This further suggestion is advanced in the *Gorgias*. Socrates asks Polus: 'Do you think men really want what they achieve in their various day-to-day actions, or do they want what they believe to be the (ultimate) aim of these actions?'[3] The conversation is continued with reference to such actions as taking medicine, undertaking commercial voyages and the like. When we go for a walk, for instance, we do so because we think it better for us,[4] and conversely, if we stand still, it is with the same end in view, our own good. In the *Lysis*,[5] it is pointed out that the value which we attach to things depends very much on their use in gaining what is ultimately dear to us.[6] Finally, this whole side of the argument is summed up in the *Laches*: 'In a word, then, when we pursue something only because of some further aim, our real purpose is directed at that *further* aim, not at the thing we are pursuing only because it is a means to another end.'[7] There is, then, in our actions an aim beyond the immediate end of each step we take, which is the real object of our whole activity, namely our own good.

---

[1] ἑκὼν ἔρχεται (*Prot.* 358 C 6 ff.).   [2] *Prot.* 358 D 1 ff.

[3] πότερον οὖν σοι δοκοῦσιν οἱ ἄνθρωποι τοῦτο βούλεσθαι ὃ ἂν πράττωσιν ἑκάστοτε, ἢ ἐκεῖνο οὗ ἕνεκα πράττουσι τοῦθ᾽ ὃ πράττουσιν; (*Gorg.* 467 C 5 ff.).

[4] οἰόμενοι βέλτιον εἶναι (*Gorg.* 468 B 2).

[5] *Lys.* 219 D 2 ff.

[6] ὃ ὡς ἀληθῶς ἐστι φίλον (*Lys.* 219 D 4 f.).

[7] οὐκοῦν ἑνὶ λόγῳ, ὅταν τίς τι ἕνεκά του σκοπῇ, περὶ ἐκείνου ἡ βουλὴ τυγχάνει οὖσα οὗ ἕνεκα ἐσκόπει, ἀλλ᾽ οὐ περὶ τοῦ ὃ ἕνεκα ἄλλου ἐζήτει. (*Lach.* 185 D 5 ff.).

This desire for our real happiness, which stands at the core of our being, is what Professor Cornford has termed our real self: he connects it with Socrates' views about the primacy of our soul over our body, which we shall be discussing in the next chapter. It is our 'true' self because the desires which we have for the good of our body or of body and soul combined are not desires for our real good, since neither of these is really one's self: only the soul can be so described.[1] It is this belief in the inherent faculty of every man to seek out and pursue his real good that is the fundamental and characterizing feature of the ethics of these early dialogues.

These conclusions, however, do not preclude a man's acting under a misapprehension of his real good: he *possesses* always the ability to apprehend correctly, but he may in fact often be mistaken. It is with the introduction of this idea, and its corollary, in Plato's works, that violence begins to be done to the normal usages of language. The passage in question is in the *Gorgias* and follows the agreement (quoted earlier) that we have an aim in all our actions beyond the immediate purpose: '"Here's another point, then: if someone kills another, thinking it will be better for him so, and in fact it is worse, I suppose such a man is doing what he thinks fit?" "Yes." "But is he also achieving his purpose, if he is actually doing what is bad for him? Why do you hesitate?" "All right; I *don't* think he's achieving his purpose."'[2] The matter at issue here is the suggestion that, if a man takes some step which is actually contrary to his own best interests, he is not only mistaken, as anyone might agree, about his own good, in supposing that this is not so, but is also failing to carry out his own wishes, since these are directed at his *real* happiness. Plato does not agree that such a man is fulfilling some mistaken wish: rather he is not fulfilling his wish at all, since he is deceived as to the object of his desire. 'He is doing what he thinks fit' but not 'achieving his purpose.' Once again the apparent paradox is reached by straining the sense of

---

[1] *Alc. I*, 130 C.

[2] οὐκοῦν...εἴ τις ἀποκτείνει τινά...οἰόμενος ἄμεινον εἶναι αὐτῷ, τυγχάνει δὲ ὂν κάκιον, οὗτος δήπου ποιεῖ ἃ δοκεῖ αὐτῷ· ἦ γάρ; ναί· ἆρ' οὖν καὶ ἃ βού- λεται, εἴπερ τυγχάνει ταῦτα κακὰ ὄντα; τί οὐκ ἀποκρίνῃ; ἀλλ' οὔ μοι δοκεῖ ποιεῖν ἃ βούλεται. (*Gorg.* 468 D I ff.).

words, by making the proposition 'he is not achieving his purpose' in large measure merely analytical. And yet there is clearly in this theory some measure of truth (in addition to a considerable measure of illumination). For any of us might well agree that if it could be shown that his actions did not tend towards his own advantage, he would admit that he was not, in fact, doing what he desired to do. This is an important point, for it leads, as we shall see, to another famous paradox: οὐδεὶς ἑκὼν ἁμαρτάνει.

The next stage, however, in our reconstruction of Plato's argument, must be one which seems to follow closely in Plato's own mind on the last, and occurs at the beginning of the same discussion of the *Gorgias*. Socrates, in his conversation with Polus, makes the surprising statement that political orators are powerless.[1] Powerless, that is to say, if by power we mean something of value to the man who possesses it. The power of politicians, like that of dictators, lies, according to Polus, in their ability to put to death, rob or exile whom they wish.[2] But Socrates draws the distinction which we have just examined, between their wishes and their suppositions about the advisability of various actions.[3] Being fundamentally at fault in the latter, they cannot achieve the former: real power is beyond them, since it implies the ability to attain their real purpose, their true happiness.

We can now apply this new point to that passage of the *Lysis* which we discussed at the beginning of this chapter.[4] It appeared there that Lysis was unable to fulfil his wishes: as we saw, in reality it was only his whims of the moment that he could not satisfy. And we can now also see that his apparent lack of power was equally only illusory: his power was as great as that of any citizen in society, where the control exercised over him does not preclude his achieving his real happiness. He is only prevented from doing ὅτι ἂν αὐτῷ δόξῃ βέλτιστον εἶναι, not from attaining ἃ βούλεται.

We have now examined the characteristics of βούλησις, as they are expressed in Plato. Before we go on to review the corollary

---

[1] *Gorg.* 466B 4f.
[2] οὓς ἂν βούλωνται (D 1), but ὃν ἂν δοκῇ αὐτοῖς (D 2f.).
[3] ὧν βούλονται and ὅτι ἂν αὐτοῖς δόξῃ βέλτιστον εἶναι (E 1f.).
[4] *Lys.* 207D 1ff.

of this theory, there is one additional suggestion to be made. We have noted the close connection everywhere in Plato between what we tend to regard as mental states, and action: as regards βούλησις, how does the good man, in the strict sense, differ from his fellows? Clearly from what has been already said, the aim of their βούλησις is the same—their true happiness. The former, however, has succeeded in fulfilling his fundamental desires, the latter has not. We may understand this, I think, as follows: whatever a man may believe to be the aim of his actions, his own valuation of various modes of life, his views are, in fact, made clear to us by what he actually does. Thus a man may declare himself bound by the Ten Commandments, but when we see him act, we can see, for instance, that instinctively he sets material gain, when it can be attained without disgrace and punishment, above the commandment 'Thou shalt not steal'. Generally we should comment that, although he *knew* that his real happiness lay in fulfilling his moral obligation, the temptation was too great for him. Plato, however, would, it seems, argue that to interpret his moral situation in this way is meaningless, since ἐπιστήμη, as we have seen, is expressed only in action. Thus the actions of such a man would appear to him ἀμαθία, a failure of moral capacity, indicating that he had not, in fact, attained ἐπιστήμη. The ascent in morality is expressible not only in terms of a man's conscious ethical commentary on life, but also in terms of his quasi-instinctive reactions to the situations which confront him. The moral man reacts invariably in a way which enables him to attain the end which he fundamentally desires, his happiness. In him, and in him alone, ἃ βούλεται and ὅτι ἂν δόξῃ βέλτιστον εἶναι are united: what he desires is what he does. This ability to react instinctively, and, as it might appear to us, unconsciously, even irrationally, to various moral situations is as much an essential in the content of Socratic-Platonic ἐπιστήμη as the explicit and conscious formulae which might express a man's intellectual attitude towards the same situations.

We may conclude our survey of the concept of βούλησις and its significance with a summary of what is said in these early works about the notorious ethical stumbling-block of οὐδεὶς ἑκὼν ἁμαρτάνει. First, the texts. The doctrine appears, fully fledged, even in the earliest stages of Platonism and is, indeed, almost universally attributed to Socrates himself. We have already seen (pp. 42 f.) that the idea lies behind part of the paradoxical impasse with which the *Hippias Minor* closes. It is also prominently found in Socrates' commentary on the poem of Simonides in the *Protagoras*.[1] In the *Gorgias*, it is referred to as agreed between the disputants.[2] In the same dialogue, it appears to be already the basis of a joke.[3]

Aristotle's comment on the theory is well known. He refers to the idea, and attributes it explicitly to Socrates, in Book VII, chapter 2, of the *Nicomachean Ethics*, where he is discussing ἀκρασία, as he terms the failure to obey moral obligation.

We may well be puzzled to know how it is possible for a man to fail in self-restraint, when he believes correctly that he is wrong to do so. Indeed there are those who claim that, if he *knows* he is wrong, the thing is impossible. Socrates, for example, thought that it went against the grain to suppose, when knowledge (ἐπιστήμη) is present, that some other motive force can overpower it and drag it around like a slave. Socrates himself, of course, was completely adamant in his denial of the idea, in the belief that the phenomenon 'lack of self-restraint' did not exist; no one, he argued, acts against his own best interest (πράττειν παρὰ τὸ βέλτιστον), if only he knows it to be so, but simply through ignorance (ἄγνοια). However, we can see that his account is at variance with the accepted facts of the case.[4]

It should be now clear that as criticism this is wide of the mark, but it may be well to analyse the meaning of the theory for Socrates and Plato. It was not their purpose, as later critics have made clear, to deny τὰ φαινόμενα, that is, to deny that people claim *video meliora proboque, deteriora sequor*. Such claims are envisaged in Plato's works,[5] but they are argued to be misleading.

---

[1] *Prot.* 345 D 6 ff.

[2] μηδένα βουλόμενον ἀδικεῖν, ἀλλ' ἄκοντας τοὺς ἀδικοῦντας πάντας ἀδικεῖν (*Gorg.* 509 E 5 ff).

[3] εὖ ἴσθι τοῦτο ὅτι οὐχ ἑκὼν ἁμαρτάνω, ἀλλ' ἀμαθίᾳ τῇ ἐμῇ (*Gorg.* 488 E 3 f.). The doctrine may also be echoed in the *Apology* (37 A 5 ff.), though I am inclined to agree with Burnet's note on this passage.

[4] Aristotle, *Eth. Nic.* 1145 b 21 ff.   [5] E.g. *Prot.* 352 A 8 ff.

The moral ἐπιστήμη which such people have in mind is a jumble of moral maxims, threats and bribes, which are the accompaniment of conventional education from childhood upwards. Such a combination of baseless discipline with parrot-like moral 'scholarship' has nothing in common with Socratic-Platonic ἐπιστήμη, which is a capability of the whole personality, determining action, in such a way that a reversal of its dictates is inconceivable.

The meaning of οὐδεὶς ἑκὼν ἁμαρτάνει is that, according to the notion of βούλησις which we have been studying in this chapter, everyone is bent on his own real good: in this field above all, reality is the demand of every man. If, then, someone is found acting in error and doing wrong, it is argued that this implies, not that his moral certainty has been overcome, but that in some way he has never achieved that sureness about his own best interest which must inevitably direct his actions (since it is only recognizable by this trait) along the right road.[1] The fault lies, not in the weakness of his 'will', but in his failure, owing to inadequacy of moral upbringing or self-education, to orientate his moral capabilities towards their true goal.

To argue thus, however, is not to say with Professor Taylor that 'bad moral conduct is therefore in all cases ignorance, intellectual error',[2] since we have already seen that ἐπιστήμη is something other than merely the conscious body of knowledge usually signified by the word. As we shall see when we reach the *Symposium*, progress in morality is emotional as well as intellectual, covers the whole extent of the personality. ἀκρασία, for Plato, is precisely the absence of a sure and personal spiritual driving-force, which, certain of its direction and foundation, is the spring of action in the really moral individual. Such a force is no more intellectual, no more emotional than faith.

We may end this chapter by reference to a passage of doubtful validity as evidence, since the dialogue in which it occurs, the *Cratylus*, seems more like parody than exegesis. Among the words for which a derivation is suggested in that dialogue is τὸ ἑκούσιον.

[1] The basic meaning of ἁμαρτάνειν is, of course, to miss one's aim.
[2] Taylor, *Socrates*, p. 141.

τὸ μὲν οὖν 'ἑκούσιον', τὸ εἶκον καὶ μὴ ἀντιτυποῦν, ἀλλ', ὥσπερ λέγω, εἶκον τῷ ἰόντι δεδηλωμένον ἂν εἴη τούτῳ τῷ ὀνόματι, τῷ κατὰ τὴν βούλησιν γιγνομένῳ.[1] The punning derivation may be intended humorously but perhaps the joke was suggested by Plato's beliefs. In any case, it serves as an illustration of them: for an action to be 'voluntary', it must be 'in accordance with one's purpose' (κατὰ τὴν βούλησιν). Conversely, the following derivation of 'necessary' (ἀναγκαῖον), connecting it with ἄγκη, describes it as 'contrary to one's purpose, so that we can define it as failure or ignorance'.[2] Here, then, we see combined, both the reason for Plato's refusal to allow that ἁμαρτία can be ἑκοῦσα, since it is παρὰ τὴν βούλησιν, and the use of the word βούλησις in that restricted sense, which this chapter has attempted to clarify.

[1] *Crat.* 420D 5ff.
[2] παρὰ τὴν βούλησιν ὄν, τὸ περὶ τὴν ἁμαρτίαν ἂν εἴη καὶ ἀμαθίαν (D 8f.).

CHAPTER IV

THE CHARACTER OF SOCRATES

τίς τῆς τοιαύτης ἀρετῆς, τῆς ἀνθρωπίνης τε
καὶ πολιτικῆς, ἐπιστήμων ἐστίν;
PLATO, *Apology*, 20B

UN Socrate qui n'eût été qu'un dialecticien plus habile eût bien
joui de quelque vogue. Il n'aurait pas retenu. Un Socrate
uniquement théoricien, philosophe au sens actuel du mot,
eût pu fonder une école proprement dite, s'attacher un petit nombre
d'élèves. Son influence ne se serait pas étendue à des esprits aussi divers
que Platon, Antisthène, Aristippe. Il n'aurait pas eu de prise sur
l'ensemble des jeunes gens qui, certes, n'avaient pas tous le goût des
raisonnements. Socrate ne dut cet empire qu'à ce qu'il fut *ami de la
sagesse*, φιλόσοφος. Il la pratiquait lui-même. Il avait le droit d'en
parler. L'usage de la vertu conférait à ses propos l'accent qui force.
Il savait toucher les âmes.[1]

So Father A.-J. Festugière approaches the question of Socrates'
influence on the youth of Athens. What sort of person was
Socrates? If we could only answer that question, we might come
near to grasping as a whole that outline of ethics various facets of
which we have been considering, since if not demonstrably
Socratic in itself, it is clearly more closely under his influence than
are the ethics of Plato's later dialogues. Obviously a complete
answer is impossible, but by examining some of the literary evidence,[2] we may be able to fill in the larger gaps in our picture.

---

[1] *Contemplation selon Platon*, pp. 68f. I should like to acknowledge here my
indebtedness to Festugière's stimulating chapter 'La vie intérieure' (*Contemplation*, pp. 61ff.).

[2] With care, however. Aristotle seems rightly to be out of favour as an
interpreter of Plato; cf. Frutiger, *Les Mythes de Platon* (p. 62): 'Le Stagirite est
un piètre exégète de l'œuvre de Platon; si nous le choisissons pour guide, nous
sommes assurés de commettre bien des bévues.' Cf. Cherniss, *Riddle of the
Early Academy*, pp. 30, 50–9. For Xenophon's accuracy, we may compare
Mem. II, 6, 35 with *Rep.* I, 335D 11f. and *Crito*, 49ff. As additional support, or
on uncontroversial matters, they may be useful.

Of the dialogues which come within the scope of this first section, five close with an exhortation,[1] which most frequently takes the form of a recommendation to persevere in the search for truth even in the face of doubt and difficulty. The despair of ever reaching a satisfactory conclusion, which would otherwise be the final note of these works, is thus explicitly set aside in favour of a determination to go further and pursue the investigation, into self or truth: 'a human life which is not submitted to the test of inquiry is not worth living'.[2] Socrates seeks always, not to accept the appearance, whether it is encouraging or dispiriting, but to arrive finally at something solid and satisfactory, which has withstood all tests of investigation. Yet, if his habit of 'irony' led Aristotle to accord him charm and a tendency to disclaim creditable characteristics,[3] it has been for others the mark either of empty frivolousness (so that a dialogue such as the *Protagoras* can be dismissed as a mere joke) or even of deceitfulness and disingenuousness.[4] The evidence is difficult to assess with an open mind and must appear to interpreters according to their several dispositions: it seems, though, certain that Socrates' aim was indeed serious throughout,[5] and the sense of urgency which appears to fill some of the discussions in these dialogues must be the genuine reflection of his own continual inquiry.

Socrates might, like Kierkegaard, have claimed to be a 'tortor heroum': no idea, however generally received, was safe from his ἐξέτασις. As a typical example of his reaction to the conventional, we may take his attitude to moral education. The *Protagoras*, a dialogue whose formlessness has often been exaggerated, contains a fairly full discussion of this topic. Socrates insists that, if ἀρετή is to be ἐπιστήμη, then it must be taught. Yet there are no teachers. Protagoras, who will not agree to this, claims that everyone is a capable instructor in morality: 'instruction and admonition begin from the earliest days of one's childhood and continue

---

[1] *Laches, Charmides, Euthydemus, Crito, Gorgias.*

[2] ὁ δὲ ἀνεξέταστος βίος οὐ βιωτὸς ἀνθρώπῳ (*Apol.* 38 A 5 f.).

[3] Aristotle, *Eth. Nic.* 1127 b 22 ff.

[4] Cf. Plutarch, *Adv. Colot.* 1117 D: πῶς γὰρ οὐκ ἀλαζόνες οἱ Σωκράτους λόγοι, μηδὲν αὑτοῦ εἰδέναι φάσκοντος, ἀλλὰ μανθάνειν ἀεὶ καὶ ζητεῖν τἀληθές;

[5] Cf. *Crat.* 413 A 1 ff., especially ἅτε λιπαρὴς ὢν περὶ αὑτοῦ.

throughout life'.[1] All take part, 'one's nurse and mother, one's slave attendant (παιδαγωγός), even one's father'. Protagoras goes on to say that education takes the form of indications that this or that action is right, of threats, commands and blows. No comment is passed on this description and it is perhaps difficult to see that Socrates is rejecting it as a real moral training, since it might seem to the majority of us to be an accurate account of what in fact happens. If, however, we notice such an obviously satirical passage as that in the *Crito* where Socrates compares the punishment meted out by the people of Athens to the threats given to children,[2] we may see in what light he viewed the conventional notion. We have already seen what he himself believed to be the nature of true ἀρετή, and we shall later consider how it is to be attained. His view of the sophists was in the main scornful. In particular, he often ridicules the disparity between their claims and their performances. He was shocked that they, the most conventional of all moralists, should claim to teach ἀρετή, 'because of the magnitude of the claim'.[3] Nor can they substantiate their claim by the evidence of saintly pupils: 'After all, the sophists, though they may be clever enough in other ways, do have one odd effect. They claim to be instructors in morality; yet they are often found accusing their pupils of criminal behaviour for not paying their fees, or failing to make some other return for the good they have received at their hands.'[4] The sophists were false prophets: Socrates himself was a true rebel, not a stage rebel, since he understood himself what he was rebelling against and had, moreover, a firm doctrine to stand in its place.

His disregard and contempt for convention is to be linked with his belief in the primacy of the spirit. Since Professor Burnet's well-known lecture on the 'Socratic Doctrine of the Soul',[5] it has been accepted perhaps without due attention that the care of one's soul was Socrates' principal teaching.[6] It is as well to realize that

---

[1] *Prot.* 325 C 5 ff.; cf. *Apol.* 24 D 9 ff., *Prot.* 319 A 10 ff.

[2] *Crito*, 46 C 4 ff.: ἡ τῶν πολλῶν δύναμις ὥσπερ παῖδας ἡμᾶς μορμολύττηται, δεσμοὺς καὶ θανάτους ἐπιπέμπουσα καὶ χρημάτων ἀφαιρέσεις.

[3] *Euthyd.* 274 A 3. [4] *Gorg.* 519 C 3 ff.

[5] *Proc. Brit. Acad.* (1915–16), pp. 235 ff.

[6] Cf. *Apol.* 29 D 2 ff.

such a teaching is only one part of Socrates' insistence on the primacy of the spiritual in every form. In the first *Alcibiades*, the question is asked: 'what does caring for oneself really mean?'[1] It is eventually answered by: 'I suppose either the phrase is meaningless, or if it has a meaning, then we must assume that a man is simply his own soul.'[2] From this follows the need for tending one's soul, but the doctrine itself depends upon Socrates' reversal of the normal scheme of values: 'One does not achieve man's true stature (ἀρετή) by virtue of money; rather money and every other human good, both personal and collective, by virtue of having attained the true stature of a man.'[3] Socrates, in his own life, combined a flamboyant zeal for living with a hardihood and contempt for pleasure which struck forcibly all who knew him.[4] 'It is not being alive that one should value most, but making a proper *use* of being alive';[5] this dictum was rigorously applied to all his thinking. Values became altered and things depended on their use for their real worth: the emphasis falls throughout on how one acts, not on what one acts with.

'In fact, to sum up, Cleinias', I said, 'perhaps we were wrong about all those things we first said were goods. We said they were goods in themselves, but it looks as if the truth is more like this: if they are in the control of ignorance (ἀμαθία), then they are worse evils than their opposites, since they are the more capable of achieving the aims of the mind that directs them, which is evil; on the other hand, if they are controlled by wisdom in their application, they are greater goods, but neither they nor their opposites have any positive value in themselves.'[6]

There are, then, for Socrates only two values, one good (σοφία), one evil (ἀμαθία),[7] since only these can affect the plane on which

---

[1] *Alc. I*, 127E 9.   [2] *Alc. I*, 130C 2ff.   [3] *Apol.* 30B 2ff.

[4] Cf. *Symposium*, speech of Alcibiades, and compare Xenophon, *Mem.* 1, 2, 1.

[5] *Crito*, 48B 5ff.

[6] ἐν κεφαλαίῳ δ', ἔφην, ὦ Κλεινία, κινδυνεύει σύμπαντα ἃ τὸ πρῶτον ἔφαμεν ἀγαθὰ εἶναι, οὐ περὶ τούτου ὁ λόγος αὐτοῖς εἶναι, ὅπως αὐτά γε καθ' αὑτὰ πέφυκεν ἀγαθά, ἀλλ' ὡς ἔοικεν ὧδ' ἔχει· ἐὰν μὲν αὐτῶν ἡγῆται ἀμαθία, μείζω κακὰ εἶναι τῶν ἐναντίων, ὅσῳ δυνατώτερα ὑπηρετεῖν τῷ ἡγουμένῳ κακῷ ὄντι, ἐὰν δὲ φρόνησίς τε καὶ σοφία, μείζω ἀγαθά, αὐτὰ δὲ καθ' αὑτὰ οὐδέτερα αὐτῶν οὐδενὸς ἄξια εἶναι. (*Euthyd.* 281D 2ff.) The whole discussion (280ff.) is in this vein; cf. also *Crito*, 46B 1ff.

[7] *Euthyd.* 281E 3ff.

right or wrong living is possible, the spiritual. To Zalmoxis, in the *Charmides*, is attributed this same fundamental doctrine: 'for he asserted that everything depends on the soul (ἐκ τῆς ψυχῆς ὡρμῆσθαι), things both good and bad, whether of the body or of the whole man';[1] and it is, of course, as important for Plato as for Socrates.

Following upon this essential primacy of the spiritual, comes Socrates' insistence on the importance of the Delphic greeting 'Γνῶθι σεαυτόν'. After Socrates' question in the first *Alcibiades* has been answered, the discussion is pursued into the meaning of the Delphic inscription itself, for only by understanding it can one attain to that proper care of oneself which is the agreed aim: 'Easy or not, Alcibiades, our situation is such that only by understanding this, can we perhaps understand what we mean by "caring for ourselves"; if we don't understand it, we shall never achieve the larger understanding.'[2] The biggest obstacle in the way of achieving this self-knowledge was the supposition in the minds of most men that they had achieved it already: for Socrates was once again establishing a new value for a concept that had become so familiar that it ceased to be an object of serious consideration. Regarding the outside world from a settled position of confident superiority had become the 'normal procedure': 'in fact, it looks to me as though you are falling foul of what I suppose is the truly human failing: you are not examining yourself, you are merely keeping an eye on the rest of the world.'[3] But this form of deception is the most dangerous possible,[4] and responsible for the majority of our mistakes in action.[5] Hence comes the usual form of Socratic 'irony', a disclaimer of real knowledge and wisdom, or at the least, a reduction of his wisdom to a claim to be free from this particular sort of self-deception: 'I feel that to this degree at least I am a wiser man, in that I do not even suppose myself to know what I do *not* know.'[6] Like Kierkegaard once again,[7] he ridicules the self-satisfied attitude of the average man in

---

[1] *Charm.* 156E 6ff.   [2] *Alc. I*, 129A 8ff.
[3] *Lach.* 200A 8ff.; cf. Xenophon, *Mem.* III, 7, 9.
[4] *Crat.* 428D 3f.   [5] *Alc. I*, 117D 7ff.; cf. 133D 5ff., 134A 2.
[6] *Apol.* 21D 6f.   [7] Cf. especially the Preface to *Fear and Trembling*.

a position of importance, and claims that to be driven out of such a position is itself a great benefit; great because to be mistaken in matters of moral import is the worst evil.[1] Refutation, then, is a gain,[2] but not one likely to appeal to most men, as Socrates himself found out. Covering his own moral earnestness with a façade of humour and satire,[3] he ran the risk of having the former quality overlooked entirely, and the satire used for its own ends, as indeed seems to have happened. Xenophon comments on his life as a whole, that he was 'capable of turning men towards the pursuit of moral excellence and uprightness'.[4] But in many cases the method of irony seems to have been its own downfall: the Athenians adduced the examples of Critias, Charmides and Alcibiades as evidence that the tendency of Socrates' teaching was indeed δια-φθείρειν τούς νέους. Xenophon's answer is to point to Socrates' own life: he was the true example of all that he taught ('...he said that his life had been made up of only one activity, namely a perennial inquiry into what was just, what unjust, and a perennial pursuit of justice and revulsion from injustice: this, he believed, was the best defence he could prepare'),[5] and we may suspect that Plato's answer would have been the same.

There is also evidence, however, that the aggressive habit of questioning all accepted ideas was tempered by a unique sense of duty. Socrates' attitude at his trial has seemed to some dishonest and priggish, but there is a remarkable passage in the *Crito* which gives us the background to this difficult question.[6] Plato makes him say, in the *Apology*: 'that injustice and the refusal to follow what one's moral superior, be he man or god, dictates, is evil and no true part of our nature (κακὸν καὶ αἰσχρόν), I am convinced',[7] a statement which might be taken in many ways, but the *Crito* gives us the sense in which it is meant. Crito, in a last attempt to rescue Socrates on the day before his execution,[8] had suggested that it would be easy to escape. After some arguments which we

---

[1] *Gorg.* 458 A 8 f.
[2] *Gorg.* 461 A 3.
[3] Cf. Xenophon, *Mem.* I, 3, 8; IV, I, I.
[4] ἱκανὸς καὶ προτρέψασθαι ἐπ' ἀρετὴν καὶ καλοκαγαθίαν (Xenophon, *Mem.* IV, 8, II).
[5] Xenophon, *Mem.* IV, 8, 4.
[6] *Crito*, 50 ff.
[7] *Apol.* 29 B 6 ff.
[8] *Crito*, 43 D 2 ff.

shall consider next, Socrates supposes that the laws of Athens, and the common good, come to debate with him. The argument which they bring forward is that Socrates has, in effect, made a contract[1] with them by the very fact of his having lived under their auspices for many years and enjoyed the various benefits which they are able to confer. Throughout this time, it has always been possible for him to leave the community in protest against the laws. But Socrates has never done this. He never left the city, even for a festival, but stayed and brought up a family: so that it is only now, when the laws' decision has gone against him, that he thinks of leaving the sphere of their jurisdiction.[2] Socrates agrees that these arguments are binding on him. If this passage represents Socrates' own arguments, or at least Plato's considered explanation of his actions,[3] it portrays a man uniquely conscientious with regard to his moral obligations.

In the same strain is his earlier argument (repeated in the Republic: οὐκ ἄρα τοῦ δικαίου βλάπτειν ἔργον, ὦ Πολέμαρχε, οὔτε φίλον οὔτ' ἄλλον οὐδένα, ἀλλὰ τοῦ ἐναντίου, τοῦ ἀδίκου),[4] that injustice is wrong even in requital or as a means of self-protection. Involving, as it must do, harm for those upon whom it is used, it cannot be right: οὐδὲ ἀδικούμενον ἄρα [δεῖ] ἀνταδικεῖν, ὡς οἱ πολλοὶ οἴονται, ἐπειδή γε οὐδαμῶς δεῖ ἀδικεῖν.[5] Again Socrates' moral earnestness is almost unparalleled, and was unacceptable even to some of his own associates.[6]

We have considered, in the preceding chapter, the meaning of Socrates' dictum οὐδεὶς ἑκὼν ἁμαρτάνει. This has proved perhaps the most unacceptable of all the Socratic 'paradoxes', as they have been called. We may suspect, however, that much of the hesitation that commentators have exhibited in face of the saying, springs from their fear that the doctrine seeks to evade moral responsibility. Such an idea is entirely false; indeed the notion of punish-

[1] ἤδη φαμὲν τοῦτον ὡμολογηκέναι ἔργῳ ἡμῖν ἃ ἂν ἡμεῖς κελεύωμεν ποιήσειν ταῦτα (Crito, 51 E 3 ff.).
[2] It is interesting to note also that another of the laws' points rests upon the disagreement between Socrates' conversation and his practice (Crito, 53 E 6f.).
[3] Cf. Croiset (Budé ed.), p. 215.   [4] Rep. I, 335D 11f.
[5] Crito, 49B 10f.
[6] Xenophon, Mem. II, 6, 31.

ment and its value plays a large part in Socratic-Platonic ethics. If we are to judge by the *Gorgias*, his views on this subject were as much suspect among his hearers as the other doctrine has been among modern commentators.

The criminal, by his crime, creates an irremediable burden of evil which renders him incapable, not only of any communion with the gods or his fellow men, but even of any stable relation with himself: 'In such a man there can be nothing to attract another man, nothing to make him a concern of god: he has nothing in common with either, and where there is nothing in common, there can be no affection.'[1] His ἀκοσμία places him outside the universe itself, since it is essentially κοινωνία that holds all together, and the universe is not called κόσμος for nothing.[2] This theme of the absence of coherence in evil natures is recurrent in Plato. It is the substance of an argument against Thrasymachus in the *Republic*,[3] and in the *Lysis* it is what distinguishes good men from evil: '...good men have much in common with one another (ὁμοίους εἶναι ἀλλήλοις) and can share affection; but evil men, as the saying indeed goes, have no common goal even with themselves· they are half-mad and utterly without stability'.[4] The burden of evil is inescapable: yet, without punishment, it is greater still. Punishment enables the criminal to repay to the universe in some measure his theft in siding with the forces which stand contrary to its own tendency. 'My own view, Polus, is that the criminal, the unjust man, is in any case to be pitied (ἄθλιος), but the more so if he does not requite his crime, if he pays no penalty for what he has done, and less so if he does pay such a penalty, to god and man.'[5] Yet, for all that punishment is necessary for the criminal, so that Socrates advises him to go to a law-court as one would in illness to a doctor,[6] its necessity is to be regretted, it appears, at least in the case of whoever must carry it out.[7]

---

[1] οὔτε γὰρ ἂν ἄλλῳ ἀνθρώπῳ προσφιλὴς ἂν εἴη ὁ τοιοῦτος οὔτε θεῷ. κοινωνεῖν γὰρ ἀδύνατος, ὅτῳ δὲ μὴ ἔνι κοινωνία, φιλία οὐκ ἂν εἴη (*Gorg.* 507 E 3 ff.).

[2] See J. P. Maguire in *Yale Classical Studies*, x (1947), p. 160 n. 33.

[3] *Rep.* I, 351 C 7 ff. [4] *Lys.* 214 C 6 ff.

[5] *Gorg.* 472 E 4 ff. [6] *Gorg.* 480 A 6 ff.

[7] *Gorg.* 469 A 9 ff.

The myth which concludes the *Gorgias* repeats in persuasive and emotional language the teachings of the rest of the dialogue. Here the purpose of punishment is declared to be twofold: 'One of two things should properly happen to a man justly punished by another: either he should gain the benefit of his own better state, or he should serve as an indication (παράδειγμα) to others.'[1] The division occurs because only in certain cases can punishment effect any improvement in the soul under punishment. Some souls are so burdened with evil as to be incurable: '...to prevent the disease of evil becoming chronic and leaving the soul beyond cure, a prey to hidden and festering sores'.[2] It is of these souls that examples are made, since nothing more beneficial is possible for them, so seriously meant were Socrates' words: 'There is something more to be pitied than a body ridden by disease: companionship with a disease-ridden soul, a soul rotted away by injustice towards god and humanity.'[3]

The reality of Socrates' emotion when faced with the ultimate problems of ethics is not to be doubted. His passionate longing for τὸ ἀγαθόν is as real as another man's practical attachment to the pursuit of wealth, power or sexual success. The doctrine of ἔρως, which reaches its culmination in the *Symposium*, appears first, in a disguised form, in the *Lysis*, certainly a 'Socratic' dialogue. Socrates explores the psychology of φιλία and places its cause in the consciousness of a lack or need.[4] Man, a creature placed between good and evil, is filled, by the onslaught of evil, with a longing for what is good, to redress the balance of his precarious existence. What is completely evil cannot long for what is good,[5] but there is an intermediate state in which the presence of evil affects us with ἔρως for the good.[6] It may even be that it is the presence of evil that gives to the good a value for us that it would not otherwise possess: 'Is it perhaps part of the

[1] *Gorg.* 525 B 1 ff.; cf. *Gorg.* 477 A 5 ff.
[2] ...ὅπως μὴ ἐγχρονισθὲν τὸ νόσημα τῆς ἀδικίας ὕπουλον τὴν ψυχὴν ποιήσει καὶ ἀνίατον (*Gorg.* 480 B 1 ff.); cf. (in the myth itself) 525 C 1 ff.
[3] ἀθλιώτερόν ἐστι μὴ ὑγιοῦς σώματος μὴ ὑγιεῖ ψυχῇ συνοικεῖν, ἀλλὰ σαθρᾷ καὶ ἀδίκῳ καὶ ἀνοσίῳ (*Gorg.* 479 B 7 f.).
[4] *Lys.* 217 ff.   [5] *Lys.* 217 B 7 f.
[6] *Lys.* 217 E 4 ff.

very nature of the good that we desire it by contrast with evil, we who are midway between good and evil? Perhaps in itself it is without value?'[1] But, whatever the cause, the reality of moral ἔρως is certain, and its psychology is explained in this dialogue in a way which makes it clear that ethical inquiry was second nature to Socrates.

There is one further subject which merits discussion, before this chapter can be concluded: it is the theory of the unity of the virtues. It is one of the best-known elements in the ethics of the Platonic dialogues, but some scholars have been doubtful about its attribution to Socrates. Professor Cornford refers to it as a consequence of the rest of Socrates' ethics 'which may or may not have been drawn by Socrates himself'.[2] The evidence is indeed slender: the doctrine certainly occurs in this first group of dialogues, since it figures prominently in the *Protagoras*, where it is established principally by means of fallacious arguments.[3] It is also the cause of the ἀπορία at the close of the *Laches*, where the coincidence of σοφία with ἀνδρεία leaves the disputants in perplexity. For what it is worth a remark of Xenophon's may be said to corroborate the attribution, since it does not seem likely to have been invented by him.[4] He remarks, in the course of a series of definitions in Book III of the *Memorabilia*, 'he [Socrates] made no distinction between σοφία and σωφροσύνη,'[5] which is consistent with the tone of such a dialogue as the *Charmides*. If a decision on this topic must be made, it seems only probable that the idea should have occurred to one who thought as deeply as Socrates on the subject of ethics. 'You will find any number of men who are marked by the height of injustice, who cause revulsion in gods and men alike, who are plunged in the most violent of passions and in the depths of ignorance, yet remain outstanding for their personal courage',

---

[1] ἆρ' οὕτω πέφυκέ τε καὶ φιλεῖται τἀγαθὸν διὰ τὸ κακὸν ὑφ' ἡμῶν, τῶν μεταξὺ ὄντων τοῦ κακοῦ τε καὶ τἀγαθοῦ, αὐτὸ δ' ἑαυτοῦ ἕνεκα οὐδεμίαν χρείαν ἔχει (*Lys.* 220D 4ff.).

[2] In his unpublished Lowell lectures, *Socrates and Plato*, pp. 42ff. Dodds (*Irrational*, p. 198 n. 34) is more positive in assigning it to Socrates.

[3] *Prot.* 329C ff.   [4] Xenophon, *Mem.* III, 9, 4.

[5] The possibility of plagiarism of Plato must be borne in mind; see Marchant (Loeb ed.), p. xvii.

says Protagoras;[1] but this is not an idea likely to appeal to such a thinker as Socrates. The theory of the unity of ἀρετή springs from much the same sort of inquiry as its identification with ἐπιστήμη, since the idea that a man may be pre-eminent in one virtue, while equally conspicuous for his lack of all the rest, must seem to place a curious meaning on the word ἀρετή. ἀρετή, for Socrates, is clearly something which must affect a whole personality. Its presence in a man may override the apparent sterilities of argument, since it stands beyond them;[2] true ἀρετή is complete and whole. Its unity seems, in this light, a simple and immediate deduction from its nature.

If we are to find our way in Plato to an understanding of his ethical development from its foundation in Socratic ideas, it can only be by grasping a firm distinction between the characters of the two protagonists.[3] That such a distinction is apparent would be widely agreed, but to define it is to invite disagreement. Since, however, it may be profitable, I will, by way of summarizing the conclusions of this first section, indicate what I believe to be the essential character of Socrates' approach to philosophy, and the differences between it and Plato's.

I have tried hitherto to show that the fundamental factor in Socratic thinking was not, as some commentators have felt, intellectual, but a quality of faith, of faith in the ability of the individual to attain a 'technique' of morality, and to achieve the practical assurance that the possession of a technical skill alone can give. A simple, even naïve faith perhaps, yet for all that subtly worked out and, because of Socrates' own apparent forcefulness, uniquely demanding attention. His aim in philosophy was to seek for certainty and assurance, not wholly of logic, but a principle of action, firmly founded upon an idealized competence. The emphasis on practice, the effect of urgency, the deliberate irony, the heightened, almost unattainable values attached to ethical concepts—all these seem real parts of his character. It is a character which seems, with modifications, to have recurred in thinkers and

---

[1] *Prot.* 349D 6ff.   [2] *Charm.* 176A 1ff.
[3] A comparable distinction is Festugière's between 'discours' and 'esprit' (*Contemplation*, p. 73 n. 2).

writers of a later date.¹ From the very first, there seems to have been general agreement that his effect had been to make philosophy an intensely human affair.² This is, indeed, an exact comment on a man for whom life was primarily moral, not intellectual, or aesthetic. To say that it was religious is again true, though Socrates' religion seems also to have been largely individual,³ a unique mixture of agnosticism and belief. He is portrayed definitively by his own final message: 'I assure you, gentlemen, that it is not death which is inescapable, but depravity (πονηρία) far more so: depravity is hotter in pursuit.'⁴

Even to sketch the differences between such a personality and Plato's is difficult and might properly be postponed to a later place. For the present, a few points must suffice. It is, I believe, a mistake to regard Plato's attitude to philosophy as not also moral and protreptic, even in his final period. But there was in him, in addition to an ever-present aristocratic ethos, an intellectual and aesthetic element foreign to Socrates, so that the theory of Forms, though first and foremost a framework for ethical certainty, is the outcome also of a systematic, scientific and even partly artistic, creative curiosity. In this he looks forward to Aristotle, the author of a system de luxe, but in his moral preoccupation he looks back also to Socrates, who stood out in his mind, not merely as creator of a theory of conduct, but, more emphatically perhaps, as himself the witness to his own faith, 'the finest, most intelligent, and moral, man of his generation'.⁵

¹ Especially, I would suggest, Kierkegaard, whose character seems most clearly to approximate to that of Socrates. But we may perhaps find parallels in the urgency of Dostoievsky, and the impossible values of Kafka.

² Cf. Xen. Mem. I, 1, 16; IV, 7; Arist. de Part. Anim. 642a; Cicero, Tusc. Disp. V, 10; Plutarch, De Gen. Soc. 582B 10f. (...Σωκράτους, ἀνδρὸς ἀτυφίᾳ καὶ ἀφελείᾳ μάλιστα δὴ φιλοσοφίαν ἐξανθρωπίσαντος), and see Pohlenz, Die Stoa, vol. I, pp. 194-5; vol. II, p. 10.

³ Cf. Xenophon, Mem. I, 3 with Plato, Apol. 42A 2ff.

⁴ ἀλλὰ μὴ οὐ τοῦτ' ᾖ χαλεπόν, ὦ ἄνδρες, θάνατον ἐκφυγεῖν ἀλλὰ πολὺ χαλεπώτερον πονηρίαν· θᾶττον γὰρ θανάτου θεῖ (Apol. 39A 6ff.).

⁵ Phaedo, 118A 17f.

PART II

THE ETHICAL SOCIETY

πολιτεία γὰρ τροφὴ ἀνθρώπων ἐστίν,
καλὴ μὲν ἀγαθῶν, ἡ δὲ ἐναντία κακῶν.

PLATO, *Menexenus*, 238c 1f.

CHAPTER V

THE APPROACH TO A FINAL POSITION

ὁ λόγος... νόμος ἐπιχειρῶν γίγνεσθαι.
PLATO, *Laws*, VIII, 838 B 4 f.

I N this and the following chapters, I shall set by the side of the ethical philosophy of Socrates, which we have been investigating, a sketch of the views put forward by Plato in his final mood of resignation, in the *Laws*. The purpose of this conjunction of the two extremes of his intellectual development is to make apparent the great differences between them, and the distance traversed in moving from one to the other: how and why this development occurred it will then be our task to discover. But before this outline can be begun, something must be said about the *Laws* as a whole.

The *Laws* represents the cadence to the parabola of Plato's intellectual history, and it has thus been only natural to see in it (and particularly in its style) the growing effects of senility.[1] Yet it would be hard to make out a convincing case for this view: indeed it may be doubted whether those scholars who, like Taylor and C. Ritter, have made an apologia for the work, have, in fact, claimed for it as much as it merits. After a careful reading, it seems clear that, uncongenial as the views it expresses may be, the *Laws* must count as one of Plato's greatest achievements. The involved and baroque prose style, which has been credited with 'uncouthness', most closely resembles, in its superb intricacy, that of the later works of Henry James, the 'major phase' according to an American critic.[2] It is certainly undeniable that the *Laws* displays an astonishing fertility of ideas, many of them new, and that it would

[1] Plato, *Laws* (tr. R. G. Bury, Loeb ed.), vol. I, p. vii. A more intelligent analysis of Plato's style in the *Laws* is given by J. D. Denniston in his *Greek Prose Style* (pp. 54 ff., 68 ff., 132 ff. and elsewhere), although on grounds of taste his verdict also goes against Plato.

[2] We may note, for example, the magnificent sentences at VI, 758 A 2, 776 A 7 ff., IX, 865 D 6 ff., XII, 947 B 3 ff. Cf. Denniston, *op. cit.* pp. 69 f.

be rash to evaluate any facet of Plato's many-sided philosophy without first seeing what he has to say of it in his final major work. Nor has Plato lost any of his psychological insight: the passage in Book VI, where he analyses the binding power of unfulfilled longing, in contrast with the tedium of unbroken companionship, is not absurdly compared with the unwinding of Marcel's history in *A la recherche du temps perdu*.[1] It is a commonplace among the apologists for the *Laws*, but one that deserves attention, that it is 'in some respects his most characteristic work'.[2] In most respects, one might be tempted to assert; it is at least, as we shall see, the logical culmination and extreme statement of those intellectual tendencies which we may be entitled to believe most characteristic of Plato. Plato the aristocrat, Plato the constructor of systems, Plato the lover of the aesthetic are all here represented in their final and most convincing forms, while the ghost of Socrates, hardly as substantial now as the ψυχαί of the Νέκυια, is no longer present even in the *dramatis personae*.

In so far as it is possible to divide the work 'along the lines of its natural articulation', the first section, which merits separate attention, is the long introductory conversation, which extends through the first two books, and although the work of legislation is supposed to begin in the third, through a considerable part of that book also. In this chapter, I propose to discuss this approach, with only very occasional reference to later parts of the *Laws*.

Much care has been expended (*pace* Bruns)[3] on this introduction, and the discussion of Spartan and Cretan theories of legislation provides a natural and satisfying first view of the questions to be discussed in the work. As the three elderly, slightly phantom figures begin their long midsummer walk across Crete, the two Dorians expound, in answer to the Athenian's question, the theory that lies behind their constitutions, the assumption that life is a 'continual, lifelong war'.[4] In the sequel, the Athenian will not accept this attitude to life, and it is dropped, but not before it has produced in us the right frame of mind for our discussion. To see life as literally a war is to raise one μέρος ἀρετῆς above the ideal

[1] VI, 776A 3 ff.   [2] *The Laws of Plato*, tr. A. E. Taylor, p. xi.
[3] I. Bruns, *Platos Gesetze*.   [4] *Laws*, I, 625E 6f.

of complete goodness, which, as for Socrates, is Plato's ultimate goal. The effect, however, of commencing the *Laws* with a consideration of this view is to stress, at the outset, the urgency of the problem of living. The notion of war lifts life from the rut of an unconscious habitual progress through time and space into an atmosphere of excitement and unrest, where actions take on significance, the greater for the consciousness in which they are carried out. 'War, which takes away the ease of situation in which we make our day-to-day decisions, is a task-master in violence',[1] but it is notoriously also a time when those who are capable of reviewing consciously their actions see more distinctly the extending consequences and the impelling urgency of their behaviour. Thus by setting the topic of his conversation in the uneasy framework of war, Plato reverts to the anxious mood of Socrates. For the war which Cleinias and Megillus envisage is not only one of city against city, individual against individual,[2] but within the person, a στάσις of element against element, in which 'victory over oneself is the first and finest of all victories, while to be defeated by oneself is of all things the most shameful, even the most evil'.[3] As a theory of life, this is rejected: it is the function of the best legislator to resolve πόλεμος, and more particularly στάσις, where he finds them, and substitute 'friendship and peace, which he must bring about by reconciliation'.[4]

But as an overture to the work it has served its purpose: the theme of struggle is thus early stated. And, indeed before the idea is finally rejected, a second strand of this complicated work[5] appears, to remain as one of the guiding principles: 'Surely perfection is the aim of all the norms of conduct ever laid down.'[6] The texture develops in this way, leading threads appearing continuously as the conversation winds its way through the theory and practice of legislation. The ideal, to be kept as παράδειγμα throughout the operation, appears early and stays to the end. The

---

[1] Thucydides, III, 82, 2. [2] 626C 11 ff.
[3] 626E 2 ff. [4] 628B 8.
[5] The principal impression left by the *Laws* is one of πυκνότης, both in language and ideas.
[6] ἆρα οὖν οὐ τοῦ ἀρίστου ἕνεκα πάντα ἂν τὰ νόμιμα τιθείη πᾶς; (628 C 6 ff.); see England's note *ad loc.*; cf. 630 C 1 ff.

aim of our legislation is no less than to produce the highest form of moral goodness in society. ἀρετή is to be the outcome, not now of personal and individual effort, but of the provisions of a legal system and the establishment of a society directed to moral ends. Thus, side by side, in this overture are visible the strands of Socratic urgency and of a new belief in the ability of external influences to produce ἀρετή. Is this ἀρετή that society sets out to achieve, we may wonder, the Socratic 'movement of faith'?

Meanwhile, the discussion of the Dorian theory proceeds, and its ideal of 'victory over self' is pronounced not to be an ideal but a regrettable necessity: καὶ δὴ καὶ τὸ νικᾶν, ὡς ἔοικεν, αὐτὴν αὐτὴν πόλιν οὐκ ἦν τῶν ἀρίστων ἀλλὰ τῶν ἀναγκαίων.[1] Then, setting the poems of Theognis against those of Tyrtaeus, the Athenian draws a distinction between Theognis' all-round hero and the ἀνδρεῖος of Tyrtaeus: a man cannot be reliable (πιστός) in the time of test 'without excellence in every direction',[2] the combination of δικαιοσύνη, σωφροσύνη, φρόνησις and ἀνδρεία. Mere possession of one form of ἀρετή is only fourth in the list of precedence. Here again we find envisaged a situation we have not met before, the explicit granting of a separate existence to one form of ἀρετή apart from the rest. Almost at once the difference becomes clearer when ἀνδρεία is referred to as attained perhaps even by mercenaries, 'the majority of whom are impulsive, unjust and insolent; perhaps the most senseless pack of men one could find'.[3] Already a different background is becoming visible to the whole discussion of ethics in this work.

While we are wondering about this change of atmosphere, the Athenian, who has already said that this introduction is intended to provide us with a standard of the excellence of laws,[4] praises the start that has been made. In approaching the question of legislation, he says, it is essential for the legislator to begin with ἀρετή; 'declaring openly that this is the aim of his legislation'.[5] Then, in

---

[1] 628C 11f.

[2] 630B 3.

[3] ὧν οἱ πλεῖστοι γίγνονται θρασεῖς καὶ ἄδικοι καὶ ὑβρισταὶ καὶ ἀφρονέστατοι σχεδὸν ἁπάντων (630B 5ff.); cf. 635D 2ff.

[4] 627D 1ff.   [5] 631A 2ff.

an important and striking speech,[1] he sets out what he feels should be the legislator's preliminary statement. Values form a hierarchy, in which τὰ ἀνθρώπινα stem from τὰ θεῖα, material goods from the facets of moral goodness which we have mentioned. The legislator must point out that all his injunctions look to these values, 'and that within them human values look to divine, and divine, without exception, to their leader, wisdom'.[2] Then appear two more of the threads which, to use one of Plato's own favourite metaphors, go to make up the warp and woof of this work: they are two of the principles on which the legislator will attain his ends. He must work towards these ends by the correction of the present system of distributing honour and dishonour, and he must give careful attention to the pains, pleasures, desires and passions which social life arouses in the people of his society. On these emotions he will depend for the effectiveness of his policy.

These two elements in his theory and practice, which in part at least combine to form one side of the legislative theory of the *Laws*, the manipulation of honour and dishonour, playing upon the emotions of the citizens in this state, though introduced here without particular attention falling on them, become, in the sequel, a cornerstone to the whole fabric of the treatise. Certainly, they present to us the greatest step so far taken away from the 'inwardness' of Socratic philosophy. Plato imagines the legislator as working, by means of his enactments, on the emotions of his subjects, and by so doing, as steering them to the attainment of ἀρετή. The title of this great work itself gives us a clue as to the direction in which Plato has moved. Νόμοι, 'laws', 'conventions': the individual has begun to disappear and the beginnings of a system show themselves. More than this, it is through the emotions that the legislator is to work: the ἐπιστήμη of Socrates, though not 'intellectual' in the received sense, as we saw, was still a matter

---

[1] Stallbaum (*Laws*, vol. I, p. 56) comments: 'Habemus igitur hic quasi designationem quandam et adumbrationem universi operis: quod mirum est praeteriisse eos, qui artem et rationem in his Legum libris omnino desiderari censuerunt.'

[2] τούτων δὲ τὰ μὲν ἀνθρώπινα εἰς τὰ θεῖα, τὰ δὲ θεῖα εἰς τὸν ἡγεμόνα νοῦν σύμπαντα βλέπειν. (631 D 4 ff.).

of intelligent behaviour, not, indeed, to be affected by pleasure and pain. The shift, then, already appears considerable.

We may be reassured, perhaps, by one remark in this speech of the Athenian. After the constitution and legal enactment has been constructed on these lines, the system[1] is to be consigned to the safe-keeping of curators, 'some of whom will go to work by means of understanding (φρόνησις), others by means of true conviction (ἀληθής δόξα): their aim will be that intelligence should reveal all these elements bound into one whole and following the dictates, not of wealth and the quest for status, but of justice and morality (σωφροσύνη)'.[2] With this the recommended pronouncement ends. In some sense, then, νοῦς is still to control the whole, and direct its activities to the requisite end. But even here there are new matters. Only some of the φύλακες are to work διὰ φρονήσεως, the rest must rely on ἀληθὴς δόξα. This is a concept that we have not met before (though chronologically, of course, Plato has earlier made use of it in the Meno, Republic and elsewhere), and which would need, on Socratic terms, some explanation: its status would be difficult to assess in a moral world where ἀρετή has been made an all-or-nothing affair, as it was by Socrates.

Before we leave the subject of emotion, we may notice an even more striking statement of the same theme: 'In any inquiry men may make about the problems of legislation, almost the whole of their investigation is bound up with the effects of pleasure and pain, both in the characters of individuals and in whole societies.'[3] We may perhaps suspect that the extremism of this remark indicates that it is a reaction from a view previously held by Plato himself. His present view of pleasure and pain is made clearer in the sentence that follows: 'For pleasure and pain are like two fountains which, in the order of things, well up continually, and it is the man who draws water only from the right one, the right amount at the right time, who alone is happy. Indeed as much is true of societies and all living creatures, as well as of men as individuals; while

---

[1] τάξις (632D 4).

[2] τοὺς μὲν διὰ φρονήσεως, τοὺς δὲ δι' ἀληθοῦς δόξης ἰόντας, ὅπως πάντα ταῦτα συνδήσας ὁ νοῦς ἑπόμενα σωφροσύνῃ καὶ δικαιοσύνῃ ἀποφήνῃ, ἀλλὰ μὴ πλούτῳ μηδὲ φιλοτιμίᾳ (632C 5ff.).   [3] 636D 5ff.

whoever draws his water unintelligently (ἀνεπιστημόνως) and when the time is not right, his is the reverse of a happy life.'[1] The most interesting point about this latter sentence is the way in which it prefigures some of the most characteristic phrases of the *Nicomachean Ethics*, a resemblance which may point to a more than superficial kinship, in some matters, between the two philosophers. For our present purpose, however, we must notice how the prime importance of these two factors is again insisted on. England comments: 'Nature provides the raw material in the form of the emotions of pleasure and pain; the educator of states and individuals moulds it by the habits which his laws and institutions induce.'[2]

'Habits': the word introduces us to a further point made by the Athenian in the conversation. He has already insisted that a 'cloistered virtue' is not only not to be commended, but is, in fact, an impossibility. Now he goes on to develop the need for 'practice in encountering pleasure' (μελέτη ἡ πρὸς τὰς ἡδονᾶς). The discussion of strong drink (μέθη), which takes up the remainder of the first book, is an illustration of this theme. As England says: 'In the course of the investigation of μέθη we are introduced to the relation of νόμος and νομοθέτης to παιδεία.'[3] Emphasis is laid throughout on the fact that natural aptitude and experience are necessary for ἀρετή, as well as ἐπιστήμη and τέχνη.[4] μέθη is a means both of attaining experience in contending with pleasures which have the advantage of being harmless, and for the legislator, of providing a test of character and progress in morals: the συμπόσια are indeed referred to, somewhat to the surprise of the Dorians, as a form of παιδεία, which is itself the key to ἀρετή: 'Where men have been well brought up, they should attain their true goodness, and when that is attained, they should be not only victorious in their wars but achieve success in all their activities.'[5]

---

[1] δύο γὰρ αὗται πηγαὶ μεθεῖνται φύσει ῥεῖν, ὧν ὁ μὲν ἀρυτόμενος ὅθεν τε δεῖ καὶ ὁπότε καὶ ὁπόσον εὐδαιμονεῖ, καὶ πόλις ὁμοίως καὶ ἰδιώτης καὶ ζῷον ἅπαν, ὁ δ' ἀνεπιστημόνως ἅμα καὶ ἐκτὸς τῶν καιρῶν τἀναντία ἂν ἐκείνῳ ζῴη (636 D 7 ff.); cf. 638 C 7 f.   [2] *The Laws of Plato*, ed. E. B. England, vol. I, p. 232.
[3] *Op. cit.* p. 234; cf. 638 E 3 ff.   [4] E.g. at 639 A 9 ff.
[5] παιδευθέντες μὲν εὖ γίγνοιντ' ἂν ἄνδρες ἀγαθοί, γενόμενοι δὲ τοιοῦτοι τά τε ἄλλα πράττοιεν καλῶς, ἔτι δὲ κἂν νικῷεν τοὺς πολεμίους μαχόμενοι (641 B 3 ff.).

One begins to feel that practice (μελέτη), not τέχνη, is now the decisive factor in the struggle for ἀρετή. Yet in fact what has happened is rather that τέχνη itself has lost much of the 'all-or-nothing' character which was given it by Socrates. The Athenian describes what a man must practise,[1] if he is to be good at anything: from the beginning of his childhood, he must live with his profession, in play as in earnest. By playing with bricks and building toy houses, for example, he acquires the preliminary instruction[2] which is necessary, and gradually his tastes and inclinations[3] are led, while he is still a child, into a love of that path of life which he must follow as a man. In this the influence of Socratic τέχνη is still evident, but with how great a difference! Throughout, this process is referred to as παιδεία,[4] but to readers of the *Gorgias* it must savour far more of ἐμπειρία. What is being here achieved is not the Socratic understanding, but the canalizing of emotion in the right direction, in children too young to be within the remotest striking-distance of ἐπιστήμη. But Plato's faith in this process is as great as that of Socrates in the power of at least some human minds to reach the 'movement of faith'.

This is the beginning, at least, of παιδεία, and that very form of it which leads to ἀρετή: 'that education which leads to the realization of a man's true capabilities, which fills a man with the passionate desire for perfection as a member of society, endowed with the intelligent ability to rule and to be ruled as justice demands'.[5] Only this, indeed, may properly be called παιδεία: other forms are merely 'mechanical (βάναυσον) and unworthy of one truly free'. In this Plato places his trust, which is complete, that by education men become good: 'We may almost say that true goodness (ἀρετή) is the result of proper education.'[6] Hence

---

[1] μελετᾶν (643 B 4 ff.).
[2] τῶν μαθημάτων ὅσα ἀναγκαῖα προμεμαθηκέναι προμανθάνειν (643 C 3 f.).
[3] ἡδοναί καὶ ἐπιθυμίαι (C 7).
[4] 643 B 1.
[5] τὴν πρὸς ἀρετὴν ἐκ παίδων παιδείαν ποιοῦσαν ἐπιθυμητήν τε καὶ ἐραστὴν τοῦ πολίτην γενέσθαι τέλεον, ἄρχειν τε καὶ ἄρχεσθαι ἐπιστάμενον μετὰ δίκης (643 E 4 ff.).
[6] οἵ γε ὀρθῶς πεπαιδευμένοι σχεδὸν ἀγαθοὶ γίγνονται (644 A 7 f.); see England's note *ad loc*.

the overriding importance which education assumes in Plato's middle and later works, never greater than in the *Laws*: it is 'the greatest of man's possessions, and most valuable for him who can make most use of it'.[1]

Thus the picture slowly forms of a society whose designer places all his hopes of the attainment of moral, the only true, goodness in the provisions of that society itself, by means of enactments and customs working upon the characters of its citizens. But for a few indications, we might think it strikingly like that sketch of moral upbringing given by Protagoras, which we have seen Socrates already reject, as incapable of leading to true ἀρετή, the product of individual endeavour. So that it is all the more striking to find, in the *Laws*, an explicit parallel drawn between the function fulfilled in the individual by λογισμός and that of νόμος in the community, the 'agreed decision (δόγμα) of society'.[2] These two, in man and in society, determine between the two advisers (συμβούλω) which everyone has in him, pleasure and pain.[3] Then, in a curious and haunting speech, the Athenian explains these remarks. We are all, he says, to think of ourselves, each living creature, as in some way puppets of the gods, constructed whether in earnest or for play. Within us, our states of mind or emotions are the strings or cords, by which we are worked, pulling us in opposite directions towards opposite courses of action: in this lies the distinction between right and wrong. The argument of this treatise demands that to one of these we should yield, the golden pull of reason,[4] but against the others fight without ceasing. This requires in us our own support, since the pull of reason is not so powerful as it is noble: to understand and believe this fable[5] will make the problem of morality clearer. This is beautiful and moving, like many of Plato's myths, and such was undoubtedly its purpose. It is also, in the peculiarity of the fable, a hint of life conceived aesthetically as a ballet of moral forces, with the essential individuality of the human struggle laid aside, one of the many contradictory visions that ensnare the religious thinker. But the

---

[1] πρῶτον τῶν καλλίστων τοῖς ἀρίστοις ἀνδράσιν (644B 1f.).   [2] 644D 1ff.
[3] 644C 6ff.; England refers to *Tim.* 69C 5ff.
[4] 645A 1; cf. *Rep.* III, 415A 2ff.   [5] μῦθος (B 1).

duty of society and the individual is clear: it is 'to acquire within us the power of grasping the truth about these forces which pull us, and to follow the lead of that truth in our life'.[1] Understanding, says Plato, of the meaning of the fable will illuminate the articulation of κακία and ἀρετή, which will in turn give us more appreciation of the nature of παιδεία: we will attempt both these tasks in the following chapters.

From now on to the close of the book, the three friends examine more closely the function of μέθη as an assistant to παιδεία. Its value is found to be that of heightening the emotions, while weakening the intellect, so that an examination can easily be made of the extent to which the emotions have been trained in the right direction, and this without danger of great harm being done. The first book ends by relating this process to the main subject of the work: 'In the understanding of human nature and the possible conformations of character, we surely have one of the most valuable adjuncts to that art (τέχνη) whose business it is to look after human character: for I imagine we might agree to describe the art of the statesman in this way.'[2] The final reference is to ἡ πολιτικὴ τέχνη.

At the very beginning of the second book, the Athenian outlines again what he believes to be τὴν ὀρθὴν παιδείαν, making clear, if that is now necessary, the importance that Plato attached to education. As the description contains one or two additional ideas, which carry our inquiry a step forward, we will examine it:

Well, what I mean is this: a child's first experiences, childish enough, are those of pleasure and pain, and it is in relation to these that moral qualities, good and bad, first appear in a man's character; whereas what we call understanding and a true outlook on the world, capable of withstanding the world's strains, is the achievement only of old age; indeed a man is lucky if he achieves it then: one who has gained these things and all that they bring with them, has reached perfection.[3]

[1] 645 B 4 ff.   [2] 650 B 6 ff.
[3] λέγω τοίνυν τῶν παίδων παιδικὴν εἶναι πρώτην αἴσθησιν ἡδονὴν καὶ λύπην, καὶ ἐν οἷς ἀρετὴ ψυχῇ καὶ κακία παραγίγνεται πρῶτον, ταῦτ' εἶναι, φρόνησιν δὲ καὶ ἀληθεῖς δόξας βεβαίους εὐτυχὲς ὅτῳ καὶ πρὸς τὸ γῆρας παρεγένετο· τέλεος δ' οὖν ἔστ' ἄνθρωπος ταῦτα καὶ τὰ ἐν τούτοις πάντα κεκτημένος ἀγαθά (653 A 5 ff.).

In this passage, the claim is made that ἀρετή and κακία exist, at least at first, in the realm of pleasure and pain. This is partly explained by the rest of the sentence: φρόνησις and ἀληθεῖς δόξαι βέβαιοι are achieved, if at all, only very late in life, and carry with them perfection as a human being and a mass of concomitant blessings. Here at once we catch a glimpse of what has caused the changes in ethical outlook that we have observed already. φρόνησις, the Socratic ideal, is still the ideal of Plato, but it has passed right out of the orbit of attainment of the ordinary man: it is perfection in humanity and such perfection can only be attained on the eve of death by a fortunate minority. True convictions (ἀληθεῖς δόξαι), which we observed for the first time earlier, have come to join it, still beyond the reach of the young, but not clearly explained as yet. How does this bear on παιδεία? We are told in the next sentence:

What I call education, then, is goodness (ἀρετή) as a child first acquires it: it is the inculcation of a right attitude towards pleasure and affection, hatred and pain, in the characters of those who cannot grasp these things rationally (λόγῳ); an inculcation so thorough that when the child achieves such a grasp, the requirements of his reason are in full accord with what he has learnt by force of habituation in the appropriate reactions. The whole of this accord (συμφωνία) between reason and habit I would call goodness: the part of it that has to do with the right upbringing of a character in its contacts with pleasure and pain, which results in producing, at the very outset, revulsion from what deserves revulsion, affection for what merits affection, and maintains these attitudes throughout life; this aspect of goodness I would distinguish from the rest and call it 'education', education, I believe, in the true sense of the word.[1]

παιδεία is thus the proper upbringing of pleasure and pain.[2] In the child, before the ability to reason has appeared, an immediate

---

[1] παιδείαν δὴ λέγω τὴν παραγιγνομένην πρῶτον παισὶν ἀρετήν· ἡδονὴ δὴ καὶ φιλία καὶ λύπη καὶ μῖσος ἂν ὀρθῶς ἐν ψυχαῖς ἐγγίγνωνται μήπω δυναμένων λόγῳ λαμβάνειν, λαβόντων δὲ τὸν λόγον, συμφωνήσωσι τῷ λόγῳ ὀρθῶς εἰθίσθαι ὑπὸ τῶν προσηκόντων ἐθῶν, αὕτη 'σθ' ἡ συμφωνία σύμπασα μὲν ἀρετή, τὸ δὲ περὶ τὰς ἡδονὰς καὶ λύπας τεθραμμένον αὐτῆς ὀρθῶς ὥστε μισεῖν μὲν ἃ χρὴ μισεῖν εὐθὺς ἐξ ἀρχῆς μέχρι τέλους, στέργειν δὲ ἃ χρὴ στέργειν, τοῦτ' αὐτὸ ἀποτεμὼν τῷ λόγῳ καὶ παιδείαν προσαγορεύῃς, κατά γε τὴν ἐμὴν ὀρθῶς ἂν προσαγορεύοις (653 B 1 ff.).

[2] τῶν ὀρθῶς τεθραμμένων ἡδονῶν καὶ λυπῶν παιδειῶν οὐσῶν (c 7 f.).

reaction to what is found pleasant or painful, which controls the child's actions, gives the educator a means of guiding his pupil in the appropriate direction. His aim, therefore, is to ensure that the child finds its pleasures, *quasi* instinctively, in the proper objects:[1] then, when it attains to reason, those things which its mind tells it it should desire, will, in fact, be already the objects of its delight. This συμφωνία of delight and ὁ ὀρθὸς λόγος (the power of reasoning about one's reactions and attitudes), when they occur together, is ἀρετή, and the first stages of its attainment are the product of education, rightly so called. It is at once clear that this level of ἀρετή is not that of Socratic ἐπιστήμη, which was the product solely of ὁ ὀρθὸς λόγος: moreover, that phrase itself is being used in an attenuated sense, as it is in English when we speak of the 'age of reason'. If ὁ ὀρθὸς λόγος were the equivalent of φρόνησις, then ἀρετή, even as here defined, would be beyond the majority of mankind, if only because one element in the συμφωνία would be absent.

Just as, in the previous book, μέθη was discussed in illustration of the need for μελέτη, so now the investigation of music which follows elaborates, by means of illustration, the idea which has just been stated, of the education of emotion in the young. In their earliest years children find great delight in the rudimentary dancing and music of jumping about and making 'all kinds of noises': thus their first education comes through Apollo and the Muses.[2] The first point established about μουσική is that it is more important that a performer should love what is good and hate what is bad, though failing artistically to express his feelings, than that his performance should be the consummation of artistic perfection, without a true appreciation of moral values.[3] In other words, that the ethical side of art must at all times override the aesthetic. From this, we move to another point of the first importance. Appreciation of artistic performances is notoriously a matter for extreme diversity of opinion: does the enjoyment of what we believe morally evil imply a like appreciation of that evil

---

[1] Aristotle, *Pol.* 1340a 15 (quoted by England) shows Aristotle's affinity with this belief.

[2] 653 D 7 ff.   [3] 654 B 11 ff.

itself? This seems unthinkable and the Athenian avoids the paradox by declaring that our reactions to art are determined[1] by its according either with our φύσις or our ἔθος or both. Any clash between temperament and upbringing will result in a similar variation between approbation and enjoyment.

The fundamental point at issue here is, as England says,[2] that appreciation of art demands a process of habituation and, moreover, that the same is the case with morality: we cannot attain to ἀρετή without the process of developing tastes and character by habit. The possibility of variation by temperament is not left out of account, but only by proper manipulation of habit-forming tendencies can Plato's purpose be achieved. Above all, the fact is stressed that serious damage to character can be caused by the secret cleavage between judgment and enjoyment. It is the function of education to prevent such a cleavage, and it is with this in mind that Plato goes on to examine the effect of 'representational' art on the development of character. Plato's views on the moral powers of μίμησις are for us among his most surprising. They presuppose on the part of the audience an amount of identification with the characters, or even the rhythms and tones, portrayed, which, though common in childhood, is not today generally thought applicable to more mature minds. We must accept, however, that Plato did feel that enjoyment of a character affects one's own moral personality.[3] Indeed, the effect of enjoyment, even if secret, is more powerful than that of conscious and overt disapprobation, so that control over the standards of artistic performance and over public taste in such matters is absolutely essential to the success of παιδεία.

The basis of Plato's canon of taste is that it should be determined from above. The judges in artistic contests must be the instructors of the audience in artistic standards; they are not there to learn from them, nor to be swayed by hysterical applause, especially if it runs contrary to their own judgment.[4] Taste, then, will be

---

[1] ἀναγκαῖον, 655E 3.   [2] 655B 9n. (op. cit. vol. I, pp. 281 f.).
[3] Note especially 656B 4ff.: τότε ὁμοιοῦσθαι δήπου ἀνάγκη τὸν χαίροντα ὁποτέροις ἂν χαίρῃ.
[4] 659B 2ff.

established by the most cultivated and virtuous, and artistic excellence will be judged proportionate to the amount of pleasure which they obtain from the performance. Pleasure, since there seems to be an intimate connection between this and well-being;[1] and the pleasure of the most cultivated, because taste must be educated to be valuable.[2]

Thus the example of μουσική leads us back once again, Plato declares, to our original position: 'Education, we see once more, is the process of pulling and leading children in the direction of reason (λόγος) and the truths which it announces through the medium of law; truths which have been established by the agreement in practical experience of men marked both by their moral stature and their advancing years.'[3] The goal to which children are to be drawn is once more that which is pronounced right by the law, and England well comments that in ἐπιεικεστάτοις καὶ πρεσβυτάτοις 'we have over again the insistence on both φύσις, natural endowment, and experience as a necessity for right opinion'.[4] Here again the means by which this is to be achieved are pleasure and pain,[5] and there is an interesting comparison (and a revealing one) between the legislator's use of games and songs to attain the συμφωνία which is his aim, and the doctor's practice of 'sugaring the pill': the triviality, only apparent, of method and the ultimate seriousness of intention are identical in the two processes.[6]

Very shortly afterwards, the Athenian re-establishes the influence of Socrates by a typically Socratic insistence on the stupidity of received values: 'What most men label as goods do not deserve the name.'[7] There follows the usual list of health, beauty, wealth and the rest, including, we may note, 'having the power of a tyrant, and fulfilling one's every impulse', an echo perhaps of the *Gorgias*, certainly of the authentic Socratic note. To this list is appended the usual commentary: 'You and I, I imagine, would agree that these things in general, though they may be possessions of the greatest value to men of justice and true religion, are the

---

[1] 657E 5f.   [2] 658E 6ff.   [3] 659C 9ff.
[4] *Op. cit.* vol. I, p. 294; he compares 655D 8.
[5] 659D 5ff.   [6] E 3 ff.   [7] 661A 4f.

most destructive of all to the unjust.'[1] Values depend on ἀρετή, as we have seen, and in the presence of its opposite, κακία, things conventionally termed good take on the opposite character. From this point, Plato moves to the concurrence of justice and happiness, which he is at pains to make acceptable, adducing the evidence of gods[2] and parents. For one who views them in the right light there is no divergence between the just and pleasant lives: this theory has, at least, the merit of being conducive to a religious life,[3] and the mental confusion, which is the present state of most of us on this subject, must be eradicated by the legislator 'by some sort of habituation, by the manipulation of eulogy and reasoned argument'.[4] The object of this attempt on the part of the legislator will be, of course, that συμφωνία which has all along been our aim: his method will be twofold. By education, to train the tastes and inclinations of his subjects, and by enactments and persuasive utterances, to remove the *a priori* logical distinction, which alone militates against the acceptance of the dogma. However it is to be done, the dogma must be accepted, since it is the truth.

But the truth, though noble and of lasting effect, is by no means easy to inculcate· καλὸν μὲν ἡ ἀλήθεια, ὦ ξένε, καὶ μόνιμον· ἔοικε μὴν οὐ ῥᾴδιον εἶναι πείθειν.[5] Perhaps this is true, but we have always a counterbalance in the plasticity of childish minds. The educator must first decide what is most beneficial to his society and then do his utmost to persuade society to treat the matter in this single manner 'in its songs, its stories and its conversations'. Thus public opinion is also to be formed by the legislator in the construction of his society, and the education which we have in mind is now described as a sort of spell to be recited continuously, with infinite variety and subtlety, until the idea that it contains is sown deep in the minds of all the citizens.[6]

The fundamental notion, then, that the legislator is to implant in his people is the identity of the pleasant and the just life. For

[1] 661 B 4ff; cf. c 8ff. The point is stressed again, despite opposition, at 662 B 2ff.

[2] With reference to εὐδαιμονία (662 D 4).

[3] πιθανός γ', εἰ μηδὲν ἕτερον, πρὸς τό τινα ἐθέλειν 3ῆν τὸν ὅσιον καὶ δίκαιον βίον (663 B 1 ff.).

[4] 663 C 1 ff. [5] 663 E 3 f.; see England's note *ad loc*. [6] 665 C 2ff.

the legislator, its rightness lies in its justice, but for his citizens, who live largely by the promptings of pleasure and pain, belief in this identity is essential to their choosing the just life, which is the entire aim of the legislator. His method is to be the now familiar one of propaganda: the ἐπῳδή which is to work upon them is simply the continual reiteration of a few ideas, notably the one we have been discussing, which have been selected by the legislator as beneficial for society. Thus it is upon propaganda, worked out in immense subtlety of detail, commencing with the earliest childhood, that ἀρετή, for the great mass of men, now depends; only the details remain to be settled.

This theme is developed during the remainder of the second book. Various additional points are made: the need is stressed, as against the Dorian methods of mass training, for individual care and attention, which is as necessary to the moral training of a man as it is to the training of a horse. Training in the mass may make for excellent soldiering but is incapable of producing all-round goodness, and of making a man 'not only a good soldier... but also capable of administering society and its local units'.[1] But music, as a field for moral education, has one drawback: its effect can be dangerous, because it is difficult to grasp and assess. Its power over moral development is not less than that of any other representational arts, but its actual effect is more subtle, and our poets are not themselves quite up to determining it and acting accordingly.[2] It is this that makes it necessary to have the canons of musical taste established by men of experience and unimpeachable moral quality. Otherwise none of them can ever become 'a magician skilled enough to lead the young towards ἀρετή by his incantations'.[3] The good legislator, by his use of μουσική with the young, and of μέθη with those who are older, can be, in truth, a moulder of characters (πλάστης τῶν ψυχῶν).[4]

The Athenian explains once again what it is that we are doing by means of this παιδεία. 'At least I am sure of this, that no living creature, however rational it is in his nature to become when

[1] 666E 1 ff.   [2] 669B 9 ff.
[3] ἱκανὸν ἐπῳδὸν...νέοις πρὸς ἀρετήν (671 A 1); cf. also 659E 1.
[4] 671 B 8 f.

mature, is ever born with that intelligence (νοῦς) in its full degree.'[1] But in the period before this proper level of intelligence has been reached, the innate delight in shouting and jumping about affords a means of guidance to the educator, so that we are not surprised to find Plato saying that 'music [i.e. vocal music and the dance], if I remember rightly, we called the beginning and end of education'.[2] Indeed, later we are told that μουσική is simply the training of the voice πρὸς ἀρετήν, which continues till it reaches the soul.[3]

So the discussion of μουσική ends, and with it the second book, with a reference to 'men of sound reason living under a sound law';[4] the equivalence of intelligence and law seems at its most complete.[5]

'In Books I and II we have been considering, under various guises, the relation of Law to the Individual—how it acquires authority, and how it helps to discipline the character through the action of pleasure and pain, desire and fear. We now pass abruptly to the political framework within which, and upon which Law acts.'[6] But in examining the genesis of society from a mythical cataclysm, Plato indicates more than once some of his fundamental views on the nature of ethics and social systems. The ultimate aim of his survey is to demonstrate how the downfall of societies has been due to their failure to apprehend the true nature of education, their failure, in fact, to produce ἀρετή among their populations by the methods which Plato himself intends to apply. At the end of the book, we discover that our theorizing has not been without purpose: Cleinias, the Cretan, is, in fact, a member of a commission charged with the drawing up of a system of laws for a new city to be founded on the island: with the principles which we have already established behind us, we can go forward with him in an attempt to produce such a scheme of legislation.

To investigate the rise of society, we must, as when we examine its tendencies in moral progress or decay, take a very long period

---

[1] 672 B 8 ff.   [2] 672 E 5.   [3] 673 A 3 ff.

[4] τοῖς νοῦν τε καὶ νόμον ἔχουσιν ὀρθόν (674 B 7).

[5] England's Appendix A to Book II contains a useful account of the structure of the first two books. There are certain items which I feel he tends to overlook, but he seems right to reject Bruns' 'Redaktor'.

[6] England, op. cit. vol. I, p. 343.

of time over which to extend our survey. We imagine, then, all but a few of humanity drowned by a great flood, and the remainder, shepherds upon the mountains, 'a handful of embers saved from the holocaust of humanity',[1] living on in ignorance of the previous ways of civilized men, and not daring yet to come down from the heights into the valleys, haunted still by memories of the flood. Their ignorance of civilization will account too for their immaturity in moral goodness and vice: the complexity of moral sensibility or the lack of it are both equally the result of the passage of time and the growing ramification of the human race.[2] 'Can we suppose...that the men of that age, who had no experience of the multitude of civilized amenities and their opposites that town life affords, could have been fully developed in their moral qualities, good or bad?'[3] Moral sophistication, it is assumed, must be attendant upon civilization and culture. The environment of these few survivors, a sufficiency of the means of life which equally prevented poverty and riches, led to their being ἀγαθοί, as did also their proverbial naïvety.[4] So, at the very outset of this study of social origins, the effect of society and environment upon morals is stressed. It is the tendency of thinkers such as Socrates to ignore almost entirely influences other than those contained in the individual himself, so that it is perhaps an indication of how far Plato has moved away from the Socratic position that he should be so much aware of the influence of environment. We have, indeed, already seen that it is one of the fundamental assumptions of the *Laws*.

Gradually the genesis of society is followed, until historical events begin to figure in the fable, principally the establishment of the cities of Sparta, Argos and Messene, at a time when the conditions of their foundation provided an opportunity unique in history, as Plato believed, for the creation of a really satisfactory political system.[5] But the external influences which affect the individual are not those which cause the dissolution of the societies

---

[1] 677B 2f.
[2] I cannot understand England's extraordinary note on 678A 9.
[3] 678B 1ff.   [4] 679B 3ff.; cf. E 2ff.
[5] 684B 5ff.

themselves. In searching for reasons for the so evident failure of these Peloponnesian communities, Plato attends to the internal structure: 'Do you seriously think that a monarchy is ever over-thrown, or for that matter, any political system brought down, by any forces except those which it harbours in itself?'[1] If we are to see in ἀρετή the consequences of social influences, the causes of social collapse are to be sought in the nature of the governments of the societies. Plato seems to regard the social unit as sufficient cause both of the rise and fall of the morality of its members, and of the vicissitudes of its own general history. His reason, pre-sumably, would be that in effect the latter is only an amplified echo of the former: a feeling for the parallelism of macrocosm and microcosm, at all levels, is frequently attested in his writings.

His feeling of surprise that a foundation of so much promise as the Dorian should have failed so completely leads the Athenian to consider the misleadingness of one's normal reaction to such a situation. We are tempted to think how fine an acquisition this or that might have been, 'if only it had been properly used at the time'.[2] But are we right? There follows a reference to the doc-trine of βούλησις, which we have already considered[3] Power, though we who possess it may be capable of directing its use efficiently, so as to conform with our wishes, is of no use. We commonly desire, and pray for, a life which is κατὰ βούλησιν.[4] It is only in the case of our friends or relatives that we are able to take the 'realistic' view and see that their wishes are not necessarily, nor even generally, to their advantage.[5] Unless βούλησις accords with φρόνησις, to desire the fulfilment of our random wishes, and even more to gain it, is fatal.[6] This leads to a recapitulation of what has been said before about the aim of the true legislator: 'He should fix his attention on ἀρετή as a whole, but first and foremost on the quality which leads the way for ἀρετή; I mean under-standing, judgment and a sound outlook, backed by a passionate

---

[1] 683E 3ff.   [2] 686D 1of.

[3] In chapter III above, especially pp. 47–51.

[4] 687E 5ff.; cf. κατὰ τὴν τῆς αὐτοῦ ψυχῆς ἐπίταξιν (c 5).

[5] Cf. Isocrates, De Pace, 106ff.

[6] It should be noted that the word βούλησις is not being used in the sense of chapter III, though the idea expressed is the same.

desire for the achievement of their demands.'[1] φρόνησις and νοῦς, accompanied once again by δόξα, are the guiding principles of society: with them ἔρως and ἐπιθυμία, following their lead, hint at the συμφωνία of Book II. In a tone reminiscent of Socrates' earnestness,[2] the Athenian reaffirms the danger of prayer misapplied. The cause of the Dorian downfall was no military incapacity, but κακία in other directions, and in particular 'ignorance in matters which are of the utmost significance to mankind'.[3] The legislator, therefore, must seek to inculcate φρόνησις and remove ἄνοια.[4]

The nature of this ἀμαθία is made clear in a speech which follows soon after. It is the state of mind occurring in a man, 'who, so far from feeling any attraction, revolts from what his judgment decides to be honourable or good, while being drawn forcibly towards what he knows to be vile and evil. This dissonance between the feelings of revulsion and attraction, on the one side, and the sober conclusions of his reason, on the other, I would describe as the nadir of ignorance.'[5] ἀμαθία, then, is the reverse of that συμφωνία which has been our aim: it has been mentioned earlier, in the discussion of μουσική, as a secret conflict between judgment and enjoyment, which it is the business of the educator to prevent, a cleavage between temperament and upbringing. The rest of this speech is perhaps even more illuminating, providing us with another clue to the cause of Plato's movement away from Socratic idealism. This ἀμαθία is the principal pointer to it, since it occurs in the popular element in the soul: 'That aspect of the personality which is the domain of revulsion and attraction (τὸ λυπούμενον καὶ ἡδόμενον) corresponds to the common people in society.' When this element is set against ἐπιστήμαις ἢ δόξαις ἢ λόγῳ..., τοῖς φύσει ἀρχικοῖς, the resultant state is the wreck of reason (ἄνοια), both in a city, when a spirit of insurrection appears, 'and moreover in the individual also, when his mind is filled

---

[1] δέοι δὲ δὴ πρὸς πᾶσαν μὲν βλέπειν, μάλιστα δὲ καὶ πρὸς πρώτην τὴν τῆς συμπάσης ἡγεμόνα ἀρετῆς, φρόνησις δ' εἴη τοῦτο καὶ νοῦς καὶ δόξα μετ' ἔρωτός τε καὶ ἐπιθυμίας τούτοις ἑπομένης (688 B 1 ff.).

[2] Cf. σπουδάζων (B 6, C 1).   [3] 688 C 1 ff.

[4] 688 E 5 ff.; see England's note on E 7.

[5] 689 A 5 ff.

with the sound advice of his judgment, and it achieves nothing; indeed perhaps the very reverse of what it intends'.[1]

Two things emerge at once from this statement: first, a reversal, apparent at least, of Socrates' emphatically stated belief in the *Protagoras*,[2] that the dictates of reason are incontrovertible. Examination of the reason for this we must leave to a later chapter: at present it is sufficient to notice that it occurs. More important, for our immediate purpose, is the remark that connects pleasure and pain in the soul with the 'common people in society'. The aim of the *Laws*, as it was that of the *Republic*, is to establish a system of society under which any member may attain to the highest degree of excellence of which he is capable. As a result of this aim, the viewpoint from which ethics is discussed is fundamentally different from, indeed in a sense opposed to, that of Socrates. The Socratic viewpoint in ethics is directed outwards from within the individual, considered not primarily as a member of society but, separately, as a self-sufficient unit of existence. This subjective approach rests largely upon the character of its originator: ethics, in the early dialogues, deals with the personal ideal of Socrates himself. ἐπιστήμη is the goal towards which Socrates himself felt that he was striving, but because his attitude towards the problem of morality was personal, it was projected outwards on man in general. For reasons which we shall discuss later, Plato regards ethics in a different light. He sees the question as though from above and is at pains to construct a theory which can stand as a guide for the whole of humanity. Not a subjective ideal impressed upon the external world, but what he felt was objectively the aim of human life. Regarding morality in this way, he sees that men in general are not capable of equal achievements, that the great mass of mankind cannot ever achieve the Socratic ideal, though this remains the object of those who are capable of it. The majority lead a life in which the mind plays little part, and personal insight into the problems of morality none at all: for they are ruled, not by φρόνησις, but by τὸ λυπούμενον καὶ ἡδόμενον. As we shall see, the final realization of this came only with the *Laws*: the influence of his great teacher wore off only slowly. But by now it has

[1] 689 B 1 ff.; cf. 691 A 5 ff.   [2] *Prot.* 352 A 8 ff. See above, pp. 16 f.

91

become clear: whatever moral ideal we establish for the δῆμός τε καὶ πλῆθος of our society, it must be attainable through the medium of pleasure and pain, and emotion in general, and it is upon these that the legislator-educator must work, since by them all but the minority live. What seems puzzling now about the ethics of the *Laws* is that no higher ideal appears to be envisaged. But that this is not so, we shall later discover.

For the present, συμφωνία remains the ideal: it is the overriding consideration, the paramount value. Without it, being τεχνικός is no title to honour, while those who possess it must be called wise (σοφοί), 'even if, as the saying goes, they can neither write nor swim'.[1] It is the indispensable preliminary of σοφία: 'For how on earth, my good friends, could there be the slightest trace of understanding (φρόνησις) in a man without accord [συμφωνία: i.e. between judgment and his emotional drives]. The thing would be utterly impossible; rather accord, in its highest and most fundamental sense, might quite reasonably be *called* wisdom (σοφία).'[2] Plato's praise of συμφωνία knows here no bounds. The greatest title to rule a community is the possession of φρόνησις, and, *pace* Pindar,[3] Plato declares it to be the natural one, 'the rule of law, unforced and unresented, and in the true sense, natural'.[4]

The fault of the Dorian communities was that they forgot the truth of Hesiod's remark: 'They are fools who cannot understand how much greater the half is than the whole.'[5] For to give men power beyond proportion is as fatal as crowding a boat with canvas, or overfeeding a body: 'The result is disaster; in the body, growth runs riot and rushes headlong into disease; in the character, the end of the process is insensate self-regard (ὕβρις) and its product, crime.'[6] For no soul is capable of bearing supreme power and remaining uncorrupted: 'In all seriousness I suggest to you, my friends, that there is no human character so endowed by

---

[1] ἂν καὶ τὸ λεγόμενον μήτε γράμματα μήτε νεῖν ἐπίστωνται (689 C 6ff.).

[2] 689 D 4ff.; see England's note on D 5.

[3] Pindar, fr. 169 (Snell); quoted or referred to by Plato at *Gorg.* 484 B, 488 B, *Laws*, 714 E, 890 A.

[4] κατὰ φύσιν...τὴν τοῦ νόμου ἑκόντων ἀρχὴν ἀλλ' οὐ βίαιον πεφυκυῖαν (690 C 2f.).

[5] Hesiod, *Works and Days*, 40.   [6] 691 C 1ff.

nature that, while it remains young and uncontrolled by some external authority, it will be able to carry the burden of supreme political power without being infected by the most deadly of diseases, loss of all reason, and so becoming an object of hatred to all who are its nearest friends; and when that happens, the result, and not long to be delayed, is utter disaster and the annihilation of all its powers.'[1] The most obvious feature about this statement is, of course, its common-sense character: we are in a world very different from that which contained the Socratic paradoxes. It brings out also Plato's latter-day devotion to τὸ μέτρον:[2] it is an expression out of the same category as συμφωνία, which we have examined already. Both words are perhaps connected with the mathematical-musical connotations of Pythagoreanism, and are part of Plato's legacy to Aristotle.

Shortly afterwards, the Athenian apologizes for saying that the legislator must make his city 'a combination of freedom, judgment and internal cohesion' (ἐλευθέραν τε καὶ ἔμφρονα καὶ αὐτῇ φίλην). If it seems that he is continually proposing new objectives for the legislator's task, we must not be surprised, 'but you must realize that when we assert that the aim of legislation is sound judgment and controlled behaviour, or understanding, or friendly relations, we are not proposing a variety of aims; it remains one and the same aim, and I hope we will not be disconcerted by any other phrases we may find ourselves using'.[3] In all the welter of detail, there is still one unchanging aim, which, however it is expressed, is the same, the ἀρετή which was stated at the very beginning of the work to be the aim of all legislation. Setting them side by side, the Athenian now examines the rise and

---

[1] οὐκ ἔστ', ὦ φίλοι ἄνδρες, θνητῆς ψυχῆς φύσις ἥτις ποτὲ δυνήσεται τὴν μεγίστην ἐν ἀνθρώποις ἀρχὴν φέρειν νέα καὶ ἀνυπεύθυνος, ὥστε μὴ τῆς μεγίστης νόσου ἀνοίας πληρωθεῖσα αὐτῆς τὴν διάνοιαν, μῖσος ἔχειν πρὸς τῶν ἐγγύτατα φίλων, ὃ γενόμενον ταχὺ διέφθειρεν αὐτὴν καὶ πᾶσαν τὴν δύναμιν ἠφάνισεν αὐτῆς (691 c 5 ff.).

[2] Cf. Democritus, fr. 233 (DK 68, B 233), and see J. E. Raven, *Pythagoreans and Eleatics*, ch. XII.

[3] ἀλλὰ ἀναλογίζεσθαι χρή, ὅταν πρὸς τὸ σωφρονεῖν φῶμεν δεῖν βλέπειν ἢ πρὸς φρόνησιν ἢ φιλίαν, ὡς ἔσθ' οὗτος ὁ σκοπὸς οὐχ ἕτερος ἀλλ' ὁ αὐτός, καὶ ἄλλα δὴ πολλὰ ἡμᾶς τοιαῦτα ἂν γίγνηται ῥήματα μὴ διαταραττέτω (693 c 1 ff.).

fall of Persian and Athenian political society: both collapses were due to the same failure to understand the true nature of παιδεία. In the one case, the Great King (since Xerxes, only so in title), in the other the people of Athens, meeting with an education from which the notion of correction was absent, became proud and ill-disciplined, so that their downfall was only a matter of time. Treated as men blessed by fortune[1] and in no need of training, it was never in their power to attain ἀρετή: 'Brought up in this fashion, there is never the slightest chance that anyone, at any period of his life, can achieve distinction by his moral stature.'[2] Education is not only itself the means to goodness, but, misapplied, can make that goodness unattainable, at any period of one's life. This is another consideration for the legislator. A man should not be viewed as extraordinary, or accorded honour, for the possession of mere physical or material superiority, nor indeed for virtue, 'where σωφροσύνη is no part of it'.[3] As Megillus seems surprised at this last remark, the Athenian questions him about his reaction to men who combine virtue in one field with extravagant vice in another: ἀνδρεία combined with ἀκολασία, professional τέχνη and σοφία with ἀδικία are rejected by Megillus, either as impossible or as undesirable. σωφροσύνη itself, as merely 'an adjunct to that quality which is the real cause for honourable distinction and its reverse'[4] is neither one thing nor the other. And so we revert to our original position: 'Our assertion, then, is that if a society is to be rescued from disaster and, in the result, judged happy, there is one indispensable requirement: that it should, within the bounds of what is possible for humanity, be scrupulously exact in its distribution of honour (τίμη) and dishonour.'[5] The usual hierarchy follows: qualities of soul, provided they have the adjunct of σωφροσύνη, qualities of the body, and, in the last place, material possessions.

Finally, the decadence of Athenian society is subjected to the same scrutiny. Once again it was the absence of correction, the

---

[1] εὐδαίμονες (694D 2ff.).
[2] οὐ γὰρ μή ποτε γένηται παῖς καὶ ἀνὴρ καὶ γέρων ἐκ ταύτης τῆς τροφῆς διαφέρων πρὸς ἀρετήν (696A 2f.).
[3] 696B 4.   [4] 696D 11.   [5] 697A 10ff.

assumption that the δῆμος was fully competent to determine its own values, even in μουσική, that led to its ruin. The lapse from respect for experts and established canons of taste spread from appreciation of μουσική to political life. νόμος, whether in music or society, is the key to goodness, and its overthrow the signal for degradation: the progress of a nation becomes a race, the race a rout, leading only to the old condition, 'a lifelong agony of inescapable misery'.[1] The description is exciting: Plato once again approaches his mood of horror at the suicidal anarchy of Greek society as he saw it. So the introduction closes, Cleinias announces the intended foundation of a new city, and the way is ready for the work of imagination, if we can now really see 'how society is best administered, and how, in his existence as an individual, a man may best live his own life'.[2]

[1] χαλεπὸν αἰῶνα διάγοντας μὴ λῆξαί ποτε κακῶν (701 C 4). The description begins at 700 A 7.
[2] 702 A 8f.

CHAPTER VI

THE SPIRITUAL HIERARCHY

νοῦν δέ γε πάντων τούτων ἡγεμόνα, πρὸς
ὃν δὴ τὰ ἄλλα πάντα...δεῖ βλέπειν.

PLATO, *Laws*, XII, 963 A 8 f.

IN the last chapter, the structure of Plato's final ethical theory was viewed externally, without any attempt at explanation from Plato's own standpoint. The object was to make clear how different the 'climate' of the *Laws* was from the earlier dialogues, by presenting an outline of the conversation of the first three books with occasional comment, and to indicate in sketch the characteristics of this new world. We saw how Socratic moral idealism had been abandoned and that the most obvious trait of the *Laws* was the 'socialization' of ethics.[1] There is a rather terrifying passage in the last book, which seems to cast this characteristic in its most extreme form.[2] Ostensibly, at least, it is concerned with the need for military discipline, and the context is legislation for the citizen army. Self-reliance must be rooted out as anathema, and the power of initiative in all matters, however serious or trivial, must be denied to all. In peace and war, it must be the instinctive act of every citizen to look to their leader, even in the smallest details, 'in a word, to produce a character by habituation which cannot even appreciate the meaning of doing something at a private venture and therefore quite incapable of it; to construct a way of life which is communal, social, and shared by all with all'.[3] The ultimate crime, in human being and beast alike, is ἀναρχία. To us, in these days, such a view has a ring of horror to it, but it is not primarily our task to correct Plato, but to understand him. We must however realize that there is no in-

---

[1] Cf. v, 730D 2ff.   [2] XII, 942A 5ff.
[3] ἑνί τε λόγῳ τὸ χωρίς τι τῶν ἄλλων πράττειν διδάξαι τὴν ψυχὴν ἔθεσι μήτε γιγνώσκειν μήτ' ἐπίστασθαι τὸ παράπαν, ἀλλ' ἀθρόον ἀεὶ καὶ ἅμα καὶ κοινὸν τὸν βίον ὅτι μάλιστα πᾶσι πάντων γίγνεσθαι (942C 1ff.).

justice to Plato in seeing in these words an extreme version, perhaps too extreme to be representative, of the social, moral and political theory of the *Laws*. The city of Magnesia ¹ is, in fact, to be a propaganda state, whose aim is to inculcate ἀρετή into its citizens by a complex and subtle 'incantation' (ἐπῳδή), extending right through life and into every department of human activity. Instead of the philosophic conversation, the picture of an old man 'whispering with three or four kids in a corner' of the *Gorgias*, the pursuit of ἀρετή is now characterized by the text of a legislator, setting out marks of honour and disgrace, working on the pleasures and pains, desires and fears of his society. This 'social' view seems now to be deeply rooted in Plato's mind: in his summary of history,² the central idea is that of the varieties of ἐπιτη-δεύματα, 'régimes', as England puts it,³ which have appeared in different societies and have been responsible for τάξις and ἀταξία. In this chapter, we shall examine the fundamentals of his teaching on society in the *Laws*, and its cause in his present view of human nature.

Towards the beginning of Book IV, Plato outlines the conditions which are essential to the establishment of the new system. In the name of the legislator he requests a dictator, not of philosophical powers of mind, but one who possesses at least σωφροσύνη, in its popular sense.⁴ (The use of the word 'popular' is, in itself, significant, since it hints for the first time that, in this dialogue, the virtues are used in two different senses.) This is the quickest and most convenient way in which the constitution may be settled satisfactorily.⁵ By his own personal example and the exercise of his powers, a dictator can take the first steps towards the goal of ἀρετή. What must be achieved, then, is the awakening of the philosophic sense in authority: this is described as ἔρως θεῖος τῶν σωφρόνων τε καὶ δικαίων ἐπιτηδευμάτων.⁶ Later it is summarized as the concurrence of supreme power with understanding and self-

---

¹ The inhabitants are called 'Magnetes' at IX, 860E 6; the name is also used at XI, 919D 3, XII, 946B 6, 969A 6; cf. VIII, 848D 3 and England *ad loc.*
² VI, 782A 5ff.
³ *Op cit.* vol. I, p. 634.   ⁴ δημώδη (IV, 710A 5).
⁵ Cf. 711C 5ff.   ⁶ 711D 6f.

control,[1] and England is right in commenting on this passage that 'the φρονεῖν indicates especially the part which might be played by the ideal law-giver'.[2] The quality of understanding is one that has so far been, remarkably enough, absent from the discussion: who is to possess it we do not discover until the end of our journey, but the outline of what is intended is becoming clear, and hardens as the conversation proceeds. The 'city of the Magnesians' is to be constructed into a hierarchy. Indeed, the word hierarchy is peculiarly appropriate, since in a sense Plato's society is to be theocratic: god is the master, the 'lord of all rational men',[3] the justifying influence over the whole fabric of society. The Athenian goes on to indicate in what way the age of Kronos was superior to the present: it was because the guidance of the whole was not in the hands of men, but of spirits.[4] Kronos was aware 'that no human character is ever capable of unchecked authority over the whole range of human affairs, without becoming a spawning-ground of senseless self-regard and crime';[5] under the dominion of mere men 'there is no escape from evil and misery' (οὐκ ἔστιν κακῶν...οὐδὲ πόνων ἀνάφυξις). So the moral of this fable is that today also we must assign control of the state to the spiritual, divine and immortal element in us, giving the name of law to ἡ τοῦ νοῦ διανομή.[6]

Law, then, directed towards the divine, is to become, as it were, the observable representative of god within society: god must rule the ideal society, and law is to be his 'vicar',[7] owing its origin to the divine and spiritual. Towards this we must strive, and against the opposite condition, the rule of a soul set on pleasure and delight. Thus in Magnesia, office is to be 'service before the gods' (ἡ τῶν θεῶν ὑπηρεσία), and is to be given to whoever is 'most marked

[1] τὸ φρονεῖν τε καὶ σωφρονεῖν (712A 1).
[2] Op. cit. vol. 1, p. 436.   [3] 713A 4.
[4] δαίμονες (713D 2).
[5] ὡς ἀνθρωπεία φύσις οὐδεμία ἱκανὴ τὰ ἀνθρώπινα διοικοῦσα αὐτοκράτωρ πάντα, μὴ οὐχ ὕβρεώς τε καὶ ἀδικίας μεστοῦσθαι (713C 6ff.).
[6] 714A 1f.; note the pun διανομή—δαίμονες.
[7] The parallelism between Plato's views in the Laws and the fundamentals of Roman Catholicism is obvious. Cf. Cornford, Unwritten Philosophy, p. 66 (where he refers to the parable of the Grand Inquisitor in The Brothers Karamazov). Dodds (The Greeks and the Irrational, pp. 223 f.) sees a closer parallel in Stalinism.

in his obedience to established law' (τοῖς τεθεῖσι νόμοις εὐπει-θέστατος).¹ By calling the authorities, as they are termed, 'servants of the law' (ὑπηρέται τοῖς νόμοις), the Athenian is not trying merely to coin a paradoxical and striking phrase, but is pointing to the root of Plato's new belief in the pre-eminence of law. God, says the Athenian in his speech to the assembled imaginary settlers of Magnesia, directs the universe in the cycle of nature, 'holding in his grasp the beginning, end and middle of all that has existence',² and right is his companion. If we would be happy, we must follow, humbly (ταπεινός),³ in procession after him. The whole message of the Laws is contained in the phrase 'assimilation to god' (ὁμοίωσις θεῷ), and in the final rejection of Protagoras' relativism, Plato asserts that god, not man, is the measure of all things.⁴

There is nothing new in the declaration of the supremacy of god, nor, indeed, in the idea of a hierarchy itself, for we have seen that the value hierarchy goes back to Socrates. But the supremacy of law, as representing god, is an unmistakable deviation from the ideal of Socrates, and we have yet to account for it. After this new faith, perhaps the most obvious feature is a feeling of weariness and pessimism that pervades the whole work. Whether or not we regard it as a newly attained 'realistic' phase in Plato's thought, we must be aware that this is conspicuously different from the tone of the early dialogues. It is intimately bound up with the attitude towards human nature, the choice of a second-best constitution, and the concept of ἀνάγκη which all appear in the Laws, and is an important symptom of the direction in which Plato has moved.

Just before the passage from Book IV, which we have been considering, a wave of doubt sweeps over the Athenian.⁵ He confesses that he was on the point of saying that no man has ever laid down a law, that our legislation is totally the product of chance and circumstance. There follows the picture of a world dictated to by war and poverty, disease, plague and the vagaries of climate, ideas almost personified in the paroxysm of despair. We have

¹ 715 C 2 ff.   ² 715 E 8 f.
³ On the force of ταπεινός, see Dodds, op. cit. pp. 215, 229 n. 39.
⁴ 716 C 4 ff.   ⁵ IV, 709 A 1 ff.

noticed, in the last chapter, an instance where the human situation was denuded of individual humanity and viewed as the playground (or sometimes battleground) of superhuman forces, toying with an insubstantial nightmare of the ghosts of mankind. It was not an isolated example: the present passage is another. There is at least one more, in Book X, where the vehicle of human life becomes a draughtboard, and god the player, making appropriate moves with the 'men' at his disposal.[1] This passage continues with a description of human existence: the individual moves in an orbit governed by the ordinance and law of destiny, but the cause and origin of that orbit is his own choice. It is the concatenation of his own past actions that makes his present unalterable: 'We hardly exaggerate if we say that each of us becomes what his own desires make him, what he is in the depths of his character':[2] a doctrine in its essentials the same as the Buddhist teaching of *Karma*. It is the burden of the irrevocable past that weighs down the Athenian, and, it seems, Plato himself.

At all events, Plato's present view of human nature is in keeping with the weariness of his general mood. In Book V, the Athenian points out that hitherto we have been considering the relation of man to divinity, in fact the divine side of man and its aspirations: we have not given our attention to the human element in humanity.[3] Yet we must attend to this as well, 'for what we say is addressed to men, not gods'. The roots of human existence are set in pleasure and pain: however else, therefore, we may seek to commend the life of moral goodness, it must appeal first and foremost to these emotions. At the very outset of our endeavour, we are in luck: the usual fate of a legislator is to have to seek to reform a society already embedded in long-standing jealousies, to which the institutions of property and finance have given rise. When faced with these consequences of human desire and degeneracy, the legislator can have small hope of success: 'What is left is little

---

[1] X, 903 B 4ff. Compare Heraclitus, fr. 52 (DK 22, B 52) and Schuhl, *Essai sur la formation de la pensée grecque*, pp. 63 f.

[2] ὅπῃ γὰρ ἂν ἐπιθυμῇ καὶ ὁποῖός τις ὢν τὴν ψυχήν, ταύτῃ σχεδὸν ἑκάστοτε καὶ τοιοῦτος γίγνεται ἅπας ἡμῶν ὡς τὸ πολύ (904 C 2ff.).

[3] V, 732 E 1 ff.

more effective than mere pious wishes, and a process of change so slight and cautious that it makes only the smallest of alterations in a vast stretch of time.'[1] The theme of εὐχὴ μόνον seems always to be at the back of Plato's mind in the *Laws*. Indeed, he is soon driven to abandon the ideal explicitly, at least as a practical aim. 'Reflection and experience',[2] says the Athenian, will show that society can never approach nearer than first remove from the ideal. An ethical and social δεύτερος πλοῦς is all that we can hope for. In some aspects, moreover, a third-best constitution may be the limit of practical possibility.[3] In the following lines, he indicates what is in fact the relationship between the *Republic* and the *Laws*. Absolute community in all the things which now provide the disrupting influences in society—attachment to women, children and the possession of property—absolute unanimity of approbation and condemnation, both secret and public, these are the signs of unity, the ultimate value in social relations. This must in any case be the παράδειγμα πολιτείας,[4] the aim of everything that is proposed hereafter, but we cannot expect to attain it. An instance follows: communal farming is not to be laid down for the citizens of Magnesia, 'since that is a demand too severe for the children of this age, brought up and educated as they are'.[5]

Necessity, the limiting factor, appears soon after in the conversation. If possible, we should never take into our society citizens whose education has been merely a bastard form of the one true upbringing; 'yet we are told that not even god can force his way against necessity'.[6] We are irresistibly reminded of the Simonides fragment which Plato himself quoted at an earlier period, in the *Protagoras*:[7] ἀνάγκᾳ δ' οὐδὲ θεοὶ μάχονται. Plato is doing no more

---

[1] εὐχὴ δὲ μόνον ὡς ἔπος εἰπεῖν λείπεται, καὶ σμικρὰ μετάβασις εὐλαβὴς ἐν πολλῷ χρόνῳ σμικρὸν μεταβιβάζουσιν (736 D 2 ff.).

[2] ἀναλογιζομένῳ καὶ πειρωμένῳ (739 A 3 f.).

[3] I agree with Taylor's explanation of this passage (*op. cit.* p. 121 n. 1); cf. 745 E 8 ff.

[4] 739 B 1.

[5] ἐπειδὴ τὸ τοιοῦτον μεῖζον ἢ κατὰ τὴν νῦν γένεσιν καὶ τροφὴν καὶ παίδευσιν εἴρηται (740 A 1 f). For a recent account of the relation between *Republic* and *Laws*, see D. Grene, *Man in his Pride*, pp. 154 f.

[6] ἀνάγκην δὲ οὐδὲ θεὸς εἶναι λέγεται δυνατὸς βιάζεσθαι (741 A 4 ff.).

[7] Simonides, fr. 4 (Diehl), quoted at *Prot.* 345 D 5.

than falling back, in his tiredness, on an idea current in his aristocratic milieu, but the fact itself is sufficient indication of that tiredness. It is true that nothing said here can detract from the
amazing vigour of the *Laws* in other directions: but the vigour
is intellectual and creative, the weariness mo refundamental. We
can say that Plato is still grappling with enormous intensity and
passion with the problems of human existence, but it is now from
a different standpoint.

This standpoint is one which recognizes humanity as naturally
prone to evil, whether through weakness or a longing for evil for
its own sake. We are no longer surprised to find Plato citing
'the general viciousness'[1] as the cause of a dilemma. In a sense,
the Athenian admits, we are justified in feeling shame for the
depravity which we seem to expect in human beings.[2] But we
are not in the position of the great legislators of the past: we
legislate as men for men, our society is not heroic, semi-divine,
nor are our laws. It is pardonable in us, then, to fear 'that some
one among our society may be found of a stony hardness, a man
whose nature is so unyielding that we will be unable to soften
him'. We may feel it impossible that any Magnesian would
commit so terrible a crime as, for instance, temple robbery. Perhaps only aliens or slaves can be dragged so deep in the slime of
evil. We will frame our law principally for them, 'but we must
be on our guard against the general weakness of human nature'.[3]
Deep in every man is the desire which drags him after evil things,
(ἐπιθυμία κακή) which haunts a man by day and wakes him by
night: 'the gnawing bite of a passion deep-rooted from the crimes
of men long dead, crimes never expiated and issuing now in this
walking shadow of the curse of evil. A man needs all his strength
to guard against it as he must':[4] the description is noteworthy.
There is a curiously Christian ring about much of the *Laws*, combined with a 'common-sense' appraisal of moral problems which,

---

[1] διὰ κάκην τὴν τῶν πολλῶν (VIII, 840D 1).   [2] IX, 853 B 4ff.

[3] ὅμως δὲ καὶ σύμπασαν τὴν τῆς ἀνθρωπίνης φύσεως ἀσθένειαν εὐλαβού-
μενος (853D 10f.).

[4] οἶστρος δέ...τις ἐμφυόμενος ἐκ παλαιῶν καὶ ἀκαθάρτων τοῖς ἀνθρώποις
ἀδικημάτων, περιφερόμενος ἀλιτηριώδης, ὃν εὐλαβεῖσθαι χρεὼν παντὶ σθένει
(854B 3ff.); see England's note, *ad loc.*

by comparison with earlier Platonism, one might be tempted to call un-Platonic. It is not doing violence to language to describe such a passage as that in Book XI which is concerned with the dangers of retail trade, as being about the powers of 'temptation' to corrupt humanity.[1] But, however we may react to it, it is essential to the understanding of the *Laws* to realize that for Plato now, 'no man's nature is so well endowed that he can see what is to the advantage of men in society, and having seen it, possess both the capacity and the desire always to do what is best'.[2] If a judge disgraces his office in the full feeling of his power, Plato can say of him now that 'by falling into crime, he reveals the essential humanity of his nature'.[3]

If mankind is thus fundamentally weak, and potentially, if not actually, corrupt, the vision of a society which is to attain ἀρετή seems to recede beyond the bounds of the possible. But there is a 'saving clause' in Plato's estimate of humanity. Within the limits of his nature, man can still achieve the solitary worthwhile aim of ἀρετή, and this by observance and fulfilment of law. We have seen already the honour paid to law in this treatise: we can now see the reason. As the Athenian says: 'Seeing the truth and, once seen, to persevere in it, is by no means a simple task; it is safest to listen to the pronouncements of law and be persuaded.'[4] Law is the visible manifestation of truth; 'and truth, whether it be among gods or men, stands at the head of all goods'.[5] Left to himself, man must go, with his imperfections, the way of all flesh, but by the aid and guidance of law, he, and society with him, may reach the culminating glories of happiness and devotion to his fellow men.[6]

Having reached this point, we may examine what is said of law and the legislator in the treatise. First and foremost, as we should

---

[1] XI, 918 C 9 ff.

[2] φύσις ἀνθρώπων οὐδενὸς ἱκανὴ φύεται ὥστε γνῶναί τε τὰ συμφέροντα ἀνθρώποις εἰς πολιτείαν καὶ γνοῦσα, τὸ βέλτιστον ἀεὶ δύνασθαί τε καὶ ἐθέλειν πράττειν (IX, 875 A 2 ff.); cf. XII, 955 D 1 ff.

[3] τὴν ἀνθρωπίνην φύσιν ἐπιδείξῃ κακὸς γενόμενος (XII, 947 E 7 f.).

[4] τὸ γὰρ γνῶναι καὶ γνόντα καρτερεῖν οὐκ εὐπετές, ἀκούοντα δὲ ἀσφαλέστατον πείθεσθαι τῷ νόμῳ (955 D 1 f.).

[5] V, 730 C 1 f.   [6] 743 C 5 ff.

expect, the legislator's decision is the ultimate canon of morality: 'To put the matter in a word, the man who will not use all the means he possesses to keep himself free from those things the legislator stigmatizes as evil and unworthy, and to follow the path laid down as good and becoming man's true nature, such a man has not understood that in so doing he drags in all the ugliness of vice the divinest thing he has, his soul.'[1] Thus submission is the paramount virtue of the *Laws*, submission to god in the character of law: 'There is more just cause for pride in honourable servitude than in ruling with honour, and the first of servitudes is that before the law; for servitude before the law is servitude before god.'[2] The task of the legislator is, therefore, not simply to produce a code of laws which will enable his society to live under reasonable conditions, but to impart, by means of his legislation, as much of the divine side of man to that society as possible. If it should be complained that the legislator seems more concerned with education than the regulation of social life, Plato will accept the charge.[3] The ideal legislator is free to choose between the outright best and the inescapable minimum.[4] The book of laws should, Plato believes, be the finest work in a country's literature, and he recommends it as a 'set book' for school use.[5] The effort towards producing a constitution as excellent as possible is required of the legislator because it is the only defence which, as Plato now sees it, stands between man and the status of a wild beast.[6] Hence the chief danger to society is to be found in any person who attempts to subvert the laws 'by dragging them into subjection to individual men'.[7]

It must seem at times in this long work that the panegyric on law knows no bounds. 'Everything in society which is marked by order and is subject to law, has good as its outcome.'[8] Indeed,

---

[1] 728A 5ff.   [2] VI, 762E 3ff.; cf. VII, 822D 4ff.   [3] IX, 857E 3ff.
[4] τό τε ἄριστον καὶ τὸ ἀναγκαιότατον (858A 2).
[5] E 4ff.; cf. VII, 811D 2ff.
[6] νόμους ἀνθρώποις ἀναγκαῖον τίθεσθαι καὶ 3ῆν κατὰ νόμους ἢ μηδὲν διαφέρειν τῶν πάντη ἀγριωτάτων θηρίων (IX, 874E 9f.).
[7] 856B 2ff.
[8] πᾶν μὲν γάρ, ὅτιπερ ἂν τάξεως καὶ νόμου μετέχον ἐν πόλει γίγνηται, πάντα ἀγαθὰ ἀπεργά3εται (VI, 780D 5ff.).

Plato goes far in many places towards making 'legal' and 'right' equivalent terms. At one point, in fact, the phrase νόμιμον καὶ ὅσιον is, as England says, a variant of the common expression δίκαιον καὶ ὅσιον.[1] But it is clear that Plato does actually recognize the limitations to which law is subject. In the first place, of course, the constructor of the system is himself as much a man as those for whom it is designed. His very ideas are not capable of the infinite range which the task of legislation ideally requires: he can only give the many problems his attention within limits, 'to the extent that a man *can* examine such things'.[2] Though the legislator is ὁ διακοσμῶν,[3] and although he is to provide the text on which the judges of Magnesia, for example, have to rely implicitly,[4] he is himself limited, not only in intelligence and breadth of mind, but also in the ability to express his views in writing: he can only aim to 'set down his laws with the utmost degree of accuracy that lies within his power'.[5] His ability is the limiting factor. Moreover, he is not in a position to envisage all the possible eventualities in his society: therefore, not only are there continual references in the *Laws* to the details which will have to be filled in by the Curators of the legal system (νομοφύλακες),[6] but the Athenian also recognizes that circumstances may arise to which the existing legal provisions will not be suited. Sometimes, because of the weakness of men, strict justice will have to be relaxed somewhat in favour of 'equity and mercy'.[7] Therefore, the scheme of legislation must be kept flexible, so that it can meet these unforeseen occurrences as they have to be met.[8]

---

[1] IX, 861D 4. [2] V, 747E 6f. [3] 742E 3. [4] XII, 957C 7ff.

[5] γράψαι τοὺς νόμους πρὸς τὴν ἀκρίβειαν κατὰ δύναμιν ἱκανῶς (VI, 769C 7ff.).

[6] There is no suitable word to translate νομοφύλακες. Of all the irrelevant connotations which are bound to be introduced, that of the periodical dusting of works of art seems the most innocuous. But it is difficult, if not impossible, to find a word in English which will suggest, as Plato definitely intends it to be suggested (see XI, 920A 6ff.), that the Curators are not only to protect the legal system from abuse and decay, but also, as 'legal guardians', to stand guard over the citizen body itself. On this point, see below, p. 120f.

[7] τὸ...ἐπιεικὲς καὶ σύγγνωμον (757D 5ff.).

[8] XI, 925E 6ff. (where an example is given). Plato also recognizes limits to the power of persuasion; cf. IV, 722B 6f.

In addition to the limitations of the written constitution, there is need of ἄγραφα νόμιμα. These traditional observances are important, says the Athenian, because if they are put into practice, they envelop the written system in a general protection, providing it with a sort of buffer against unfettered human desires and inclinations. If they are not observed, the situation of the written law is that of a building the supports of which collapse while it is still being constructed.[1]

But by far the most serious drawback to the supremacy of law is the fact that, once in use, it is beyond the control of the legislator, and subject to the world of chance and change. All change from the ideal (for change of what is *bad* is allowed for) is to be deplored, and the more so, says Plato in his despondency, because the human mind can become acclimatized to any way of life, as the body will accept, in time, any diet.[2] In its inception the guarantee of the value of law is that it was cast by a mind which could see further than the mass of men, and was in closer contact with the divine. But a legal system is not merely an object for exhibition; it is a rule of life, and life under the moon, in the grip of decay. Not only must there be a static hierarchy of gods, legislator and mankind, but the hierarchy must be carried into the structure of society itself. Towards the end of the *Laws*, Plato begins to outline the fabric which will preserve the system of law, the only reason for the claim that Magnesia is a city further on the way to the true end of human society than any other. As before, it is headed by the divine, followed by the protective element, which exercises its control over the descending scale of magistrates, executive and legal, civil servants and troops, down to the citizen body itself. The basis of this fabric we will now consider.

The possibility of moral and happy living hinges on the relationship which society has with the divine. Plato has more to say about this in Book x. Belief in the existence of gods, and gods both interested in the fate of mankind, and incorruptible in their surveillance of human life, is the foundation of society, and its defence is declared to be 'the finest and most effective prelude, to

---

[1] VII, 793 A 9 ff.   [2] 797 D 9 ff.

support our whole legislation'.[1] The theme of this book, and one of the most important in the whole work, is this: 'The greatest of all issues...is whether or not we view the gods as they are and thereby live well.'[2] The basis of his belief Plato finds in the primacy of the spiritual over the material, which he supports by a powerful and involved argument. This is, in effect, the central core of Platonism, and if ever we have to call on the assistance of the gods, says the Athenian, now is that time.[3] At the end of the argument, soul is declared the universal cause of all phenomena: 'If, in all seriousness, we lay it down as our belief that soul is prior in existence to body, body a mere late-comer on the scene, and that, in the nature of things, soul is governor, body the subject, we shall be in the right: our statement will be definitive and final, and will comprise the whole of truth.'[4] The solemnity of language, as so often in Plato, sets its own value on this pronouncement. But there is a warning contained even in this statement of belief: we must not create for ourselves 'darkness at noon', by attempting to grasp directly the nature of real wisdom: we are still held by the limitations of human nature (897D 8 ff.).

There is confirmation for our view that relation to god is the most important single problem for society, in the fact that, with the question of belief in god, the Nocturnal Council first appears. For this council is the protective element in society which we have mentioned: it is to consist of the most distinguished and venerable members of the community, and supersedes the council of Curators as the highest committee in Magnesia.[5] Its claim to superiority lies in the higher value that understanding has than habituation in

---

[1] x, 887B 8 ff. The relation between religion and the structure of Magnesia in the *Laws*, especially Book x, is considered by F. Solmsen, *Plato's Theology*, pp. 131–74.

[2] μέγιστον δέ...τὸ περὶ τοὺς θεοὺς ὀρθῶς διανοηθέντα 3ῆν καλῶς ἢ μή (888B 3 f.).

[3] 893B 1 f. On the primacy of ψυχή in *Laws* x, see Solmsen, *op. cit.* pp. 131–48.

[4] ὀρθῶς ἄρα καὶ κυρίως ἀληθέστατά τε καὶ τελεώτατα εἰρηκότες ἂν εἶμεν ψυχὴν μὲν προτέραν γεγονέναι σώματος ἡμῖν, σῶμα δὲ δεύτερόν τε καὶ ὕστερον, ψυχῆς ἀρχούσης, ἀρχόμενον κατὰ φύσιν (896B 10 ff.); cf. E 8 ff.

[5] One among many pieces of evidence that the *Laws* was left unrevised at its author's death may be found in the fact that the relationship between the elements of the hierarchy seems to fluctuate and is never made fully clear.

a tradition. Without it, there can be no civilization or finality.[1] Life within a system has value only in so far as that system was constructed by men of understanding. To possess understanding is, therefore, to rise superior to the system (since personal understanding is more complete than second-hand discipline), and, for the system to remain excellent, it must be in the hands of men who have travelled beyond it and attained the wisdom of those who established it. This the Nocturnal Council is to do: with it a new dimension opens in the structure of society, and the way in which this new light suddenly floods into the closed atmosphere of the *Laws* at the very end of the treatise is one of the most impressive features of the work. Their principal task is to test and fix the system when they believe it sufficiently perfected.[2] It is a point worth noticing that, with the introduction of the Nocturnal Council, the influence of Socrates is once again apparent: the mention of personal understanding brings with it the marks of the great exponent and possessor of that quality. The central part of this final movement of the *Laws* is taken up with a demonstration that the natural protector of the structure of society is that element in it which is fully aware of the aim of its system of legislation:[3] the Socratic ring of this argument is unmistakable, particularly in a work from which it has been notably absent. 'If our settlement of this territory is to achieve its goal, there must, even at this stage, I believe, be some element in it which can grasp the true nature of what we have called our aim as builders of society. More than that, such an element must know how that aim is to be attained, and what advice, whether, first and foremost, of the laws, or, secondarily, that of men, is well or ill given.'[4] Only the 'social' atmosphere and the mention of law blend the Socratic with what we now see to be the essentially Platonic tone of the *Laws*.

From now on the hierarchy and its organization become more explicit and more clear. The virtues themselves, and the whole world

[1] XII, 951 A 7ff.   [2] 957 B 1 ff.   [3] 961 D 1 ff.

[4] δεῖ δὴ καὶ τὰ νῦν, ὡς ἔοικεν, εἴπερ μέλλει τέλος ὁ κατοικισμὸς τῆς χώρας ἡμῖν ἕξειν, εἶναί τι τὸ γιγνῶσκον ἐν αὐτῷ πρῶτον μὲν τοῦτο ὃ λέγομεν, τὸν σκοπόν, ὅστις ποτὲ ὁ πολιτικὸς ὢν ἡμῖν τυγχάνει, ἔπειτα ὅντινα τρόπον δεῖ μετασχεῖν τούτου καὶ τίς αὐτῷ καλῶς ἢ μὴ συμβουλεύει, τῶν νόμων αὐτῶν πρῶτον, ἔπειτα ἀνθρώπων (962 B 4 ff.).

of the spirit, look to the leadership of the mind,[1] and the fabric of society merely reflects this fact. Its structure is compared to the human body in an important speech by the Athenian. The trunk is the citizen body at large, while the head and its organs of sense are represented by the younger Curators. Within the head, their seniors, who compose the Nocturnal Council, perform the functions of the mind, so that these two groups between them compose the salvation of the state.[2] Finally, the scheme is summarized: 'Is it not a matter of the greatest value to us to know, so far as a man *can* know these things, that the gods exist, and that they are the evident possessors of the highest power? This was a question we discussed in all earnestness, and while it is enough that the great majority in our society should share in this knowledge merely by conforming to the tradition which our laws enshrine, those who have a part to play in its preservation must be allowed to include no one who has not exerted every ounce of his strength to gain every evidence there is of the gods' existence.'[3] In effect, a summary of the whole work.

So the erection of the hierarchy proceeds to its culmination. I have called it a 'spiritual hierarchy', because the criterion of advancement within it is the liberation and flowering of the spirit as Plato sees it. For all but the few, law is the horizon of intellectual and moral life.[4] Perhaps the greatest tragedy of the *Laws* is that it sets the final seal of doom on the Socratic approach: when Plato describes the Nocturnal Council condemning to death the man who, setting himself outside the tradition of the state, refuses to keep his views privately to himself, it is not only ironical but tragic that we seem to hear an echo of Socrates' judges.[5] Yet it is the logical and necessary outcome of an approach which sets the general good of society above the individual and his minor concerns.[6]

---

[1] 963 A 8 f.   [2] 964 E 1 ff.

[3] μῶν οὖν οὐχ ἓν τῶν καλλίστων ἐστὶν τὸ περὶ τοὺς θεούς, ὃ δὴ σπουδῇ διεπερανάμεθα, ὡς εἰσίν τε καὶ ὅσης φαίνονται κύριοι δυνάμεως, εἰδέναι τε εἰς ὅσον δυνατόν ἐστιν ταῦτ' ἄνθρωπον γιγνώσκειν, καὶ τοῖς μὲν πλείστοις τῶν κατὰ πόλιν συγγιγνώσκειν τῇ φήμῃ μόνον τῶν νόμων συνακολουθοῦσιν, τοῖς δὲ φυλακῆς μεθέξουσιν μηδὲ ἐπιτρέπειν, ὃς ἂν μὴ διαπονήσηται τὸ πᾶσαν πίστιν λαβεῖν τῶν οὐσῶν περὶ θεῶν; (966 c 1 ff.).

[4] For a summary of its function, see IX, 880 D 8 ff.

[5] XII, 952 C 5 ff. See Dodds, *op. cit.* pp. 223 f.   [6] XI, 923 B 4 ff.

CHAPTER VII

THE FUNCTION OF EDUCATION

φημὶ κατὰ πάσας πόλεις τὸ τῶν παιδιῶν γένος ἠγνοῆσθαι
σύμπασιν ὅτι κυριώτατόν ἐστι περὶ θέσεως νόμων.

PLATO, *Laws*, VII, 797 A 7 ff.

HAVING already now examined the thematic structure
of the *Laws* from one angle, we may turn to the application in detail of the principles which we saw at work
over the whole treatise. An obvious illustration will be the theories
of education which figure so largely in the *Laws*. We will investigate first the few pronouncements on education outside Books II
and VII, and then look at Book VII in some detail.[1] In the main,
we shall be discussing in this chapter the education envisaged for
the general mass of citizens, and the methods by which law and
education are to direct their lives towards ἀρετή. The education
of the protective element is not discussed at great length, and only
in the last book: we will glance at it at the end of this chapter.

We have seen already that the relative positions of various
officials were left obscure by the lack of revision.[2] A case in point
is that of the Minister of Education: he is elected with great cere-
mony and those who elect him are instructed to bear in mind 'that
this office is by far the most significant of all the high offices in our
society'.[3] This perhaps represents a period in the writing of the
Laws before the Nocturnal Council had been decided upon,
although it is, of course, true that the Minister of Education, and
any of his predecessors in office who may be alive, are *ex officio*
members of the Council, and he may still remain the most important single magistrate. The reason for his pre-eminence is given
in the same speech. In all growing creatures, the first shoots are

---

[1] Book II has already been analysed in chapter V (pp. 80–7). On education
in the *Laws*, see also R. G. Bury's article in *Revue des Études Grecques*, Vol. 50
(1937), pp. 304 ff.

[2] See above, p. 107 n. 5.   [3] VI, 765 D 8 ff.

the most important: if they are set on the right road of development, the biggest single step has been taken 'towards the true development of their natural qualities'.[1] Moreover, of all creatures, man has the greatest potentialities for good and evil, and the direction in which he develops these depends on the correctness, or otherwise, of his education and upbringing. The legislator cannot, therefore, afford to make education a side-line in his task: it is the kernel of his whole work that the official in charge of education should be the most excellent of the entire citizen body.

The function of education itself is to produce a character best suited to the organization of society, that is, best able to carry out the injunctions of law. Education moulds the inner life of the members of society to conform with their legally imposed outer life. The aim of the educator is, indeed, very like that of the 'shrewd and subtle-minded man' of Critias' famous fragment.[2] Critias suggested that the gods had been invented to control the private thoughts and actions of men, which were beyond the reach of law: this is certainly the purpose of education in the *Laws*: 'We must now turn to those things which law cannot achieve, but which the formative effect of praise and blame can do, towards making all in our society more easy to control, more receptive to the legal injunctions we are about to enact.'[3] Its methods will be rather those of example and incantation (ἐπῳδή)[4] than direct teaching:[5] an attempt to get right inside the child's mind and inculcate a moral attitude as strong as Socratic ἐπιστήμη itself; the aim, in fact, of propaganda. For the basis of the society of Magnesia requires that the emotions and inner subtleties of the mind be brought into line with the sanctions of law quite as much as the conscious surface.

At the outset of Book VII, we are told that the privacy of the home renders unnoticed the fact that a host of unimportant inci-

---

[1] πρὸς ἀρετὴν τῆς αὐτοῦ φύσεως (765 E 4.) The use of ἀρετή here gives a good indication of its basic significance.

[2] Nauck[2], p. 771, ll. 9 ff.

[3] ὅσα μὴ νόμος, ἀλλ' ἔπαινος παιδεύων καὶ ψόγος ἑκάστους εὐηνίους μᾶλλον καὶ εὐμενεῖς τοῖς τεθήσεσθαι μέλλουσιν νόμοις ἀπεργάζεται (v, 730 B 5 ff.).

[4] See Dodds, *op. cit.* p. 226 n. 20 and Schuhl, *Essai*, p. 252 n. 2.

[5] 729 C 2 ff.

dents, occasioned by the emotions of childhood, may go to produce a character of a tendency opposed to that of the legislator, which makes the child incompatible with his companions.[1] Such an occurrence is a fundamental obstacle to the legislator's achievement of his aims. Slowly, imperceptibly, his citizens are set against the observance of law, 'since they have acquired the habit of breaking the law in a host of trivial misdemeanours' (ἐν τοῖς σμικροῖς καὶ πυκνοῖς ἐθισθέντων τῶν ἀνθρώπων παρανομεῖν). For unless the private and personal life of the individual is properly regulated, one may look in vain for any strength in the foundations of public law.[2] The process of character building starts almost from the moment of birth: continual childish frights, for example, habituate the infant in timidity, and they must be avoided by rocking the child rhythmically and inducing calm.[3] If fear is allowed to achieve a grip on the baby, 'we would all agree that this tends towards producing a habit of cowardice'.[4] The key to this very early stage in education is ἄσκησις, habituation from the earliest moments in the desired way of life. At this stage, conscious mental processes are not observable and cannot be affected consciously. Yet Plato believes that it would be a monumental error to suppose that for this reason education cannot yet begin. In most men, the powers of the conscious mind develop late or not at all. Consequently the lives of most men are not directed consciously by the intellect, but by the intimate workings of their emotional character. This can be affected from the start, and not to do so is, in most cases, to lose all hope of ever directing the pupil's life effectively. The general aim, at this point, is to create an equable temper in the child, and thus to foster εὐψυχία.[5] The two extreme approaches to the question of upbringing, spoiling or enslaving the child, have both equally disastrous results. It is, in these early years, essential to protect the child from unpleasant experiences, such as fear, but it is merely mischievous to do this by providing for it a steady stream of pleasant experiences. This is

---

[1] VII, 788A 5ff. [2] 790B 2ff.
[3] 790C 5ff.
[4] τοῦτο δέ που πᾶς ἂν φαίη δειλίας ἄσκησιν...γίγνεσθαι (791B 7f.).
[5] 791C 8ff.

to encourage a false luxuriating in emotion, at the most dangerous period, the beginning of life.[1]

The Athenian's speech lays great stress on the need for producing contentment, the mean state. If it did not sound ridiculous, he would lay it as a duty on pregnant women to avoid undue emotion, whether of pleasure or pain. 'My own view of the question is that the right life for man is neither the pursuit of pleasures, nor, indeed, a headlong flight from pain, but contentment with the mean state (I mentioned it just now, and called it a gracious existence); that is a temperament which an inspired tradition makes us all assign to god himself, and we are right.'[2] As so often in Plato, the language of this speech underlines the seriousness of what he is saying. The key to his teaching here (and to much of the educational theory of this book) is to be found in the words: 'The character of all of us at that age is most solidly founded upon habit.'[3] What Plato is here trying to implant in the children's minds is the tradition of ἄγραφα νόμιμα: every society makes its indelible brand on the personality of its members, by the insistent effect of environment, a fixed horizon and propaganda of a disorganized kind. Plato is setting out to give this traditional mark a direction and purpose, and to regulate its application.

Having taken education back a stage from the conscious process of instruction to the sphere of habituation in the earliest years, he now finds the roots of character in this apparently trivial world of games and play. Because the vast majority of men do not realize that games are for children both the factor determining character and the means of expressing it, the continual change of personality, which goes on when no established standard of games exists, escapes their notice.[4] The setting up of standards is the first essential

---

[1] 792 C 2 ff.
[2] ὁ μὲν γὰρ ἐμὸς δὴ λόγος οὔθ' ἡδονάς φησι δεῖν διώκειν τὸν ὀρθὸν βίον οὔτ' αὖ τὸ παράπαν φεύγειν τὰς λύπας, ἀλλ' αὐτὸ ἀσπάζεσθαι τὸ μέσον, ὃ νυνδὴ προσεῖπον ὡς ἵλεων ὀνομάσας, ἣν δὴ διάθεσιν καὶ θεοῦ κατά τινα μαντείας φήμην εὐστόχως πάντες προσαγορεύομεν (792 C 9 ff.).
[3] κυριώτατον γὰρ οὖν ἐμφύεται πᾶσι τότε τὸ πᾶν ἦθος διὰ ἔθος (792 E 1 f.). Once again there are affinities with Aristotle; cf. such passages as *Eth. Nic.* 1103 a 16 ff.
[4] 797 A 7 ff.

in the world of children, as it was seen to be in adult society. The desire, perpetually seizing the young, for 'something new' is disastrous, because they carry it with them into adult life: we cannot expect the habits of childhood to be put away with increasing age. This is really the core of Plato's interest in education, and of the way in which he meets the subject: both are derived from his sensitivity to the correlation of microcosm and macrocosm,[1] even when the difference between the two worlds is only that between child and man. In both cases we must expect the same principles to hold true, and we cannot hope to solve the problems of adult social living by ignoring the essentially similar ones of childhood. If adherence to the tradition is a virtue among men, it is one among children also. All that we must remember is that the scale is different: otherwise the principles are the same.

As we saw in the last chapter, change is bad because humanity can become acclimatized to any system, however bad, by habit. We must therefore be on the look-out for a decline in standards of play, both in outward forms and, more seriously, in 'moral' approbation and disgust: 'The lesser changes, in outward appearances, would certainly cause harm, but frequent alterations in what, in their inner characters, children praise and blame, if they occur, would, I believe, be of the utmost seriousness and would need to be very carefully guarded against.'[2] This is particularly true in the case of music and poetry, and the fixing of standards in these fields demands the careful consideration of the legislator. We must accept it as axiomatic that the poets themselves are incapable of judging between good and evil, and need guidance.[3]

In accordance with his view of the human ability to become acclimatized, Plato believes that any style of music will give pleasure to the man who has been brought up in it: the standard of choice between the styles is not therefore one of pleasure, but of moral effect. The subjection of music to order and system will not make it more pleasurable, but its moral effect will now be for the good, where it was previously for the bad.[4] This passage also introduces a distinction in the field of ἀρεταί, which is of con-

---

[1] Notice especially 798 B 6ff. [2] D 1ff.
[3] 801 B 10f. [4] 802 C 4ff.

siderable importance in later Platonism, though we have not met it before. There now appear to be two great classes of virtue, the male or active group (here called ἀρρενωπόν) and the female, passive group (θηλυγενέστερον).[1] It is important, because it is akin to the fundamental distinction in Plato's social ethics between the obedient, emotional class, and the constructive, intellectual, protective element. It is also noticeably incompatible with the strict unity of virtue as Socrates envisaged it, and is part of the 'common-sense' structure of the later years: it may even be the root of that structure, while it is certainly a good description of it.

The passage ends with a vindication by the Athenian of his treatment of character:

I feel as though I were playing the part of a shipbuilder: for when a shipbuilder begins his work, his first step is to lay down a keel (τροπιδεῖα —there is a pun here on τρόπος, character), and indicate the outlines of his ship. I am doing much the same thing in my attempt to outline the different types of lives, with all their distinguishing marks, which answer to different types of character: these characters are in fact the keels of our lives, and I am trying to lay them down by considering what equipment, what characters will be best for us in this, the voyage of our life.[2]

The goodness of one's life is determined by τρόπος, the keel upon which the rest is built: attention to it is the most necessary part of education. The discussion is now at its most serious, and it is no accident that Plato now connects childhood with maturity in yet another way. We cannot afford to dismiss play as beneath our serious intentions, for the whole of human life is play before the gods.[3] In ourselves, we are worth nothing: as the puppet theatre of heaven, we attain our only value. Thus the worlds of childhood and adult life are bound together and the difference in value, in ultimate seriousness, between them disappears. We must recognize our role (τρόπος again) and perfect our play before god—but to do this we must abandon completely our current view of ourselves: τούτῳ δὴ δεῖν τῷ τρόπῳ συνεπόμενον καὶ παίζοντα ὅτι καλλίστας

---

[1] E 5 ff. See below, pp. 214 f.
[2] 803 A 3 ff. (I read σκοπῶν with England and Taylor).
[3] B 3 ff.

παιδιάς πάντ' ἄνδρα καὶ γυναῖκα οὕτω διαβιῶναι, τοὐναντίον ἢ νῦν διανοηθέντας.¹ In the present passage, we are taken back to the great fable of the first book,² and more echoes of the introduction follow. The value set on war, as the Athenian points out, is mistaken because there is in war neither παιδιά nor παιδεία of any worth, and these are what we find supremely serious.³ In play, dedicated to the gods, we fulfil all the potentialities of our nature, 'for we are for the most part toys, but with a little touch of reality in us, too'.⁴

Play and education (and the two expressions seem inextricably mixed, in derivation and use, for Plato) are the essentials of life. Thus education is compulsory for every citizen.⁵ A familiar theme soon follows: the greatness and urgency of the task. If the training for the great games leaves no time for other occupations, 'the life which we say (and rightly) is spent in training body and soul alike in an all-out effort to become truly a man' requires twice the effort or more, if it is to succeed.⁶ The day is hardly long enough for this activity: 'Indeed the man who is most concerned with the task of right living and right conduct, keeps awake all the hours he can.'⁷ Schools will open at dawn, for children must not live without supervision. They are the most difficult to handle of all wild animals: the flow of their minds has not yet been canalized, so that they need every kind of check.

In the middle of his description of education in Magnesia, Plato includes a satirical account of 'education' via the works of the poets: the learning by heart, the anthologizing, 'dinning their ears with reading aloud and cramming them with information'.⁸ The satire is obvious, but we cannot fail to be struck by the way that the method of this conventional education resembles Plato's

---

¹ 803 C 6 ff.   ² I, 644 D 7 ff.   ³ VII, 803 D 2 ff.

⁴ θαύματα ὄντες τὸ πολύ, σμικρὰ δὲ ἀληθείας ἄττα μετέχοντες (804 B 3 f.).

⁵ D 3 f.

⁶ ὁ περὶ τὴν τοῦ σώματος πάντως καὶ ψυχῆς εἰς ἀρετῆς ἐπιμέλειαν βίος εἰρημένος ὀρθότατα (807 C 4 ff.).

⁷ ἀλλ' ὅστις τοῦ ζῆν ἡμῶν καὶ τοῦ φρονεῖν μάλιστά ἐστι κηδεμών, ἐγρήγορε χρόνον ὡς πλεῖστον (808 B 6 ff.).

⁸ πολυηκόους τ' ἐν ταῖς ἀναγνώσεσιν ποιοῦντας καὶ πολυμαθεῖς (810 E 11 ff.). The whole passage begins at 810 E 6.

own. In fact, of course, it is only the content to which he now objects. In a later passage, he puts forward the basis of his attack on the poets: the whole system of the Laws is 'a representation in action of the noblest and finest of lives: we may rightly call it drama, in the most proper sense of the word'.[1] Thus the legislator and the dramatist are both poets, and rivals in the greatest drama of all, 'one which only a true system of law can, in the nature of things, produce'.[2] Plato has come to see that the methods of conventional education are effective, indeed the only ones which offer a chance of influencing human nature. He has adopted them as his own, but for different ends: the convention which they are to sow in the mind of society has the merit, in Plato's eyes, of being true, as it is based, not on the lowest common denominator of human intelligence, but on a vision of the truth by the highest faculty. By our music and our poetry we must work enchantment, 'exhorting all to follow us in the achievement of man's true stature, by taking their part in this dramatic representation'.[3] But it is now clear to us from this survey of education that in the quality of the tradition is the only difference between the aim of Plato and that of Athenian society. Uniformity, as complete as may be possible, is the intended outcome in both,[4] and the conventional man is the ideal of social ethics, however high the convention. The ethical society seeks to mould its members into the pattern of its existence: here lies, of course, one other important distinction between the two forms. Athenian society stumbles towards its aim, without direction, and produces the conventional man almost by accident. Plato is fully conscious of his intention and certain of his method: with him education and propaganda are made essential parts of the legislator's task.[5]

We have already seen that the value of the tradition depends upon the quality of those who originated it and are now its

---

[1] μίμησις τοῦ καλλίστου καὶ ἀρίστου βίου, ὃ δή φαμεν ἡμεῖς γε ὄντως εἶναι τραγῳδίαν τὴν ἀληθεστάτην (817 B 4f.).

[2] ὃ δὴ νόμος ἀληθὴς μόνος ἀποτελεῖν πέφυκεν (817B 1ff.). I suspect a pun on νόμος, law, and mode, or tune, in music.

[3] προκαλούμενος ἑκάστους εἰς ἀρετῆς ἕπεσθαι κτῆσιν συνακολουθοῦντας διὰ τῶν μιμήσεων (812c 6ff.).

[4] 816c 7ff.   [5] IX, 857E 3ff.

protectors. We would therefore expect that some higher education would be designed to enable the protective element to attain that point outside the system from which they can direct and preserve it. Not much is actually said of this education but it is clearly envisaged. At the first mention of the Nocturnal Council, we are told of their need for μαθήματα which will help them in their work of understanding the laws.[1] Later we are explicitly informed that they must have superior insight, both in theory and in practice, into the problem of ἀρετή: τοὺς φύλακας ἀκριβεστέρους τῶν πολλῶν περὶ ἀρετῆς ἔργῳ καὶ λόγῳ κατασκευαστέον.[2] This, it is agreed, requires a more careful education than the general mass are to receive: this element must proceed 'to a form of education more exacting than the one we described earlier'.[3] As the dialogue ends, the three friends are on the point of setting out the scheme of education which this highest level of society must pursue: the greatest effort of all still remains to be made.[4]

[1] XII, 951E 5 ff.   [2] 964D 3 ff.   [3] 965B 1 ff.

[4] 969A 3 f. It is somewhat surprising that the dialogue ends thus abruptly, without any indication of the form that this higher education is to take. Yet the close of the *Laws* seems too effective not to have been designed. Perhaps it may be an acceptable explanation of these facts to suggest that Plato, at the time of finishing the *Laws*, thought of the Nocturnal Council as pursuing a course of study almost identical with that of the Guardians in the *Republic*.

CHAPTER VIII

THE ETHICAL STANDARD

WITH the structure of the *Laws* now seen in its proper perspective and its significance understood, we can turn to the effect that this new outlook has had on some of the characteristic ideas of the ethics of Socrates, in particular on the meaning of ἀρετή. The word meant for Socrates, as we have seen, essentially a moral capability which directed action: the quality of *controlling* human life may be said to have been the essential criterion of Socratic ἐπιστήμη. But equally important, in view of the way in which Plato's thought later moved, was the fact that ἐπιστήμη was a personal insight reached by each man for himself by means of inquiry and discussion. We have now to see what is the ethical standard of social ethics. Or rather what are the standards, for it is at once obvious that in the hierarchical society there will be more than one standard. There are, in fact, two: the moral ideal of the general body of citizens, and the ideal of insight beyond the system which the protective element must gain. Most of the *Laws* is obviously concerned with the first of these, but in the final analysis it is the second which is more important and enough is said of it for us to see what Plato envisaged as the task of the Nocturnal Council in reaching true ἀρετή.

First, the standard of the average human being. The outlines we have already seen: how it is the product of environment and how education is concerned with producing a character which will be suited to the achievement of it.[1] Plato's views on the effect of environment on character are far-reaching. His first concern in establishing the state of Magnesia is that it should not be situated in a position where commercial activity, particularly at sea, is unavoidable. As it is about ten miles from the coast, in rather difficult country, and capable of producing its own food, the Athenian says in relief: 'From the point of view of achieving ἀρετή, then, it will

[1] Cf. ἀρετῆς τε καὶ παιδείας (VI, 757C 5.).

not be beyond all mending.'[1] For the effect of trade is to split society into rival interests and produce 'warped and unreliable traits of character'. The economic structure of society is one of the principal points of Plato's attention. Extremes of riches and poverty, with their effects of luxury and shameless beggary, are destructive of moral character.[2] The fact, therefore, that it is impossible in Magnesia to gain excessive wealth is conducive in no small degree to σωφροσύνη.[3] But other conditions, though less obvious, are equally essential: climate and diet have an effect which we must not ignore,[4] and the consequences of physical condition alter, as certainly, one's moral outlook.[5] All this we may regard as a realistic approach to ethical problems, as 'facing the facts' and forming theories only in accordance with them. But Plato seems to take his awareness of what may loosely be called environment further than realism demands. There is a curious passage in Book VI where he warns married men against having intercourse with their wives when drunk: the drunkard is a clumsy lover: 'his offspring, one must presume, will be capricious and unreliable, with nothing straight-set in either character or body'.[6] However, this feeling that heredity, of a sort, is an important influence on character is tempered in the case of the families of criminals: he insists more than once that the disgrace of crime should not descend to the relatives of the criminal,[7] though any family which contains capital offenders in three consecutive generations must be banished.[8] It is, in any case, true that environment is not allowed to become an autonomously decisive influence in the sphere of ethics. For the system of the *Laws* is in itself the conscious construction of an ethical environment, and even where ἀνάγκη makes a displeasing feature unavoidable, the Curators are to protect their society, as far as possible, from the consequences of it:

...our Curators of the law must be curators not only in the sense that they will watch over those whom it is easy to keep an eye on, in

[1] IV, 704D 3ff.   [2] XI, 919B 6ff.
[3] VIII, 836A 1f.   [4] V, 747D 1ff.
[5] 728E 4f.   [6] VI, 775B 4ff.
[7] IX, 855A 2ff., 856C 8ff. Compare *Theaet.* 173D 6ff. and see Schuhl, *Essai*, pp. 35f.   [8] 856D 1.

case they become criminal and break the law, those, that is, who by the favourable circumstances of their birth have been properly educated and brought up, but even more carefully must they keep on their guard against men of very different circumstances, who follow callings which provide a powerful drive towards making criminals of them.[1]

It is worth noting that the characters which an undesirable environment will produce are twice described as ἄπιστα, unreliable. Reliability we have seen to be one of the characteristics of Socratic τέχνη: it is still a feature of the ἀρετή of the average man in the *Laws*, the ἀρετή δημώδης or δημοσία, as it is now called.[2] We have now to see in detail what constitutes this ἀρετή, and how it is attained. Archer-Hind, in an appendix to his edition of the *Phaedo*, gave an account of δημοτικὴ ἀρετή. It was not, he said, a contemptible thing for Plato,

since it is worth the philosopher's while to pause in his study of the truth, that he may implant it in the hearts of men: it is indeed the highest that the great mass of mankind can hope to attain.... Again this is no longer an ethical code which the multitude frame for themselves; it is one which the philosopher frames for them: nor does he construct it on utilitarian grounds: they receive it, not because they know why it is good, for they are without knowledge of the good, but because the philosopher convinces them that it is for their advantage to do so; that by submitting to its restrictions they avoid great evils. As they hold it, therefore, it is utilitarian; as he conceives it, not so: thus they are still, though in a far more refined sense, δι' ἀκολασίαν σεσωφρονισμένοι. Plato acknowledges that the morality of the multitude must be utilitarian, since none other is attainable save by the highly trained metaphysician.[3]

This description is based almost entirely on the *Republic*, but with very few modifications it will fit the δημοσία ἀρετή of the *Laws*. It is now, I think, clear that Plato's method of inculcating this

[1] ...τοὺς νομοφύλακας χρὴ φύλακας εἶναι μὴ μόνον ἐκείνων οὓς φυλάττειν ῥᾴδιον μὴ παρανόμους καὶ κακοὺς γίγνεσθαι, ὅσοι γενέσει καὶ τροφαῖς εὖ πεπαίδευνται, τοὺς δὲ μὴ τοιούτους ἐπιτηδεύματά τε ἐπιτηδεύοντας ἃ ῥοπὴν ἔχει τινὰ ἰσχυρὰν πρὸς τὸ προτρέπειν κακοὺς γίγνεσθαι, φυλακτέον μᾶλλον (XI, 920A 6ff.).
[2] IV, 710A 5ff., XII, 968A 2.
[3] Archer-Hind, *op. cit.* pp. 151f.

moral background has grown more subtle: it is no longer merely by convincing at a conscious level, but by feeding the growth of the mind at all levels with the more sophisticated equipment of propaganda, that the necessary viewpoint is to be produced.

It is still, however, of vital importance to bear in mind that the acceptance, unconscious or otherwise, of this particular background is principally utilitarian. 'Passionate sensations of pleasure, revulsion and desire are basic characteristics of human nature: they are precisely like pulleys or strings which operate upon every mortal creature, inevitably and with fundamental effect.'[1] If, therefore, we are not to frighten all away from it even in their youth, it must be shown superior in pleasantness and avoidance of the unpleasant. This is the inescapable dispensation of human nature,[2] and the basis of all our choosing. We must accept a view of life which admits that we are naturally confined to these limits; we must realize what naturally governs our choice of life: if we assert that our wishes are set on other objects, we can only say this 'owing to ignorance, and inexperience of life as it is actually lived'.[3] Plato is in fact even more specific: the whole of human life, he says, hangs on three needs and desires, and it is by the right manipulation of these needs in man that virtue can be attained. The three needs are for food and drink, which enter the field first, and for sex, the most violent and powerful of the three.[4] 'These are three diseases which afflict humanity: we must divert them away from the goal of so-called pleasure towards the good, in its highest form; we must try to hold them in check by three weapons, the forces of fear, law and expounded truth (calling to our aid too the Muses and the gods of festivals), and so abate their growth and onslaught.'[5]

Although human needs are here reduced to these three, there is another which Plato has constantly in mind, the desire for honour and respect. τιμαί (marks of honour) figure largely in the *Laws*.

[1] ἔστιν δὴ φύσει ἀνθρώπειον μάλιστα ἡδοναὶ καὶ λῦπαι καὶ ἐπιθυμίαι, ἐξ ὧν ἀνάγκη τὸ θνητὸν πᾶν 3ῷον ἀτεχνῶς οἷον ἐξηρτῆσθαί τε καὶ ἐκκρεμάμενον εἶναι σπουδαῖς ταῖς μεγίσταις (v, 732E 4ff.).

[2] 733C 1f.

[3] διά τινα ἄγνοιαν καὶ ἀπειρίαν τῶν ὄντων βίων (D 5).

[4] vi, 782D 10ff.   [5] 783A 4ff.

Another of the dangers of the maritime state was the impossibility of awarding τιμαί rightly, for the preservation of the state was in the hands of the most worthless section of society: 'Yet how could any system of governance achieve its proper aim, if it is deprived of this weapon?'[1] The true ἰσότης is one which, realizing that the members of society are not of equal value, distributes τιμαί corresponding to real worth (τῷ μὲν γὰρ μείζονι πλείω, τῷ δ' ἐλάττονι σμικρότερα νέμει):[2] this is, in fact, the essence of justice as it affects social relations.[3] The task of achieving this social justice the legislator attempts in the preambles to his laws. The ground has been prepared by the system of education, which has moulded characters to suit the attainment of ἀρετή. On top of this, the legislator formulates his preambles to raise a conscious moral structure by means of persuasion, backed by sanction.

The need for persuasion is always stressed. The use of it distinguishes the free from the constrained and servile legislator.[4] Great emphasis is laid on it, for example, throughout the closing pages of Book IV. The effect of law on a man is that he should be 'persuaded, or driven by fear, into obedience'.[5] It is only reluctantly that Plato invokes sanctions: it is usual to find after the preamble some such remark as: 'Those who are already persuaded the law can leave in silence, but, now that the prelude is over, it must raise its voice and cry aloud to the unpersuaded.'[6] If persuasion could achieve all that is required, Plato would be satisfied, but there are limits to the powers of persuasion 'in the face of the mass of the uneducated'.[7]

Plato's treatment of sex may stand as typical of his attitude to a difficult moral and legal problem.[8] First, he attacks, in persuasive

---

[1] IV, 707 B 3; cf. V, 740 D 7f., 743 E 6ff.

[2] VI, 757 B 7ff.

[3] This is how I take the words at C 6f., in preference to Taylor's version.

[4] IV, 719 E 7ff.

[5] πειθομένῳ μὲν δὴ καὶ πάντως φοβουμένῳ (IX, 870 E 4f.). Cf. IV, 715 C. A difficulty here is that πείθεσθαι, with its double connotation of 'being persuaded' and 'obeying', is almost impossible to translate into English.

[6] τῷ μὲν πειθομένῳ τὸν νόμον ἐᾶν σιγῇ δεῖ, τῷ δὲ ἀπειθοῦντι μετὰ τὸ προοίμιον ᾄδειν μέγα (854 C 7ff.).

[7] ἐπὶ τὸν ἄπειρον παιδείας ὄχλον (IV, 722 B 6f.).

[8] VIII, 835 D 3–842 A 3.

language, the habit of homosexual relations, carefully analysing the psychological variations on love that may arise. He then suggests that if homosexuality could acquire the same aura of, as it were, sacrilege that surrounds incest, it would be easy to stamp it out. Horror of incest is a part of the normal moral background of every person: it is learnt, almost from the cradle, says Plato, at every hand, from the fool and the tragic poet alike. We have to establish a similar tradition of horror at homosexuality: we must castigate it as wholly unnatural and tantamount to deliberate racial murder. For sexual restraint as a whole, we have the example of great athletes, who denied themselves this so-called 'exquisite pleasure' to gain their victory: ours is the greater victory and we have as much need of endurance. The law then demands that men should not behave worse than birds and animals who mate only with one partner. But Plato realizes that the power of sex may be too great: a second law therefore lays down that *discovery* in the act shall bring marks of disgrace. Three influences are invoked to check the appetite of sex: fear of god, the desire for distinction, and the sublimation of love to the spiritual plane. The final statute legislates for a better and a worse eventuality. If the best prevails, it enjoins that no man should have sexual relations with any of either sex, except his wife: if the worst, that homosexuality be prohibited completely, while relations with other women, if they become known, be cause for disgrace and loss of citizenship, for the man will have proved himself truly an alien. So the powers of persuasion and sanction are mixed to meet the situation.

Persuasion is thus the first weapon of the law. We are not surprised, then, to find that obedience to the law (or 'being persuaded by the law', see p. 123 n. 5.), its converse, is in fact the essence of δημοσία ἀρετή. 'I can only wish them to be as amenable as possible to persuasion, when it directs them towards fulfilling the true nature of a man,'[1] says the Athenian, and throughout ὁ πειθόμενος is commended. In the same way, the criminal is hard to persuade (δυσπειθής)[2] and 'unpersuaded by law and by god' (τὸν ἀπειθοῦντα ἅμα νόμῳ καὶ τῷ θεῷ).[3] In obedience to the

---

[1] βουλοίμην ἂν αὐτοὺς ὡς εὐπειθεστάτους πρὸς ἀρετὴν εἶναι (IV, 718 C 8 ff.).
[2] IV, 708 D I.   [3] V, 741 D 3 f.; cf. 745 A 3 f.

law, the average man can live in accordance with divine truth, for law is the visible representation of such truth. It enables him to answer with certainty the question which would otherwise be beyond him: 'What line of conduct is agreeable in the sight of god and follows his way?'[1] In fact, of course, he will accept this path of god, not for its truth, but for its pleasantness, as Archer-Hind observed, and because he has absorbed it with the air he has breathed and the food he has eaten, almost since his birth. This is the ethical standard which Plato calls δημώδης ἀρετή: it is not, he believes, to be despised. It is the highest that the majority of men can reach, and higher than most in fact do reach. For the tradition which it observes is higher than any which exists now: it is the culmination of achievement for the ethical society.

Before we climb the scale and inspect the highest ἀρετή of all, something must be said about Plato's attitude to crime in the *Laws*. We shall, on grounds of probability, expect that his view of κακία has grown more complex, as has his view of ἀρετή. And we shall be right. It is complicated, not only by the opposed tendencies of legalism and philosophical ethics, but also by the fact that his combination of a new realism and the idealism that he inherited from Socrates makes his judgments sometimes a little difficult to correlate. Personal and social ethics are at work simultaneously on the same ground: the result is a somewhat intractable confusion, even apparent self-contradiction, in his pronouncements on the subject of evil.

In Book v, he advocates indignation as the right attitude to evil-doing, but indignation mixed with gentleness:[2] this seems to be the substance of his own approach. Without indignation, the soul cannot repulse evil in stern combat. But in the face of those whose crimes are not beyond cure, we must remember that 'no wrongdoer is ever so of his own will'.[3] In its context, the remark seems here more the statement of an attitude, the concrete realization of πραότης, than the precise formulation of a theory, though

---

[1] IV, 716 C 1.
[2] V, 731 B 3 ff.: θυμοειδῆ μὲν δὴ χρὴ πάντα ἄνδρα εἶναι, πρᾷον δὲ ὡς ὅτι μάλιστα.
[3] πᾶς ὁ ἄδικος οὐχ ἑκὼν ἄδικος (731 C 2 f.).

it is followed by the usual argument: no man willingly accepts the ultimate evil (as he sees it) for his most precious possession. Such a possession is his soul, and into it the criminal has admitted the ultimate evil. So he is a creature for our pity: but our pity can only have scope where the disease is curable. In such a case, indignation must be held in check, but for the incurable we must set free our anger. This passage states no more than the frame of mind in which we should regard evil, and states it well. But the theory of πᾶς ὁ ἄδικος οὐχ ἑκὼν ἄδικος appears elsewhere and in different contexts.[1]

In Book ix, we find the most comprehensive account of Plato's view of evil at this period. He still holds to his idealist attitude, but is clearly aware of the difficulties it contains for him in the present stage of his philosophy. In explanation, he adduces the obvious lack of agreement among men on questions of right and wrong.[2] In particular he realizes that his own attitude raises considerable difficulties in connection with the usual distinction between voluntary and involuntary crime. It is difficult to summarize the answer which he gives to this problem, but we shall not be misinterpreting him if we say that he retains the usual distinction in the case of *effects* of criminal intentions (βλάβαι), but treats all the *intentions* themselves as involuntary.[3] Thus the action to be taken by law is of two sorts: damages must be made good,[4] and the law must make every effort to cure, by teaching and constraint, the deranged mental state of the criminal. As usual, the law will operate by means of pleasure and pain, honour and dishonour. Where the incurable criminal is met with, there is nothing for him but death: it will be no evil to him and will rid society of an evil man, besides providing a warning 'pour encourager les autres'. This is the only case where the death penalty is permissible. In this way, Plato extricates himself from the difficulties of his position: his distinction is between the inner

[1] Especially v, 734 B 3 ff., IX, 860 C 7 ff.
[2] 861 A 9 f.: ταραχή τε καὶ ἀσυμφωνία.
[3] Professor Taylor's explanation of this passage as being the first instance of the distinction between torts and crimes seems an unaccountable misinterpretation (*op. cit.* p. xlix).
[4] 862 B 6 ff.

situation in the soul, where only ethical considerations apply, and the external effect, which must be regulated by legal rulings. He sums up the ethical teaching of the whole passage:

I would most certainly give the name 'wrong' to the despotism of self-assertion, fear, pleasure, revulsion, envy and desire over the soul, whether it has harmful results or not; on the other hand, a conviction of acting for the best (wherever that best may be taken to lie, either by society or by individuals), if it succeeds in controlling a man's character and directing his actions, such a conviction, its results and all submission on the part of individuals to its governance, must be termed 'right', even if its consequences are unfortunate: for it is directed towards the highest form of human life. Yet one must admit that the majority of men take such consequences to be what they call 'involuntary' wrongdoing.[1]

His first point might have been made by Socrates: the concern of ethics is solely with the intention, whatever may be its outcome in practice. But he goes beyond Socrates in distinguishing the cases of a man merely overcome by human passions and desires, and that of one whose wrong is more philosophical, consisting in a misconception of the moral law, a sophistication of his original position parallel to that which has taken place with regard to ἀρετή.

None of this, however, affects his legalistic attitude to crime. ἄκων continues to be frequently used in a purely legal sense.[2] The idea of premeditation also enters into the discussion: unpremeditated crimes of passion are said to constitute a sort of no-man's-land between the intentional and the unintentional.[3] Moreover, Plato is as certain as Socrates ever was of the need for the individual's responsibility for crime: it is the worst wrong a man can do

---

[1] τὴν γὰρ τοῦ θυμοῦ καὶ φόβου καὶ ἡδονῆς καὶ λύπης καὶ φθόνων καὶ ἐπιθυμιῶν ἐν ψυχῇ τυραννίδα, ἐάν τέ τι βλάπτῃ καὶ ἐὰν μή, πάντως ἀδικίαν προσαγορεύω· τὴν δὲ τοῦ ἀρίστου δόξαν, ὅπῃπερ ἂν ἔσεσθαι τοῦτό γ' ἡγήσωνται πόλις εἴτε ἰδιῶταί τινες, ἐὰν αὕτη κρατοῦσα ἐν ψυχαῖς διακοσμῇ πάντα ἄνδρα, κἂν σφάλληταί τι, δίκαιον μὲν πᾶν εἶναι φατέον τὸ ταύτῃ πραχθὲν καὶ τὸ τῆς τοιαύτης ἀρχῆς γιγνόμενον ὑπήκοον ἑκάστων, καὶ ἐπὶ τὸν ἅπαντα ἀνθρώπων βίον ἄριστον, δοξάζεσθαι δὲ ὑπὸ πολλῶν ἀκούσιον ἀδικίαν εἶναι τὴν τοιαύτην βλάβην (863 E 6ff.).

[2] VIII, 845 E 2, IX, 865 A 4, D 3, 867 A 1, 874 E 5ff., etc.

[3] 878 B 4ff.

himself, he says, to try to shift the responsibility for his own actions on to others or on to external circumstances.[1] In fact, the worst consequence of wrongdoing is that it brings in its train its own revenge (τιμωρία) (not δίκη, which would be a benefit), in the shape of isolation from all but the evil, isolation not imposed by others, but arising out of the disease in the criminal's own nature. This is a clear echo of Socratic ideas, but the question of responsibility and punishment is also considered from the legal point of view, and the care and critical attention which this requires from both legislator and judge is emphasized.[2] As we have seen, it is recognized that criminals may be incurable:[3] they can then only be examples (παραδείγματα) to others.

Such is the complicated view of evil which we find in the *Laws*. It remains now only to attempt an appreciation of the final achievement, to be attained by the Nocturnal Council. We have seen that the long work ends abruptly, giving us the impression of a catapult wound and ready to hurl us still further into the heart of the ethical problem: it is perhaps the most exciting conclusion of any in Plato's works. For, at the end of the *Laws*, what is envisaged as the task of the Nocturnal Council is nothing less than an analysis of the ethical Forms as acute and searching as that of the μέγιστα γένη (*Sophist* 254 Bff.). The problem is cast in a form which reminds us irresistibly of the metaphysical problem of the One and the Many: 'Bear in mind that you must not only tell me how four things, and those real, can be one: when you have shown me that they *are* one, then you must ask me in return how they can be four.'[4] They will have, somehow, to understand the four cardinal virtues both as four individual ἀρεταί (justice, self-control, understanding and courage), and as also, in some way, one. In other words, the very core of the problem of the right and good must be examined and understood. The One and the Many, even the Forms themselves, are introduced:[5] the organiza-

---

[1] v, 727 b 4 ff.; cf. xi, 934 a 1 ff.
[2] Compare v, 728 b 2 ff. with xi, 934 a 1 ff.
[3] Other instances are v, 735 b 7 ff., ix, 854 a 3, e 5 ff., xii, 944 d 2 f., etc.
[4] 964 a 3 ff.
[5] 965 b 7 ff. On this point, see Cherniss, *Riddle of the Early Academy*, pp. 5, 88 nn. 17, 18.

tion (συντάξασθαι) of the whole ethical division of the Forms is to be reviewed. In this way, the Nocturnal Council can advance to their final position, the vision of ethical truth and the consequent ability to distinguish 'those things in this world of change which are intrinsically good, and those which are evil'.[1] So the ideal of the protective element places them outside the system, at the pinnacle of human achievement: they will have accomplished what not even Plato, perhaps, claimed to have attained, a complete grasp of, and a conscious ability to explain, the heart of the matter, the meaning of ἀρετή.[2]

Plato has recently been more than once attacked for holding his final position. Professor Walbank has roundly accused him in rhetorical terms of

the blackest treason to that flowering of the human spirit which we call Hellenism, treason, too, in its most gifted exponent, and explicable only as the outcome of a motive of irresistible compulsion. That motive was unquestionably the maintenance of privilege, the preservation of an oligarchic and paternal form of society with power and responsibility concentrated at the top. In the interest of such a social order and its perpetuation Plato is prepared to purge and censor most of the finest products of Greek genius. He had set out with the purest motives; he followed the light as he saw it. But what he did not see was that obscurantism cannot be confined to the lower orders; like a plague arising among city slums, it sweeps outwards and upwards until it has infected every rank of society. When that happens, society must either root it out, or perish.[3]

For us, there is much truth in this and perhaps a lesson to be learnt, but we may doubt whether it contains as much for Plato. It used once to be common criticism of the *Republic* to accuse it of much the same sins, but the patient efforts of scholars to understand the work in the light of its own background, not ours, have put such remarks largely out of court. The *Laws*, which has an exceedingly

---

[1] τά τε καλῶς γιγνόμενα καὶ τὰ μὴ κατὰ φύσιν (966 B 4 ff.).
[2] 966 A 5 ff.
[3] *Journal of Hellenic Studies*, vol. LXVI, p. 15. Professor Dodds' valuable article on 'Plato and the Irrational' (*ibid.* vol. LXV, pp. 16 ff.) also seems to me to treat Plato somewhat harshly at times.

contemporary atmosphere, is only now receiving its share of critical attention. Such tirades as Professor Walbank's seem, at least, to imply ignorance of the historical and philosophical circumstances of its time. Socrates, sensing the break-up of his own society, was at pains to establish a secure foundation for the individual's life, independently of society, in the creation of a self-sufficient canon of behaviour. In the half-century that passed between the death of Socrates and that of Plato, this became too little as a prerequisite for purposive life: it was Plato's task to construct a whole society that might weather the storm that now was upon them for the first time and without parallel in previous history. We should be able to sense the enormity of his aim. That, in our eyes, he failed, is not surprising: what is more surprising is the extent and imaginative clarity of the work which he produced. First and last, the *Laws* remains one of Plato's greatest achievements, but it is not likely ever to be a popular one: the final comment lies with Plutarch's wry remark: 'There are few of us who read Plato's *Laws*, but thousands upon thousands who have used, and still use, the laws of Alexander.'[1]

[1] Plutarch, *De Alexandri fortuna*: Or. I, 328E 5 ff.

PART III
THE GROWTH OF
A REALITY PRINCIPLE

CHAPTER IX

THE 'MENO': ΟΡΘΗ ΔΟΞΑ

THE progress of Plato's thought on ethics from the *Meno* to the *Laws* is most obviously one of growing complexity and depth, and it will be the first task of this last section to bring out the stages of this progress. But within the greater complexity, we must not fail to notice that the emphasis on depth and subtlety is in itself both the symptom and the cause of that change of emphasis that we have examined in the previous two sections. Socratic ἐπιστήμη was a simple, undifferentiated, indeed largely undefined, inward ability of the whole personality, an understanding of moral demands. It was the implications of this ideal that exercised Plato's mind throughout the great dialogues of the middle period, and, as they became clearer and more compelling, caused him slowly to revise his own beliefs. In the *Meno*, we see the beginning of a process which, in one continuous sweep, brings us almost imperceptibly to the final period of resignation, a shadow in such late dialogues as the *Timaeus*, substantial and, perhaps, forbidding in the *Laws*.

M. Croiset places the *Meno* in its context admirably when he says: 'Par la nature du problème examiné, le *Ménon* se rapproche des deux dialogues précédents [*Protagoras* and *Gorgias*]; ce serait pourtant une erreur de croire qu'il reprenne simplement la même question sous une autre forme: en réalité, il y introduit des idées nouvelles fort importantes et il ouvre dans ses dernières pages des perspectives qui vont loin dans la philosophie platonicienne.'[1] He is right to stress at the outset the newness of some of the ideas which the *Meno* contains. With one of these, the dialectical method of ὑπόθεσις, we shall not here be much concerned, but the concept of 'right conviction' (ὀρθὴ δόξα),[2] in its ethical bearing, calls for some discussion. The passage in which first mention of this

---

[1] Croiset, *Ménon* (Budé ed.), p. 227.
[2] Or ἀληθὴς δόξα: the terms are interchangeable.

new concept occurs is sufficiently well known.[1] Conversation has been brought to a standstill; ἀρετή, which had earlier been confidently identified with ἐπιστήμη, is in danger of being abandoned as an imponderable: for the identification has, on examination, fallen to the ground. The major premise of the syllogistic argument which proved that ἀρετή was to be identified with ἐπιστήμη, had been that what is useful is always ἐπιστήμη, a proposition with which we are familiar from the early dialogues.[2] Socrates now suggests that this proposition is not, in fact, true; that there is something else which, for all practical purposes, is as valuable as ἐπιστήμη. This new importation is ὀρθὴ δόξα. The distinction between two modes of knowing, which appear here under the names of δόξα and ἐπιστήμη, has also occurred before, but the emphasis was there rather different. We can recognize it in the contrast between πίστις and ἐπιστήμη in the *Gorgias* which was discussed earlier.[3] However, the purpose of that contrast was specifically to undermine the pretensions of πίστις to equality with ἐπιστήμη. Considerations such as this have recently led a French scholar, M. Goldschmidt, to put forward a new interpretation of this dialogue.[4] We must examine his case before proceeding to a positive assessment of the meaning of ὀρθὴ δόξα.

M. Goldschmidt's suspicions are aroused by the argument which disposes of the identification of ἀρετή solely with ἐπιστήμη. It is based on a demonstration that there is no universally recognized teacher or student of ἀρετή and that it is impossible to conceive of a 'knowledge' which is not taught and learned. 'Mais c'est là un critère tout extérieur et accidentel.' M. Goldschmidt quite rightly points out that, on this argument, solid geometry, which is part of the advanced system of education in the *Republic*, would have to abandon its title to ἐπιστήμη, for Socrates explicitly remarks that no one teaches or studies it.[5] The argument is, therefore, not cogent and casts suspicion on what follows. Socrates, suggests

---

[1] *Meno*, 96D ff.   [2] *Meno*, 88E 4ff. See, for example, above, p. 59.
[3] *Gorg.* 454D 1ff. See above, pp. 24f.
[4] In his interesting, but at times over-ingenious book, *Les Dialogues de Platon*, pp. 117ff.
[5] *Rep.* VII, 528A 6ff.

M. Goldschmidt, is not actually making positive contributions either here or later in the dialogue. He has realized that the identification of ἀρετή and ἐπιστήμη was accepted by Meno without his realizing the full consequences; the rest of the dialogue is a 'tentation' of Meno, which consists in allowing him to accept false suggestions made by Socrates. The passage concerning ὀρθή δόξα, then, is no more than the culmination of this process, reducing Meno to the absurd position of giving δόξα a value equal to that of ἐπιστήμη.

M. Goldschmidt argues his case well, but his preoccupation with form leads him, at times, to fail in understanding its correlative, content. He is, of course, right in observing that Meno has not understood the identification of ἀρετή and ἐπιστήμη in its full sense. The argument used against this proposition occurs elsewhere,[1] and always indicates, as M. Goldschmidt says of it here, that ἐπιστήμη has been taken in some wrong sense. But it is not necessary to deduce from this that the concept of ὀρθή δόξα is, in some way, a mirage. Indeed, unless M. Goldschmidt is content to argue that Plato changed his mind later, it is quite impossible to accept his interpretation. In the *Republic* and the *Laws*, if not here, ὀρθή δόξα is, regretfully perhaps, but none the less seriously, accepted as an ethical δεύτερος πλοῦς for the mass of mankind. In this case, at least, we must accept the traditional interpretation as a basis for further discussion of the passage.[2]

Although most of what the *Meno* has to say about ὀρθή δόξα occurs towards the end of the dialogue, there is some other evidence, by implication at least, to be found earlier. In a pause during the well-known geometrical discussion between Socrates and Meno's slave, Socrates describes the slave's present state of mind to Meno.

Soc. A man may lack knowledge, then, on some subject, and still possess true convictions about the very subject where he has no knowledge?

Meno. It looks like it.

---

[1] *Prot.* 319D 7ff., *Alc. I*, 118D 6ff.

[2] For a statement of it, see, for example, R. C. Lodge, *Plato's Theory of Ethics*, pp. 31ff.

Soc. At present, in our friend here, these convictions have been stirred up into life, like a dream; but if he were to be questioned on this point, repeatedly though with variations, I firmly believe that he would gain knowledge about it as accurate as anyone possesses.[1]

From this, we can form a preliminary picture of ὀρθὴ δόξα, and more can be learnt from the context in which this passage occurs. ἀληθεῖς δόξαι are said to have been aroused in the slave 'like a dream' (ὥσπερ ὄναρ): E. S. Thompson, in his edition of the *Meno*, has rightly observed that the opposition of dreaming and waking vision (ὄναρ and ὕπαρ) is often used by Plato as a metaphor for that between ἐπιστήμη and δόξα.[2] The reference is of course partly to the instability of dreams and newly acquired opinions, partly to their apparent strangeness. But by repeated question and answer on the same lines, δόξα can actually be converted into ἐπιστήμη. There is a difficulty here. The context shows us that the ἀληθεῖς δόξαι of the slave are concerned with the particular geometrical figure which Socrates has drawn for him, or, if any abstraction has taken place, with any figure of the same dimensions. ἐπιστήμη on the other hand, must be concerned with Forms, and Forms alone, and for the present we have no explanation at hand of how this change of object occurs. In the *Republic*, the same problem is raised even more acutely, as we shall see. Its ethical relevance is this: ὀρθὴ δόξα is introduced, as is later made clear, as a moral *pis aller*. If we are to accept the implications of the present passage, the 'true conviction' will be about individual moral actions and decisions: between this and ἐπιστήμη of moral Forms there is so far no apparent mediation. But we will postpone discussion of this point until it reappears in the *Republic*.

Nothing is said here of the metaphysical status or value of ἀληθεῖς δόξαι: when we turn to the passage, referred to earlier, at the end of the dialogue, we find that it is their practical use that

---

[1] Σω. τῷ οὐκ εἰδότι ἄρα περὶ ὧν ἂν μὴ εἰδῇ ἔνεισιν ἀληθεῖς δόξαι περὶ τούτων ὧν οὐκ οἶδε; Με. φαίνεται. Σω. καὶ νῦν μέν γε αὐτῷ ὥσπερ ὄναρ ἄρτι ἀνακεκίνηνται αἱ δόξαι αὗται· εἰ δὲ αὐτόν τις ἀνερήσεται πολλάκις τὰ αὐτὰ ταῦτα καὶ πολλαχῇ, οἶσθ' ὅτι τελευτῶν οὐδενὸς ἧττον ἀκριβῶς ἐπιστήσεται περὶ τούτων (*Meno*, 85 c 6 ff.). Cf. 86 A 6 ff.

[2] *Op. cit.* p. 140. He refers to *Rep.* V, 476 D, VII, 533 B–C, 534 C, and *Laws*, XII, 969 B.

is insisted upon. The example taken to illustrate the equivalence in practical value is the well-known one of the man who has a correct opinion about the way to Larissa, 'without having gone there, or knowing how to'. His correct opinion will take him to Larissa as satisfactorily as the knowledge of the other man in the illustration, who has made the journey before.[1] From beginning to end of this passage, the explanation of the phrase ὀρθὴ δόξα is attached to practicality. What is stressed throughout is the equivalence, from a practical point of view, of the ὀρθῶς δοξάζων with the φρονῶν, so that the keynote is: 'As a guide to successful action, true conviction is nothing inferior to φρόνησις.'[2] Only one factor operates against the usefulness (ὠφέλιμον) of ὀρθὴ δόξα: its instability.[3] But here again δόξα can be transformed into ἐπιστήμη, by αἰτίας λογισμός.[4] It is important to notice that, for all their practical equivalence, it is stated by Socrates, with considerable emphasis, that the two must not be thought identical.[5] These two ideas, partly complementary, partly in conflict, of the equivalence in use, and difference in objective fact, of ἐπιστήμη and ὀρθὴ δόξα, stand side by side in the Meno without any very coherent explanation of the relation between them. For even a hint of that, we must wait: in several respects, the Meno has the appearance of being a 'curtain-raiser' to later dialogues, especially the Republic.

Several questions stand out from this context. First, and most obviously, what is ὀρθὴ δόξα? On this point it is necessary to differ, at least in emphasis, from the traditional view. According to this, it is an essential element in the Platonic concept of ὀρθὴ δόξα that it should consist in 'accepting information on the dogmatic authority of the parent, teacher or advocate, without independent examination of the evidence'.[6] If we revert to the example of Meno's slave, it becomes obvious that, in fact, this is not a necessary condition of ἀληθεῖς δόξαι. The purpose of the conversation

---

[1] This seems to be implied in εἰδὼς τὴν ὁδόν and the contrast with the phrase quoted above: ἐληλυθὼς δὲ μὴ μηδ᾽ ἐπιστάμενος (97A 9ff.).

[2] δόξα...ἀληθὴς πρὸς ὀρθότητα πράξεως οὐδὲν χείρων ἡγεμὼν φρονήσεως (97B 9ff.). Cf. 98C 1 ff.   [3] 97E 2ff.   [5] 98B 2ff.

[4] On αἰτίας λογισμός, see below, pp. 139f.

[6] Lodge, op. cit. p. 32. Cf. Robin, Platon, p. 258; Joseph, Essays in Ancient and Modern Philosophy, p. 71; Moreau, Construction, p. 82.

with the slave is to demonstrate that these δόξαι are present in every person and may be brought to the light by the unaided reflection of the subject, not needing to be implanted by any 'authority'. It is irrelevant to our present purpose that it may seem to us that the δόξα is, in fact, at least suggested by Socrates' leading questions: as far as we can judge, that was not how it appeared to Plato. That the state of mind of the slave is described as ἀληθὴς δόξα only, not as ἐπιστήμη, is determined, not by the source of his views, but by their innate character. The slave, having found that his original, spontaneous answers to the problem were obviously wrong, has discovered the right answer by concrete demonstration. His certainty, *in this particular instance*, is as sure as that of Socrates, based as it is on personal examination of the sufficient evidence. It differs from that of Socrates only in that it is essentially bound to the particular case, and not, like his, linked to a general rule (i.e., in this case, Pythagoras' theorem). The other illustration of the distinction between these two modes of cognition, the case of the road to Larissa, is less satisfactory. For, in this instance, the state of mind of both men is bound up with the individual case, and in neither does it depend on insight into the Forms. The state of mind of the φρονῶν, therefore, is not strictly speaking ἐπιστήμη here, and the illustration, like others in the *Meno*, tends rather to confuse the issue.[1] On the evidence contained in the *Meno*, then, the status of ὀρθὴ δόξα is determined by its inherent connection with the concrete example, and we have yet to find a satisfactory account of its relation to true ἐπιστήμη which might enable us to see how one can become the other, or, the same process seen from another angle, ὀρθὴ δόξα lose its metaphysical limitations. For these, as it appears in this dialogue, are intimately connected with its object, a particular case among concrete phenomena, and it is not at all clear how any other state of mind can be possible, having the same object.[2]

[1] Cf. Robinson, *Plato's Earlier Dialectic*, p. 120. If this seems a somewhat summary dismissal of a (presumably) carefully chosen example, we should remember it is being used for a particular purpose, to underline the *practical* value of ὀρθὴ δόξα. For this type of *ad hominem* example, see H. Cherniss, *A.J.P.* LIII (1932), pp. 233 ff.

[2] Except, of course, ψευδὴς δόξα.

Another question also arises from this passage, closely connected with the one which we have been discussing. It concerns the exact nature of αἰτίας λογισμός, a phrase almost as dark and shadowy as ὀρθὴ δόξα. It may be translated perhaps 'chain of causal reasoning' (Thompson; Croiset has 'un raisonnement de causalité', Cornford 'by reflection on the reason'[1]): this would be in agreement with a further remark in which Plato explains that 'ἐπιστήμη differs from ὀρθὴ δόξα in being tied fast'[2] and with the whole Daedalus passage. The Larissa illustration is no more helpful in answering this question than it was earlier: there is nothing in the state of mind of the φρονῶν there which can be said to correspond to αἰτίας λογισμός (he is distinguished only by personal experience): but we have already had reason to suppose that this illustration is inherently unsatisfactory. Reference to the earlier context makes the phrase clearer: the 'cause' which stabilizes knowledge of the geometrical example is the fact that the latter is a case of a general law (i.e. that the square on the hypotenuse of a right-angled triangle is equal to the sum of those on the other two sides). In other words, the αἰτίας λογισμός is the same criterion as before: it consists in elevating the object of cognition from particulars to Forms, and, in addition, by some process not so far made clear, bringing the particular instance into relation with the Form, as effect to cause.[3]

This view is confirmed by another remark about αἰτίας λογισμός. It is said to be identical with 'recollection' (ἀνάμνησις):[4] in what sense, we can determine, not by what is said at this point, but by reference to the earlier passage in which ἀνάμνησις is discussed. It is there introduced to overcome Meno's eristic disbelief in the possibility of gaining knowledge.[5] Socrates disposes of this difficulty by asserting that in previous cycles of existence, the soul has already gained all knowledge, and what passes for learning is in fact the recovery of this knowledge within the mind. This is

---

[1] *Mind*, n.s., XLI (1932), p. 50.
[2] διαφέρει δεσμῷ ἐπιστήμη ὀρθῆς δόξης (98 A 7f.). See Thompson *ad loc.* for the meaning of δεσμῷ.
[3] Cf. *Ep.* II, 313 B 4ff. and Novotný, *Platonis Epistulae, ad loc.*
[4] *Meno*, 98 A 3 ff. See Cornford, *Principium Sapientiae*, p. 59.
[5] 80D 5ff.

possible because all nature is related:[1] one essential truth remembered, the soul can progress through nature (φύσις) until the whole is recaptured. The meaning of φύσις here is not absolutely clear, but it must include the Forms, and the progress through nature is the tracking down of relation, between particulars and Forms, perhaps even (though this is more doubtful) between the Forms themselves. This coincides with what we discovered about αἰτίας λογισμός earlier. ἀνάμνησις and αἰτίας λογισμός are identical because both consist in plotting the relation of facts within the schematic structure of the universe. This relation in itself is sufficient 'cause', and the plotting of it provides the 'chain of causal reasoning'.

We shall discuss the importance assumed by the concept of ὀρθὴ δόξα in connection with later dialogues: for the present, all that is necessary is to place it in relation with what has gone before. It has already been suggested that the early dialogues do contain hints of Plato's later ethical development.[2] The significance of ὀρθὴ δόξα which is of most importance in this work, is its use as a moral *pis aller* for the bulk of mankind, and we can certainly find hints of the need for this in the early dialogues. There is a revealing insistence in these works on the difficulty and length of the task of achieving ἐπιστήμη. When Euthydemus and his brother claim the ability to impart the ἐπιστήμη of which ἀρετή consists, Socrates is startled into disbelief 'because of the boldness of the claim'.[3] In the Laches, he insists on the absurdity of suggesting that courage is a widespread virtue, since it is an ἐπιστήμη which very few men possess, because of the difficulty of acquiring it.[4] Finally, in the Gorgias, the consideration which conclusively proves that rhetoric can only induce persuasion, not knowledge, is the shortness of time at its disposal and the composition of its audience: 'We would agree, I think, that so vast a matter cannot be adequately explained to a large crowd in a short time.'[5]

---

[1] συγγενής (81 D 1).
[2] See above, p. xiii.
[3] *Euthyd.* 274 A 3 f.
[4] *Lach.* 196 B 5 ff.
[5] οὐ γὰρ δήπου ὄχλον γ' ἂν δύναιτο τοσοῦτον ἐν ὀλίγῳ χρόνῳ διδάξαι οὕτω μεγάλα πράγματα (*Gorg.* 455 A 5 f.).

The *Meno*, however, is the first place where the second-best appears in conjunction with ἐπιστήμη as something of value. We have found a parallel to this conjunction in that between πίστις and ἐπιστήμη in the *Gorgias*, but there, as we saw, the presence of πίστις was needed merely to show off, by its dinginess, the supreme value of ἐπιστήμη. Here it appears as a value in itself, and, in the future, assumes a position of central importance.

THE 'REPUBLIC':
ΑΡΕΤΗ, ΠΑΙΔΕΙΑ AND THE SOUL

'The *Republic*...is a sad book.'   LORD RADCLIFFE

APAINTING by Paolo Ucello shows two angels and two devils fighting for the soul of a dead woman: in Christian terms, this is the situation around which the *Republic* is built. Its focal point, the moment from which it extends both forwards and backwards, is the beginning of Book II. There Glaucon and Adeimantus together appeal to Socrates to convince them, in effect, of the primacy of moral demands, and, in setting out the sort of argument that he must refute, show by the seriousness of their language and the cumulative effect of their repeated statements of 'what is commonly held about the nature of justice and its origin',[1] how vital Plato felt the accomplishment of this task to be. More perhaps than any other of Plato's works, the *Republic* is difficult to understand in terms of its structure and form; and yet some such attempt must be made, for it is by misconception of its formal intention that the various misinterpretations, current and abandoned, of the *Republic* as a whole have been arrived at. The construction of the 'ideal state' with all its ramifications, occupies so large a part of the whole work that it is sometimes difficult to remember that this construction itself is only part of Socrates' answer to the plea of Glaucon and Adeimantus, but only by bearing this in mind, and so setting the 'ideal state' back into its context, can we possibly understand the *Republic* as a complete work.

Formally, both in the social structure of the city state which it portrays, and in the larger scheme of its subject-matter, the *Republic* resembles a pyramid: as the field of vision becomes narrower, so the detail and the length of treatment become

[1] II, 358 C 1 f.

greater, so that the discussion of the mental vision of the philosophers, the smallest (to change our metaphor) of the Chinese boxes, is described in greater complexity than any of the earlier and more extensive topics of the previous books. Like many of the longest and most complicated works of literature, moreover, its beginning is one of calculated innocence. The visit to the Peiraeus, the invitation to Polemarchus' house and the setting of the room, with its circle of stools focused on the ageing business man, Cephalus—the effect of all this is intentionally to play down what follows, to insist on the insignificance of its origin. Disingenuous perhaps, but deliberate. And the subject of conduct, which is to be the centre of the whole massive conversation, is introduced in a similar, naïve manner, with the unphilosophical reflections of Cephalus on the 'lessons' of his life. Yet, in the opening speech of Cephalus, an important point is made, which has bearings far beyond its context: this is his insistence that happiness depends, not on environment and possessions, but on character.[1] It would not be a perversion of the *Republic* as a whole to describe it as an investigation of human character with a view to discovering the sources, actual and possible, of moral action. Cephalus' contention foreshadows Plato's own beliefs and acquires great prominence in the sequel.[2] The conversation with Cephalus contributes other themes which also are to reappear: the violence of passion,[3] the attractions of property and wealth,[4] and the typical conventional morality of 'telling the truth and paying one's debts', which Cephalus puts forward as his own just before he leaves the discussion to Socrates and Polemarchus.[5] All this is introduced in a manner calculated to disarm; the *Republic*, though it stands at the heart of Plato's philosophy and carries discussion

---

[1] I, 329D 2ff.: ὁ τρόπος τῶν ἀνθρώπων.
[2] Cf., for example, IV, 443C 9ff.
[3] I, 329C 7ff. This is pre-eminently a sign of conventional moral views in Plato's works; cf. *Prot.* 352A 8ff. Another indication of the conventional moral presuppositions in Book I is given in the phrase τὸ τοὺς φίλους...εὖ ποιεῖν καὶ τοὺς ἐχθροὺς κακῶς (332D 7ff.), where εὖ ποιεῖν is not originally intended in the 'Platonic' sense to which it is reduced at 335B–D.
[4] 330B 8ff.
[5] 331B 1ff. Cf. Joseph, *Essays*, pp. 3f.

into its most involved problems, approaches its task in a manner which seems to deny the importance of what follows.

We have already examined the argument with Polemarchus in another context:[1] here it will be enough to make once again, because its lessons seem not yet to have been learned, the point that the late H. W. B. Joseph was, I think, the first to make. It concerns both the argument with Polemarchus and the following one with Thrasymachus. Mr Joseph was at pains to show that the first book of the *Republic* was not a gross example of fallacious argument, and that Plato was not 'taken in by quibbles...that any freshman can detect'. He insisted that the purpose of this first book was to expose the false assumptions inherent in conventional thought about ethics, and maintained that 'the false assumptions are so many forms of a single error, that of supposing that the practice of justice (or righteousness) consists in the performance of specifiable acts'.[2] Thus Book I is a preliminary skirmish in the field of human conduct and moral virtue, as it is generally understood and discussed; for, as Joseph said, it is common enough at all times to find the problem of conduct discussed in terms of particular actions or decisions. 'Is it just (or right, or ethical) to do x?' is a question which occurs often enough in moral discussions. Plato's point is that moral virtue cannot be defined or determined by reference to 'right' acts, even if we make it a condition that these acts must be done in the 'right' spirit. It was, as we have seen, a cardinal point with Socrates that ἀρετή was a matter of inward vision or capacity, not to be specified by the actions to which such a vision gave rise, since the ethical context of these actions is inextricably part of the world of sense and change, which causes it to happen that an action right at one moment will be wrong at another; part, in fact, of the insoluble problem of what E. M. Forster has called good-and-evil. Although there is a close inherent connection between ἀρετή and action, the one cannot be deduced from the other, nor explained in terms of it.

The opening book of the *Republic*, then, in its function as prelude,[3] rejects all attempts to define ἀρετή by reference to

---

[1] See above, pp. 44 f.   [2] Joseph, *Essays*, p. 6.
[3] προοίμιον (II, 357 A 2).

individual morally correct actions. The rest of the work develops the implications of this rejection. If justice is not the carrying out of acts which can be specified as right in themselves, what then is it? Glaucon and Adeimantus express the general view in saying that justice is a form of social self-defence, imposed by the great mass of the undistinguished, to protect themselves against suffering from the ruthless self-assertion which they, in common with everyone else, would prefer to practise, if they could only do so without meeting the consequences. But since universal self-assertion would reduce them to a state of misery, they have abandoned this active preference and fallen back on the second-best, passive 'collective security'. The other side of the same picture is presented by Adeimantus, in his description of justice as entirely a matter of outward appearance and reputation. These two views are traced back to their source in conventional moral education, to the constantly repeated threats and exhortations of all those in a position of command over children,[1] who think of moral virtue only in its outward form. The really just man understands all this, and feels sympathy with the moral dilemma of the average man, realizing that 'a few men here and there may be granted some sort of divine inspiration or achieve ἐπιστήμη: they will be repelled by injustice and will have no part in it, but the rest will be just only against their own wills, forced to attack injustice by their inability to be men, or by old age or by some other weakness which makes them incapable of *being* unjust'.[2] We may note, not only that it is just such a feeling that gives rise to the *Republic*, but also that there is a curious echo here of the Socratic 'paradox', οὐδεὶς ἑκὼν ἄδικος:[3] this is the corresponding paradox of Thrasymachus.

It is also the paradox against which Glaucon and Adeimantus invoke Socrates, in support of their natural integrity against the plausibility of these ideas. Once again, there is a hint of the sequel in their plea: if it could really be understood by all men that justice,

---

[1] 362E 1 ff. Note *Odyssey*, XIX, 109 ff., quoted here: even the gods only reward justice by μέθη αἰώνιος.

[2] πλὴν εἴ τις θείᾳ φύσει δυσχεραίνων τὸ ἀδικεῖν ἢ ἐπιστήμην λαβὼν ἀπέχεται αὐτοῦ, τῶν γε ἄλλων οὐδεὶς ἑκὼν δίκαιος, ἀλλ' ὑπὸ ἀνανδρίας ἢ γήρως ἢ τινος ἄλλης ἀσθενείας ψέγει τὸ ἀδικεῖν, ἀδυνατῶν αὐτὸ δρᾶν (366 c 6 ff.).

[3] Cf. also 360 c 6.

in itself, was the highest good they could look for, then 'they would not have to be on their guard against each other's injustice; each would be his own best moral guardian'.[1] Here, in effect, is the whole teaching of the *Republic* summed up; as much is hinted at in the use of the word φύλαξ (guard or guardian). It is because they have achieved this full understanding that the philosophers, the true φύλακες, are able to be not only their own moral guardians, but Guardians also of the whole of society.

So far the discussion has been largely negative, with only occasional clues to the positive ideas that will be suggested later. This positive movement in the *Republic* begins with the introduction of the idea of society, to stand as a magnified example of the individual. The use of this 'political analogy' has been both attacked and defended,[2] but its significance in the present context has not perhaps been appreciated. Whatever the logical validity of such an analogy, its use implies certain ideas in Plato's mind, ideas which in turn indicate a movement away from the Socratic ethical position. For if society is analogous to the individual, justice in society (and this is, in fact, Plato's whole point) must be analogous to justice in the individual. This, however, is an idea which could never have occurred to Socrates, for the ethical 'movement of faith', which we have seen Socratic ἐπιστήμη to be, could not possibly be achieved by society. Its characteristic features, particularity and inwardness, cannot be those of whatever moral virtue society as a whole might be said to possess. Moreover, the fundamental point which Plato wishes to make with regard to society is that it comes into being because of the innate differences and deficiencies of human individuals: however natural, it is essentially a union of heterogeneous elements.[3] This, in itself, might refer to no more than economic deficiencies, but,

[1] οὐκ ἂν ἀλλήλους ἐφυλάττομεν μὴ ἀδικεῖν, ἀλλ' αὐτὸς αὑτοῦ ἦν ἕκαστος ἄριστος φύλαξ (367 A 2 ff.).
[2] See Murphy, *Interpretation of Plato's 'Republic'*, pp. 68 ff.; Joseph, *Essays*, pp. 41 ff.
[3] 370 A 8 ff.; cf. Joseph, *Essays*, p. 108 and n. 3 on that page, where Joseph refers, in addition to this passage, to 374 E 4 and III, 395 B 3–6. He believes that *Laws*, III, 689 C 6–E 2 implies some change of opinion: in the context, however, nothing of the sort seems actually intended. See above, pp. 90 ff.

146

for Plato, the deficiencies in moral and intellectual powers are even more important; the two sorts of deficiency are indeed considered parallel.[1] ἀρετή, therefore, regarded as something observable in a social group must be different from Socratic ἐπιστήμη: what it is, in fact, will be the principal topic of the next few chapters.

The adoption of society as an analogy for the individual indicates further the lines on which Plato will conduct his inquiry. He will obviously not be trying to delimit the notion of justice by specification of just acts: no analogy would be necessary or useful for this. Nor will he be investigating justice from the point of view that Glaucon and Adeimantus put forward as the prevailing one: rewards and advantages can be concerned only where *relations* with other groups are involved, and Plato will be considering inter-society relations only in so far as they bring about certain adjustments in the internal structure of his society.[2] The rewards of justice, therefore, will not be expected to enter into the discussion, so long as it takes society as the basic unit for its examination. Whatever justice is, it must be something internal, since the society in which it is being sought is thought of, at this stage, almost as existing in a vacuum. We are not, therefore, surprised to find that Glaucon suggests that justice is perhaps to be found in the relations between the elements in society.[3] This seems a promising, if rather obvious, lead into a positive discussion, but, inexplicably (as we are tempted to believe), it is dropped and the growing complexity of society adopted instead as a theme.

The reason for this, as we discover, is to allow the first appearance of the φύλακες: as society becomes more complex, more luxurious, its demands and wants outstrip its ability to supply them, and the obvious step is for it to attempt to secure more for itself by plundering a neighbour's territory. For the purpose of his present argument, Plato assumes that the neighbouring cities have a similar need for expansion, and the φύλακες enter naturally

[1] See M. B. Foster, *Political Philosophies of Plato and Hegel*, pp. 28f. and App. A.
[2] By being, for example, the primary cause of the existence of φύλακες (in the first sense of the term) (373 D 1 ff.).
[3] 372A 1 f.

as a protective element, in the literal sense.[1] According to the principle of 'one man, one task—that to which he is best suited', the φύλακες are to be specialists and, for their task, must be shown to have suitable characters. (We should note, perhaps, here that the use of the word φύσις, to denote what I have called 'character', is the connecting link by which Plato is enabled to pass from the technical sense of specialization to the moral and philosophical sense; φύσις may equally well be used of natural technical aptitudes and innate moral tendencies. The transition is, perhaps, more obviously invalid in English.)[2]

Instead of reverting to the question of justice in society, Plato now begins an inquiry into a suitable education for the φύλακες. Once again, the reason for this, though obscure at first, is not hard to find. Consideration of the sort of education which the military class requires slowly makes it obvious that a further, higher[3] stratum in society will be necessary, in the first place to lay down the limits of this education and its components. M. B. Foster shows this connection well, in saying of the soldier-guardian in the *Republic*:

> In order that the civic virtue of Andreia may be produced in him, it is necessary that the proportion [between humane studies and bodily exercises] should be right, but not that he should be convinced of its rightness, or aware of what makes it right. . . . But the trainer who is to produce this character must himself possess a further excellence beyond that which it is the object of his training to produce. He must *know* the proportions in which the elements of education are to be mingled in order to produce the character required. Thus the production of a class of fighters in the state necessarily presupposes the existence of a further class which is competent to prescribe their training, and this is the class of rulers in the strictest sense.[4]

---

[1] Some of the obscurities of development in the *Republic* result from the fact that Plato is setting out his ideas in the reverse order to that in which he thought of them; i.e. he assumes the need for φύλακες in the sense of Book VII, traces their origin to the need for defence, and hence to expansionism. This also explains in part the apparent haphazardness of exposition with regard to education.

[2] 374E 4, etc. Cf. Foster, *op. cit.* pp. 28 ff. and App. A.

[3] In the sense of 'more responsible'.

[4] Foster, *op. cit.* pp. 11 f.

Though we hear no more of them until Book III,[1] the philosopher-kings are a necessary part of society from this point onwards.

We have seen also, in examining the *Laws*, that the prominence assigned to primary education, such as is discussed during the rest of Book II and much of Book III, has important ethical implications.[2] It is unimpeachable evidence of Plato's belief, at this period, in an irrational basis for at least social morality. Indeed, before the consideration of primary education begins, it is explicitly stated, in connection with the soldier-guardians, that the courage which they must exhibit implies a particular *emotional* character.[3] There will be no need here to discuss in detail what the educational syllabus of these early books of the *Republic* may be said to mean in terms of Plato's ethical development. As in the *Laws*, education is only a special instance of environment, and it is the moral effect of environment as a whole which Plato is most concerned to bring out. The resulting discussion is remarkably similar to the corresponding passages in the *Laws*.[4] We may confine ourselves to noticing a few instances. There is a familiar ring about Plato's insistence that the first stages of the development of anything are the most important, because moulding and information are then at their easiest and may be most complete.[5] The sort of ἀρετή to which this education of sentiment must give rise can only be the πολιτικὴ ἀρετή which we remember from the *Laws*: thus it is natural to find that σωφροσύνη is said, for the majority, to be mere obedience to superior judgment and control over their own lower passions and desires.[6] Primary education is designed to effect such a state of mind; this aim is the sole criterion of what is good and bad in education. The good is 'that which has a part to

---

[1] III, 412 B 8 f.   [2] See above, pp. 111 ff.
[3] 375 A 11 f.
[4] This in itself is sufficient to show that Murphy is wrong in supposing that Plato abandoned his views on the evocative powers of what Murphy calls 'aesthetic and sentimental education' (see Murphy, *op. cit.* pp. 43 f.).
[5] 377 A 12 ff.; cf. *Laws*, VI, 765 E 3 ff., II, 672 B 8 ff., etc. For other examples of similarity of treatment, cf. IV, 424 B 1 ff. with *Laws*, VII, 797 A 7 ff.; 441 A 7 ff. with *Laws*, II, 653 A 7 ff. For contrast, 425 B 7 ff. is at variance with the whole spirit and practice of the *Laws*.
[6] III, 389 D 9 ff.

THE GROWTH OF A REALITY PRINCIPLE

play in the achievement of σωφροσύνη';[1] the bad is anything that tends to mar this building of character. When Plato comes to summarize his intentions in this universal education of personality, he sets out a sort of aesthetic formalism of morals. By dwelling on the close parallelism between εὐσχημοσύνη, grace and delicacy of surroundings, and ἀρετή itself,[2] he is able to compare ugliness of environment (which includes both moral and aesthetic ugliness) to the presence of poisonous weeds in a pasture, by imbibing which unawares the φύλακες would fill their souls with a mass of evil.[3] Thus here, as in the Laws, Plato's treatment of environment, and in particular of education, shows how far he has moved, in his presuppositions about ἀρετή, from the 'Socratic' position of the early dialogues. The claims made for education are not perhaps as all-embracing here as they are in the later work; yet at one point Plato insists that, given the right start that education on the suggested lines will provide, the progress towards ethical perfection will be in the nature of a cycle of cumulative effect (as we might say, a snowball process or a chain-reaction), so that education may be considered as sufficient cause of the attainment of ἀρετή.[4]

The concept of ἀρετή which begins to emerge from these early books of the Republic is sufficiently like that of the Laws, and sufficiently unlike that of the early dialogues, not to require further specification. As far as ἀρετή is concerned, the difference between Republic and Laws is a difference merely of degree, not of fundamental outlook. Chronologically, of course, the present passage contains the first full-length exposition of the new moral theory: hence the considerable length of treatment which precedes the definition of the four cardinal ἀρεταί in Book IV. But before we reach this culminating point of the first section of the Republic, we have to discuss the preliminary theory, that of the soul.

In the state, σοφία and ἀνδρεία have been assigned to particular elements, while σωφροσύνη and δικαιοσύνη have been found to

---

[1] 390A 4; cf. B 3, C 8, etc.
[2] On this correspondence in Plato's thought between moral, aesthetic and mathematical values, see Cornford in Mind, n.s., XLI (1932), pp. 187f.
[3] 401 B 1 ff. Environment compared to a fast dye (430A 1 ff.)
[4] IV, 423 E 1 ff. Cf. III, 401 D 5 ff.; IV, 424D 7 ff., 425 B 10ff.

lie in the right relationships of all the elements. Thus if, as was originally assumed, justice in society and soul are essentially the same, the same three elements as in society must exist in the soul also.[1] Their existence is established by an examination of various cases of a conflict of motives, after which Plato asserts that there are three types of motive or drive (τὰ αὐτά...ἐν ἑνὸς ἑκάστου τῇ ψυχῇ γένη).[2] What we have here to discuss is the relevance of this new theory to Plato's ethical beliefs: we are concerned with the details of the theory only in so far as they reflect on the whole subject of Plato's ethics. In the first place, we must see in what way the theory is relevant to our present subject. It has, for instance, been supposed that Plato's recognition of a conflict of motives implies an abandonment of some of Socrates' characteristic ideas; in particular, of the theory of βούλησις, discussed in chapter III.[3] But the mere recognition of mental conflict and a discussion of its psychological mechanism cannot be said to imply this at all. Socrates 'recognized' mental conflicts, from a psychological aspect, but the terms of his theory were sufficiently abnormal to make such conflicts irrelevant as evidence. What is important about the present passage is that it shows Plato displaying a positive and hitherto unexampled interest in the empirical psychology of moral decisions. This in itself only confirms what we have already noticed in the earlier books, namely that the ethical framework is no longer Socratic, but already tends towards the final position taken up in the *Laws*. It must, of course, be remembered that the differentiation of rational and irrational motives in the soul is made necessary by Plato's theory of individual-social correspondence. But this in itself is not a self-obvious fact, or even a straightforward deduction from empirical evidence, but rather an

---

[1] It may be noticed that the differentiation of the φύλακες into two strata, one ruling, one obeying (at 412B 8f.), is treated quite without explanation as something only to be expected. See above, pp. 148 f.

[2] 441 C 5 f. For excellent accounts of ψυχή in the *Republic*, see Joseph, *Essays*, pp. 41–81; Murphy, *op. cit.* pp. 24–44 (especially pp. 36 ff.). No suitable word has been found to translate Plato's μέρη, γένη, εἴδη, etc., of the soul. 'Parts' is obviously misleading (see Murphy, *loc. cit.*); perhaps 'aspects' (εἴδη) or 'types of motive' (γένη) are less harmful.

[3] E.g., by Murphy, *op. cit.* pp. 48 ff. As a corrective, see Joseph, *Essays*, p. 56.

aspect of Plato's new attitude to ethical theory. In earlier dialogues, of course, Socrates is pictured as striving towards definition of moral concepts, but the important fact in all these cases is that no such definition is ever reached. Although it is generally believed that Socrates aimed at explicit definition,[1] such definitions as are offered are all negatived; no positive definitions are offered and accepted. ἐπιστήμη for Socrates (*qua* 'capability', i.e. implicit) is not definition: perhaps only with Plato does the aim become explicit specification, as the metaphysical framework becomes overt. But even here, in the *Republic*, the definitions of ἀρεταί which we are offered seem more in the nature of illustrations, like the parables in Books VI and VII.

Perhaps we are more likely to maintain perspective in examining the definitions of Book IV, if we remember that the full investigation of ἀρετή, by what Plato calls the longer road, has not yet been attempted. Definition of ἀρεταί is conceivable, even possible, because we are not yet at grips with ἀρετή in the full sense. This is made clear by the context: courage (ἀνδρεία), for example, exists solely in virtue of the irrational drive towards self-assertion (τὸ θυμοειδές), which Socrates has allowed to children and animals; yet we cannot believe that nothing higher is visualized, even if not described.[2] We may also, at first, be surprised to find that the ἀρεταί are treated as plural, but even here there are hints that such plurality is not final. In spite of the four distinct definitions of ἀρεταί, wrongdoing is collected under one head as 'confusion and aberration among the drives in the soul'.[3] Confusion is increased by a statement of Socrates, made only a page or so later, to the effect that 'ἀρετή has only one aspect, whereas there are innumerable aspects to its opposite, four of which deserve particular mention'.[4] We may at least infer from this lack of agreement that Plato's definitions of ἀρεταί in Book IV are not his final word on the

---

[1] By Robinson, for instance: *Plato's Earlier Dialectic*, pp. 49 ff.

[2] 441 c ff.; cf. A 7 ff. ἀνδρεία is also connected with δόξαι at 429 B 8 ff.

[3] 444 B 6 ff.

[4] ἐν μὲν εἶναι εἶδος τῆς ἀρετῆς, ἄπειρα δὲ τῆς κακίας, τέτταρα δ' ἐν αὐτοῖς ἄττα ὧν καὶ ἄξιον ἐπιμνησθῆναι (445 C 5 ff.). The four εἴδη τῆς κακίας mentioned here are of course the corrupt constitutions of Books VIII and IX.

subject; later we shall see that this is the case.[1] At present, we shall avoid some prevalent misunderstandings by recognizing that what we have so far discussed is merely an interim statement, which leaves out of account much of what is most important in Plato's ethical construction in the *Republic*.[2]

[1] See below, pp. 178f.

[2] On this point, see J. Moreau, *La Construction de l'Idéalisme Platonicien*, pp. 234 ff., especially pp. 252-4.

CHAPTER XI

THE 'REPUBLIC': ΔΟΞΑ AND ΕΠΙΣΤΗΜΗ

THE *Republic* often gives the impression of great effort resulting only in anticlimax and disappointment, and never more than at the end of Book IV. It seems that the definitions of ἀρεταί are too feeble and too circumscribed to be the adequate end of any quest. The immediate reaction, only natural, is to believe that one has been cheated by Plato and the plan of the conversation into accepting the unsatisfying for true value. Perhaps from the previous chapter we can now understand how this sense of expectations unmet is wholly intended by Plato; we have avoided the longer road,[1] and the cost must be paid in disappointment. That we have not, in fact, arrived at the goal which we hoped to reach is at once implied in Socrates' words when the discussion begins again on the second and more difficult section of the quest. The discovery of the real nature of justice is referred, in spite of the definition only recently concluded, to the future once again.[2] But the realization, by the reader, that we have still the greater effort to make, that what follows is still a continuation of the same subject, but in a higher key, is now hindered by a conscious device. In the next section of the *Republic*, the decisive step is to be taken towards a real attempt to reach the goal; but this is obscured by a pretence on Plato's part that all that is involved is a demonstration of the possibility that the model society sketched in during the previous books might come into existence.[3] It has already been suggested that the plan of the *Republic* is difficult to plot; one of the most obvious causes of this is Plato's habit of disguising his trail. In the earlier dialogues, as we saw, it was the conclusion that was most often obscured in this way. At this period, it is the articulation of the dialogue itself; yet structure and sense are so inextricably mixed that, even now, we

[1] We are expressly told so at IV, 435D 3.
[2] V, 472B 7. Cf. VI, 504D 6ff.   [3] V, 471C ff.

154

can say that Plato is covering up his meaning in hindering an understanding of the structural course of the conversation. His purpose, if we may interpret him, is presumably to prevent the reader from supposing that he had discovered that σύγγραμμα of his philosophy which, in the Seventh Letter, he denied had ever existed.[1]

If we avoid the false trail laid for us by Plato, we will be able to see the real importance of this second section of the Republic. It is considerably shorter than the first, but in it are made the fundamental distinctions from which the rest of the construction proceeds. The opposition between δόξα and ἐπιστήμη, already outlined in the Meno, is here described with greater confidence, even if, as we shall see, the difficulties inherent in the theory are not, perhaps, more successfully avoided. It is on this distinction that the ethical system of the Republic at bottom stands. In this chapter we shall consider the concept of δόξα as it appears here, and, for the sake of completeness, two passages in other dialogues where light is thrown on this theory.

When he is challenged by Glaucon to prove the feasibility of his suggested ideal, Socrates first puts forward the characteristic belief that the achievements of thought may grasp hold of more of truth than those of action;[2] then, hesitantly, states the famous paradox of the Republic: unless philosophy directs society, there will never be relief from evil.[3] If we imagine ourselves readers of Plato's works in their chronological sequence, this is, in a sense, a new paradox; but only in a sense, for if we remove the word 'society' from it, and substitute 'the individual', it is only a restatement of Socrates' central idea, that ἐπιστήμη is ἀρετή. For the philosophical ideal of Plato in the Republic is only a sophisticated version of Socratic ἐπιστήμη. Yet, of course, in the substitution of society for the individual, the one necessary step is taken which transforms the personal morality of Socrates into the search for the ethical society which occupied the rest of Plato's life. It should not be

---

[1] Ep. VII, 341 C. [2] 473 A 1 ff.
[3] 473 C 11 ff.: κακῶν παῦλα. Cf. VI, 501 E 2 ff., and contrast Laws, IV, 713 E 3 ff. (above, p. 98); the similarity in language and the difference in what is said between these two passages is remarkably instructive.

difficult to see, however, that the one has developed out of the
other. In the dialogue, the paradox produces as much bewilder-
ment as if, in fact, it was quite without philosophical parentage.
In the face of it, Socrates is forced to make his conception of the
philosopher clearer, and the passage which is our chief concern in
this chapter opens.

This phase of the conversation is one of the most carefully
formulated in the whole of Plato's works, and we must, at the
start, realize the cardinàl importance of the conclusions reached in
it to the whole of his philosophical development. Socrates begins
his assault on the convictions of his hearers by producing a definition of the philosopher as a man with a passion for every sort of
knowledge.[1] But, for Glaucon at least, this raises problems, which
concern the status of devotees of culture, who rush from one drama
festival to the next in their fevered search for fresh experience.
Thus, at the outset, the 'humanist' is contrasted, and unfavourably
contrasted, with the true philosopher. For Socrates will not
allow, any more than Glaucon, that the man of general culture
can fall within the definition of philosopher. The reason for this
exclusion is set out at great length. We will not be succumbing to
the current fashion of seeing the traces of Isocrates and the need to
combat his plausible heresies in every other line that Plato wrote,[2]
if we explain the seriousness and length of the following argument
by understanding it as Plato's reply to the 'humanist fallacy', of
which we may take Isocrates as representative. N. R. Murphy
sums up the argument by saying: 'Against them [i.e. the humanists]
Socrates has to show that acquaintance with particular cases and
with the varied types that are found in experience, without reflection on their essential nature, will not produce understanding
but only what he rather mysteriously calls δόξα.'[3] We have now
to unravel this mysterious doctrine.

As Murphy has pointed out,[4] there are two distinct lines of

[1] 475 C 6ff.
[2] See, for example, R. S. Bluck, *Plato's Life and Thought*, pp. 34–5, 64, 66, 76,
112–14. For a sane account of Isocrates' place in the present argument, see
Murphy, *op. cit.* pp. 99 ff.
[3] Murphy, *op. cit.* p. 101.   [4] Murphy, *op. cit.* pp. 104 ff.

argument in the section from 474B to the end of Book V. The first mentions the Forms, the second, while presupposing a distinction between the world of phenomena and another, more 'real' world, implies this in no other sense than as an epistemological necessity. In the first, the Forms are assumed as common ground between Glaucon and Socrates, and, on this premise, Socrates quickly defines the philosopher as one who has a clear view of the Form itself, in addition to the things which share its character; the man of culture as one who believes in the existence of beautiful things, but will not allow that of anything that might be called 'Beauty'. The first is granted true insight (γνώμη), the second conviction (δόξα) only.[1] But it is suggested that our cultured opponents may not accept this plain statement, and a longer and more complex argument is then set out to win them over and persuade them gently.[2] This argument draws up a correlation between states of mind and their objects in each case. It is agreed by Glaucon, as spokesman for the artistic devotees of common sense, that so sure a state of mind as knowledge must have an object as stable, as 'real' as itself. At the opposite end of the scale, pure mental blankness has as its object an equal purity of non-existence. If there exists a state of mind and a field or object which can be said to fall between these two extremes, it might be asserted of both that simultaneously they were and were not. The concept of δόξα is introduced, but before the analysis can be pressed to its logical conclusion, Socrates interpolates a discussion of the word 'faculty' or 'capacity' (δύναμις) as that which produces an ability to do something.[3] The purpose of this is not entirely clear, but because of it the conversation makes a detour during which the correlation of mental state and mental object is drawn even more clearly.[4] The argument here becomes very involved: δυνάμεις are distinguished both by their effect (ὃ ἀπεργάζεται) and by 'that against which each is drawn up' (obviously a military metaphor).[5] Knowledge and belief are both δυνάμεις; but, since they are different, they must have different fields or objects. The

---

[1] 476D 5f.   [2] E 1f.
[3] 477C 1ff.   [4] E.g. at 478A 3f.
[5] 477C 9ff. For the metaphor, cf. τέτακται (B 7).

object of δόξα, then, is not what is real, nor, since belief can also be distinguished from pure mental blankness, is it what is quite unreal. Moreover, it is only common sense to hold that belief must have some object other than complete non-existence. Belief is a state of mind which can be placed somewhere between ἐπιστήμη and ἄγνοια (or blank ignorance). Its field of operation must also lie between the wholly real and the wholly unreal; what such a field of operation might be, may emerge if we ask our opponents whether any of their 'beautiful' objects is ever fully entitled to the predicate; whether, in fact, another observer might not call it ugly. Similar contradictory predicates, we find, may be asserted of any of the objects in this world. The just action does not *really* exist in this world, which is the world to which our opponents restrict their thinking. Here we may note, following Murphy,[1] that it is the 'just-action' which, in this passage, is said not to exist in full reality; the content of the world of phenomena, in other words, is described as unreal in so far as no predicate that is wholly true can be asserted of it. The argument here is epistemological, not metaphysical, even if we believe that Plato's religious inclinations might well render him liable to challenge the reality of objects in the world of sense;[2] here it is the validity of predication, and in particular of moral predication, that is in question. Thus we find that, when the argument is summarized, it is the conventional notions about the things of this world that are said to roll adrift between the poles of pure reality and unreality: 'We have discovered, it seems, that it is the mass of conventional views that most people hold about the nature of what is good and other such subjects, that pitch and toss somewhere between the poles of pure being and pure non-existence.'[3] Here, then, is the field of objects, intermediate between the extremes, that is 'drawn up' against δόξα, the state of mind similarly intermediate. The devotees of culture have set their heart on the fluctuating values

---

[1] Murphy, *op. cit.* pp. 108 ff. I do not, however, follow Murphy in restricting Plato's views on predication to what we would now call relative terms.

[2] See E. R. Dodds, *The Greeks and the Irrational*, pp. 214 ff.

[3] ηὑρήκαμεν ἄρα, ὡς ἔοικεν, ὅτι τὰ τῶν πολλῶν πολλὰ νόμιμα καλοῦ τε πέρι καὶ τῶν ἄλλων μεταξύ που κυλινδεῖται τοῦ τε μὴ ὄντος καὶ τοῦ ὄντος εἰλικρινῶς (479 D 3 ff.).

of this semi-reality, just as the philosopher has set his on the true values of the world of Forms; 'so we may fairly call them lovers of belief rather than of wisdom—not philosophical, in fact, but philodoxical'.[1] So, at last, we have distinguished the philosopher from this other claimant to the post of ruler in the true society.

But we are by no means out of the wood yet; indeed Socrates admits as much almost at once. He confesses that we might have got a clearer view if we had not had other subjects stretching out before us.[2] From our point of view, too, as readers, there is much that calls for answer in this argument and in the belief that lies behind it. We have yet to understand what quality of mental state is represented by δόξα, i.e. what it feels like to be δοξάζων. The correlation of state of mind and object is even more fraught with philosophical difficulties, unless we can discover some way in which δόξα and ἐπιστήμη can be distinguished without necessarily implying a distinction of objects.

We saw in the *Meno* that only by considering their respective objects could δόξα and ἐπιστήμη be adequately differentiated. Yet we found there the new concept of ὀρθὴ δόξα, which for practical purposes was given equal value with ἐπιστήμη. The same concept appears in the *Republic*, and with it the same problems. Its first appearance is in Book III. Socrates, after mentioning casually the necessity for a division among the φύλακες into a ruling and a subordinate class, asserts that the former must be those who are capable of preserving the inward conviction[3] that they must always act with the interests of the community in mind. They must be proof against beguilement or robbery, where their convictions are at stake. This true inward conviction is described, in a mysterious and ambiguous phrase, as 'viewing things as they really are' (τὸ τὰ ὄντα δοξάζειν).[4] It is equated with 'the possession of truth' (ἀληθεύειν), and, immediately afterwards, called ἀληθὴς δόξα. There follows an account of how such belief can be lost, which makes it clear that what is in question here is not Socratic ἐπιστήμη, which according to the *Gorgias* is to be distinguished from πίστις by being unshakable.[5] This, even if there were no

---

[1] *The Republic of Plato*, tr. F. M. Cornford, p. 184. [2] VI, 484 A 5 ff.
[3] δόγματος (413 C 6). [4] III, 413 A 7 ff. [5] *Gorg.* 458 E ff.

other argument against it, would prevent us from using this passage as evidence that Plato did not seriously intend his account of the correlation of mental states and objects. If we attempted to do so, we would have to set aside an extremely careful argument in favour of a phrase in a wholly different context; and in interpreting this phrase we should have, moreover, to rely on that most unreliable of guides to Plato's meaning, his use of terms. It should by now be axiomatic in any study of Plato that an argument about his meaning which turns on a rigid interpretation of his terminology is at once suspect, in particular if such an argument is used to discredit a normal, common-sense understanding of Plato's intention.[1] The phrase, connecting as it does δόξα with τὰ ὄντα, i.e. the real world (of Forms), remains an anomaly by the standards of Book v; but we should not seek to reinterpret or discard it simply for that reason. To understand Plato we must be ready to accept anomalies.

Moreover, the context supplies us with a clue to the vocabulary. It has already been shown that Books I–IV go no further into the problems of ethics than the level of unintegrated definition of moral terms. Thus at this stage of the discussion, the φύλακες, even of the ruling category, cannot be said to possess more than δόξα. The conception of a state of mind going beyond δόξα, and the elaboration of the distinction between them, has not yet entered into the conversation. Within the terms of Book III, there is nothing, no higher form of moral awareness than ἀληθὴς δόξα, which might be used as a definition of ἀληθεύειν. We are not, therefore, assisted by this passage to resolve the dilemma of Book v, which is, indeed, essentially the same dilemma as that of the *Meno*.

During the discussion of ἀρεταί in Book IV, references to δόξα are frequent.[2] On the other hand, ἐπιστήμη is used only of the σοφία of the φύλακες, a concept so far insufficiently precise and

---

[1] This is a hoary problem; it should be necessary to do no more than refer, for example, to H. C. Baldry's article on 'Plato's "Technical Terms"' (*Classical Quarterly*, XXXI, 1937, pp. 141 ff.). But examples of arguments that depend on too rigid interpretation of terminology are to be found in two recent books: Sir D. Ross, *Plato's Theory of Ideas* (e.g. p. 21) and N. R. Murphy, *Interpretation of Plato's 'Republic'* (e.g. ch. VIII *passim*).

[2] E.g. IV, 429 C 1, C 7; 430 B 3, B 5, B 7; 431 C 6.

only later given its real significance and thereby its real title to be called ἐπιστήμη. δόξα itself is compared to a dye, a dye designed to be as 'fast' as possible.[1] The comparison is a telling one: not only does it imply the result of conscious application, it is also an 'unnatural' state, the sophistication of an almost colourless innocence. We are reminded of the 'city of swine' and the fawn dullness of their way of life. δόξα, the dye of belief, is a protective coating intended to weather the storm of experience. We find also, immediately after the simile of the dye, that δόξα is distinguished from two other states of mind. First from that primary state of innocence, which we can find exemplified only in children or animals (for the world with which we are faced is inevitably the world of experience), and secondly from some higher, but unspecified state.[2] This is indicated by the first use in the Republic of the adjective πολιτική applied in what is obviously a restrictive sense to certain moral virtues: here it is left unexplained, accompanied only by a vague promise of further consideration later.[3]

The supposition that Plato intends to stand by the consequences of his correlation theory of mental state and object gains support from a passage somewhat later in Book IV.[4] It is there said that forms of ἐπιστήμη take on different characteristics as their objects vary. This is part of a general pronouncement of the same order about all correlatives. We cannot infer from this that the theory of Book V is actually implied here; Plato explicitly rejects the possibility that knowledge of good and evil, for example, is itself good and evil.[5] It is, however, evidence that Plato already feels that states of mind are correlative, in some sense at least, with their objects, if only in the obvious sense that medical knowledge, for example, can be differentiated from mathematics by reference to its object. The epistemological theory of Book V is perhaps a psychological, if not a logical, deduction from this limited statement.

The usage of Book V is on the whole confirmed by the frequent occurrence of δόξα and related words in the remainder of the Republic, in a sense which agrees with the definition that we have

---

[1] 430A 1 ff. [2] 430B 6 ff. [3] C 3 ff.
[4] 438D 11 ff. [5] E 1 ff.

been considering.[1] We must therefore believe in Plato's firm acceptance of the consequences of his theory. δόξα is 'more shadowy than true understanding (γνῶσις)';[2] to say that it is also the state of mind of one who regards the unreal moral entities of this world (unreal in a moral sense) is no more than an equivalent of that statement. So long as the object of thought is an action or a moral judgment about an action, the thought itself can never be more valid than δόξα; ὀρθὴ δόξα, if it happens to be right, but never more. The distinction is still far from clear. There appears to be more in the theory than a mere realization that good and evil are inextricably involved together in the actions of this world. It is not the possibility of rightness of judgment *as such* that Plato seems here to be denying, for the mysterious concept of ὀρθὴ δόξα involves it in some degree at least. We may perhaps escape this particular dilemma by the assumption that 'correctness', as applied to δόξα, is correctness within the inescapable limits of the phenomenal world, and that there exists no one-to-one correspondence between the ὀρθότης of ὀρθὴ δόξα and that of ἐπιστήμη (which is always ὀρθή). To say this is to abandon, as we have been already almost forced to do, the 'road to Larissa' illustration of the *Meno*, which cannot in any case be accommodated to the correlation theory of the *Republic*.[3]

But there remains an almost insoluble, and altogether more important, philosophical predicament which this theory forces upon us. As an interim judgment, we may describe the purpose of the *Republic* as the creation of an ethical equipment to withstand the onslaught of experience; yet we must at once admit that this purpose has already been undermined by Book v. The culmination of this effort of creation occurs only later, in Book VII; the ruling element in the φύλακες is to achieve a basis of moral perspicacity which goes beyond any ethical understanding so far contemplated in the *Republic* for any part of society. It is to be

---

[1] See, for example, VI, 490 B 1, 493 A 8, C 2, 496 A 7, 503 A 2, 506 C 6ff., 508 D 8; VII, 533 B 4, 538 C 6; IX, 574 D 5, 584 E 8; X, 602 A 8.

[2] γνώσεως μέν...σκοτωδέστερον (V, 478 C 13 f.).

[3] See, however, VI, 506 C 7ff., with its apparent echo of the 'road to Larissa' illustration.

attained by a complex and carefully planned training, culminating in the vision of moral reality. But on the premises of Book v, it is impossible that any understanding of the moral Forms should ever strengthen the validity of judgments about those moral phenomena which must always be the material for thought and decision in the world of action and experience. By establishing the uncertainty of δόξα as necessarily the condition of a mind grappling with experience in time, Plato seems to have cut away the foundation of his whole effort in the *Republic*. The philosopher returned from his vision of the Forms to direct society is once again plunged in the swirling twilight world of compulsion which he hoped to control by the informing power of his moral understanding; in that world Plato has already resigned his hopes of achieving an ultimately satisfying power of moral decision-making.

It may be thought that such a view runs contrary to the commonsense understanding of what Plato intended. It is certainly possible that Plato was not aware of the implications of his own theory; perhaps even probable that he was not, at the time of the *Republic*. But the theory recurs in a later dialogue, the *Timaeus*.[1] Its reappearance there gives weight to another theory of Plato's state of mind at this period. In many ways, the *Timaeus* marks the turning-point on the way to Plato's final surrender to despair: the fact that a theory which made the construction of the *Republic* an impossible dream should occur again at the beginning of Plato's final period of pessimism, may mean that it was in part the realization of the implications of this view that brought him to the edge of despair. Once Plato accepted, as it seems he did, the belief that in this world and about this world no certainty can be achieved, the way was open for the full feeling of despair; indeed there was hardly any alternative.

There is a further appearance of ὀρθὴ δόξα which may be noted, in the *Symposium*,[2] a dialogue which was probably written at about the same time as the *Republic*, perhaps a little before.[3] ὀρθὴ δόξα

---

[1] *Tim.* 27D 5ff. Cf. 51D 3ff. These passages are more fully discussed below, ch. xiv.   [2] *Symp.* 202A 2ff.

[3] On the relative dates of *Symposium* and *Republic*, see Ross, *Plato's Theory of Ideas*, pp. 5f. But part of Ross' case for the *Symposium*'s being earlier than the

is there placed in the same category as love (ἔρως), as intermediate between wisdom and ignorance. It cannot be the former—'how can something irrational be equated with ἐπιστήμη?'[1]—nor yet the latter either—'how can something which chances upon the truth as it is, be called ignorance (ἀμαθία)?'[2] In the context, it serves no more than to demonstrate the existence of intermediate concepts between such extremes as wisdom and ignorance, beauty and ugliness, but its connection with ἔρως is instructive. Perhaps it contains the clue to Plato's answer to our dilemma. ἔρως, the stream of desire, is a connecting link between the physical world and the Forms. It enables the soul (another such intermediate) to move from one world to the other, and prevents that too insistent dichotomy which would imprison the human spirit in one or other world. It is perhaps part of that common-sense apparatus of reasonable optimism that Plato possessed at this time. The soul *can* range and its discoveries *can* influence its behaviour, even outside the world in which they were made. ἔρως is the common principle, the common light which makes possible the 'journey' of the soul; so long as the common principle is there, perhaps the distinction between δόξα and ἐπιστήμη is unreal. Yet there remains the correlation theory of the *Republic*, the *Timaeus* and the general despair and pessimism of the last dialogues.[3]

Republic is an assumption that I cannot share, viz. that the speech of Diotima in the *Symposium* represents her own views and does not give us a true 'philosophical' picture of those of Plato or Socrates (Ross, p. 21). I cannot myself think that there is any very solid evidence for a *precise* dating of the *Symposium*.

[1] ἄλογον γὰρ πρᾶγμα πῶς ἂν εἴη ἐπιστήμη;

[2] τὸ γὰρ τοῦ ὄντος τυγχάνον πῶς ἂν εἴη ἀμαθία;

[3] I hope it is clear from this account that what is doubtful here is not the possibility of the soul's ever 'escaping' from the world of sense; such a possibility is guaranteed by the whole conception of the *Republic*, and in particular by such passages as VII, 524E 6ff., where mathematics is described as one of τῶν ἀγωγῶν...καὶ μεταστρεπτικῶν ἐπὶ τὴν τοῦ ὄντος θέαν. What is in doubt is whether Plato thought that such contemplation of reality could have any effect, any relevance in solving the moral problems of the physical world, and if so, how.

CHAPTER XII

THE 'REPUBLIC':
SUN, LINE AND CAVE

Many complain that the words of the wise are always merely symbols and of no use in daily life, which is the only life we have. When the wise man says: 'Go over', he does not mean that we should cross to some actual place, which we could do anyhow if it were worth the effort; he means some miraculous beyond, something unknown to us, something that he too cannot define more precisely, and therefore cannot help us here in the least. All these symbols merely express that the incomprehensible is incomprehensible, and we have known that before. But the cares we have to struggle with every day: that is a different matter.

Concerning this a man once said: Why such reluctance? If you only followed the symbols you would become symbols yourselves, and thus rid of all your daily cares.

Another said: I bet this is also a symbol.

The first said: You have won.

The second said: But unfortunately only symbolically.

The first said: No, in reality; symbolically you have lost.

Franz Kafka

THE commentator who turns to the symbols and allegories of Books VI and VII is faced with one of the most hotly disputed passages in all Plato's works. Scholars have for years exerted themselves to express in more and more subtle definition the essence of what Plato meant in these books; but the controversy continues and we must suppose that no wholly satisfactory account has been suggested. The reason for this is perhaps to be found in the fact that Plato was more aware, it seems, than any of his commentators, of the limitations both of his own powers of expression and of the expressibility of the truth as he saw it; all is said that could be expressed; what is not said goes unexpressed because Plato felt it inexpressible.[1] Thus to seek to reduce the allegory and the symbol to neat controlled exposition, with nothing of what Plato said overlooked, and nothing of what he *should* have said omitted, is a dangerous undertaking in which we

[1] VI, 509 C 9f.

are certain to fail, if only because Plato himself could not have done it, and moreover did not attempt it. He used instead the compulsion of symbol; to understand him we must yield to that compulsion.

Some general points must therefore be made about the whole passage to be discussed. Comment and criticism, to be valid or illuminating, must be consonant with the material to which it is applied. Some agreement is thus needed about the nature of the whole passage. One of the most sensible of all Platonic scholars, P. Frutiger, has denied the title of myth to this central core of the *Republic*, at least in the restricted sense of the term at which he arrives.[1] But the allegorical nature of the whole is admitted even by Frutiger; he calls the description of the Form of the Good, symbolized by the sun, 'mysticisme, ce mysticisme que connaissent plus ou moins tous les métaphysiciens lorsque leur pensée atteint l'absolu';[2] the parable of the cave he describes as allegory. We may grant that there are mystical overtones in Plato's description of the Good; but we shall be nearer the truth in calling the account of the sun ('the offspring of the Good')[3] symbol.[4] The difference between this passage and the rest of 502 C to 521 C seems to be that here Plato is using his vivid sense of the sun's pre-eminence and power to hint at that, on so much higher a plane, of the Form of the Good; whereas in the parable of the cave he has consciously constructed an image of his own to express what he already felt to be the nature of the difference between the worlds of sense and thought. His feeling about the Good derives, in part at least, from his instinctive awe of the sun; in the cave parable, on the other hand, though the influence of his (and our) awe of the sun is still present, it is in general his conscious thoughts about reality and unreality which give power to the imagery. Thus it is more appropriate to call this latter parable allegory, not symbol. But whatever distinctions between these two concepts we may

[1] Frutiger, *Les Mythes de Platon*, pp. 101 ff. and 116 ff. For his sense of myth, see pp. 35 ff.
[2] *Op. cit.* pp. 121 ff.   [3] ὁ τοῦ ἀγαθοῦ ἔκγονος (508 B 12 f.).
[4] On the distinction between symbol and allegory, see R. Mason, *The Spirit above the Dust*, pp. 50 ff; also Owen Barfield, *Poetic Diction*, p. 201; Erich Heller, *The Disinherited Mind*, pp. 164 ff.

later make, it is more immediately relevant to reach a decision about the overall character of the passage. Clearly it falls outside the limits of normal logical exposition. There seems to be more than the usual 'Socratic reticence' in the pleas of inability to meet the scope of his subject which we find at the beginning of our section of the dialogue.[1] We must accept the fact that the whole of what follows is, in greater or less degree, philosophical prose-poetry; we must realize that any attempt to extract from it a satisfactory logical paraphrase is doomed to failure from the start. We might as soon extract coherence of outlook from Pindar. The terms of our discussion, then, must be those appropriate, for example, to the philosophical poems of Empedocles; analysis must not be pushed beyond its (very real) limits.

Such difficulties as are actually inherent in our passage are mostly due to the complexity of intention which it exhibits. There is no single purpose to direct it, and at times the various aims that Plato has in mind tend to conflict with one another and produce some obscurity. To make a convenient division, we may distinguish between the philosophical purpose, and the formal or aesthetic. The latter may well be clearer after we have discussed the former.

In general it will perhaps be agreed that structurally there should be no break between 502c and 521c: the fact that the division between Books VI and VII occurs during this passage is, as Cornford pointed out, unfortunate, being 'an accidental expedient of ancient book production'.[2] More particularly, the diagram of the divided line is, at first at least, no more than an expansion or clarification of the imagery of the sun.[3] The two should therefore be treated as intimately one.

[1] See, for example, 506c 2 ff.
[2] Cornford, *op. cit.* p. v. Cf. P.-M. Schuhl, *Fabulation Platonicienne*, p. 46. My general account in this chapter is greatly indebted to Mr J. E. Raven, who has allowed me to see an unpublished article of his on this subject. I approach the subject from a very different standpoint, but my agreement with his view is such that if his article had been in print, I would have referred the reader outright to it. (Since this note was written, Mr Raven's article has appeared in the *Classical Quarterly*, n.s., III (1953), pp. 22 ff.)
[3] This is explicitly stated at 509c 5 ff.

Our passage opens as part of the justification by Socrates of his statement that philosophers must rule society. He is arguing that, though difficult, we cannot say that this is impossible. The difficulty rests principally with the shortage of characters suitable for selection as rulers.[1] For, of those whose innate moral character brings them to our notice, few will be capable of that course of moral training which is to reach the highest study (μέγιστον μά-θημα).[2] In explaining what this highest study is, Socrates reminds us of his warning about the necessity, sooner or later, of taking the longer road.[3] Now is the time when we must travel this longer road, in order to get behind those interim definitions of moral virtues which were put forward in Book IV. Thus the Form of the Good is first introduced as the goal of that 'longer road' which has been at the back of our minds all this time. But it is a goal that can only be hinted at, not even described in such a rough sketch as was possible of the ἀρεταί of Book IV.[4] Partly, of course, this hesitation is due to Plato's known views, expressed in the *Republic* as elsewhere, of the need for a lengthy training, not possessed by anyone present at this discussion, before the Good can be adequately apprehended. But partly also this refusal to express the ultimate, to do more than describe an image of it, an offspring of the Good, is an indication that what we have here is symbol, not allegory. To quote a parallel from another context, the White Whale in *Moby Dick* is not a figure chosen because it neatly subsumes the character of a concept already fully grasped and comprehended, as is the Slough of Despond, in *Pilgrim's Progress*, for example. It is an image chosen from Melville's actual experience because it leads on the mind to the imaginative apprehension of something beyond, the power of evil, something not more adequately seized even by Melville himself, except as it is mirrored and imaged by the whiteness of the great whale. This is the essence of a symbol, and by this criterion the sun, in our passage, is a symbol; a symbol that leads on the mind to conceive, however imprecisely, the Form of the Good.

Plato will venture little enough explicitly of it. The Good is

[1] 503 B 7ff.   [2] 505 A 2; cf. 503 E 4, 504 D 2 ff.
[3] 504 B 1 ff.; cf. IV, 435 C 9ff.   [4] 506 D 6ff.

168

that which exists as the *raison d'être* of the ideal society as envisaged by Plato; in grasping its reality, the φύλακες will not only be fulfilling the anxious aim of every individual,[1] they will also be establishing that one necessary condition for their direction of society. In knowing how and why the institutions over which they preside are good, they will become φύλακες in the real sense at last.[2] Socrates, however, refuses to be like those who glibly say that the Good is pleasure or knowledge; but at the urgent request of Glaucon he consents to describe what he believes to be an image of the Good, the sun. He begins by drawing the now familiar distinction, as he says, between the world of the multiplicity of phenomena and that of the Forms.[3] From the senses in general, sight is selected and it is shown that, alone of the senses, sight requires, in addition to its own effective working and the presence of a visible object, the existence of light to make its potentialities actual. The principal source of this light is of course the sun, which can be distinguished both from the eye that sees and the visual sense; and is both cause of vision and an object of it. Moreover, the symbol of the sun helps us to understand, if not to solve, the problem of the last chapter. In the light of day alone is clarity of vision possible; by night, the same eyes seem almost blind. So with the mind: an object standing in the light of truth and reality can be seen by the mind in full clearness; but the wayward phenomena of this world make the same intelligence seem capable only of δόξα.[4] At this point, symbol seems to blend with allegory; but we must be careful. We are accustomed to read, and to say, that in the image of the sun, the visible world and the mechanism of its visibility *stand for* the world of thought and the apprehension of truth. But the main purpose of distinguishing symbol from allegory is to avoid this misleading form of statement. A symbol, as we have seen, does not *stand for* something grasped with equal clarity; it does no more than *hint at* something as yet unformulated; that is why it is used. So that, in discussing the image of the sun, we should not seek to find even that degree of reciprocal relation that allegory admits. To do so would be to fall into the cardinal

---

[1] 505D 5 ff.   [2] 506A 4 ff.
[3] 507A 7 ff.   [4] 508C 4 ff.

error of supposing to ourselves that Plato uses the vivid image of the sun for an equally vivid theory of ultimate reality. By avoiding this incorrectly imagined situation, we shall not succumb to the temptation of *arguing* from the image to the theory; we shall be content, as Plato was content, to let the symbol *suggest* the reality. Thus when Plato describes the Good as, like the sun, cause of illumination and truth, but more valuable than them both, cause also of reality,[1] yet not reality, even beyond reality (ἐπέκεινα τῆς οὐσίας),[2] we shall not be misled into supposing that he had already apprehended an exact metaphysical status for the Good. Adam's account, in his note on this passage, of the various interpretations suggested is a record of the absurdities into which this fallacy has led scholars. All that Plato himself is committed to, is the belief that the Good, in the realm of thought and reality, has a position akin to that of the sun in the world of sensation; he cannot be taken further.

The symbol has been placed before us, but Socrates admits that the comparison is incomplete. To carry it further, he begins to draw a diagram, based on a vertical divided line.[3] With the introduction of this diagram the confusion of purpose begins to be apparent. But before we discuss this question, we must attempt a summary of what we find in the text.[4] The vertical line is divided unevenly, the upper section being the longer, and each section is then subdivided in the same proportion. The four sections thus obtained are said to contain,[5] as far as their relative clarity and obscurity is concerned, the following, starting from the

---

[1] On the sense in which the Form of the Good is 'cause of reality', see the interesting discussion by H. Cherniss in *American Journal of Philology*, LIII (1932), pp. 236f.

[2] 508 E I ff.

[3] Vertical, to suggest the ascent to truth (Cornford, *op. cit.* p. 217; Joseph, *Knowledge and the Good*, p. 24). This seems to have gone unnoticed by, e.g. Ross, *op. cit.* p. 45.

[4] 509 D ff. See the diagram in Cornford, *op. cit.* p. 217.

[5] The text says that each section will *be* the following (ἔσται); Cornford misleads in translating this 'will stand for'. If we must introduce the notion of 'standing for' at all, then the sections of the Line stand, not for the things they are said to be or contain, but for something beyond, just as the Sun stands (though as we have seen, the phrase misleads) not for itself, but for the Good.

bottom: (A) images, i.e. shadows, reflections, 'and everything of that kind, if you understand' (πρῶτον μὲν τὰς σκιάς, ἔπειτα δὲ τὰ ἐν τοῖς ὕδασι φαντάσματα καὶ ἐν τοῖς ὅσα πυκνά τε καὶ λεῖα καὶ φανὰ συνέστηκεν, καὶ πᾶν τὸ τοιοῦτον, εἰ κατανοεῖς);[1] (B) originals of the images in (A) (τά τε περὶ ἡμᾶς ζῷα καὶ πᾶν τὸ φυτευτὸν καὶ τὸ σκευαστὸν ὅλον γένος). The distinction between sections (C) and (D) is based, not so much on a difference of content, but on a difference of method within them. Both are subdivisions of the world of the mind: in (C) the mind uses the contents of (B) as images for its discussion and always leaves some things assumed, without trying to relate them to a first principle. In (D), on the other hand, the discussion moves in the opposite direction and concerns itself with the discovery of an unhypothetical first principle, confining its attention, also, to the field of Forms and making no use of images. The procedure of (C) is explained in terms of mathematical method, the assumptions suggested being those of odd or even numbers, or of three types of angle (i.e. assumptions of existence), and the images being visible figures which represent the concepts under discussion. (D) is the procedure of dialectic, in Plato's sense, which rejects all use of sensible objects and tries to derive all the terms of its discussion, the Forms, from a single principle (ἡ τοῦ παντὸς ἀρχή).[2] Plato allots four states of mind to cover the four divisions of the line: conjecture or imagining (εἰκασία) for (A), conviction (πίστις) for (B), discursive thought (διάνοια) for (C), and true insight (νόησις) for (D).[3] These are to be arranged 'as the terms of a proportion, assigning to each a degree of clarity and certainty corresponding to the measure in which their objects possess truth and reality.'[4]

Because it was unrecognized, the confusion of purpose that has been mentioned earlier is behind much of the confusion of scholarship on the subject of this diagrammatic 'clarification' of the sun

[1] 509E 1 ff. For a translation of the bracketed passages, see Cornford, p. 219.
[2] 511B 7.
[3] On the distinction between διάνοια and νόησις, see Cornford in *Mind*, n.s. XLI (1932), p. 51.
[4] Cornford, *Translation*, p. 221. There is an obvious reference here to the correlation theory of Book V.

image.[1] One point, in particular, has for long been a crux of scholarship.[2] The diagram is at first described as representing the contrast between visible (ὁρατόν, ὁρώμενον) and intelligible (νοητόν, νοούμενον).[3] But only a few lines later, in parenthesis as it were, the contrast is referred to as being between the objects of *opinion* and knowledge (τὸ δοξαστὸν πρὸς τὸ γνωστόν).[4] This transference brings to the fore an uneasiness that has been at the back of our minds since we first began to examine the diagram of the line. For though the line is introduced as a continuation and expansion of the sun image, it is difficult for us to accept it, as we were able to accept the sun, as a symbol in the true sense. A line, even a vertical line, does not have those unconscious associations that make the sun so effective a symbol. And of course our suspicions were well founded: the diagram is the unhappy playground of a struggle between symbol and allegory. It is this that gives rise to the substitution of δοξαστόν for ὁρατόν: the latter is correct while we regard the organization of the visible world as symbolizing, as suggesting to us, another world, that of reality and truth that lies behind it. Or at least, correct up to a point: here, the validity of the symbol is destroyed when it is no longer allowed merely to suggest. The line, as Plato has described it, is continuous; it is not, as the usage of the symbol requires, two parallel lines, the configuration of the one suggested by that of the other. In fact the organization of the upper section, the world of the mind, is as clearly visualized as that of the lower (perhaps, as we shall see in the sequel, even more clearly visualized). But if the line diagram is an uneasy symbol, it is not wholly satisfying either as allegory. The introduction of the word δοξαστόν shows us that Plato, simultaneously with the symbolical associations of the visible world, has in his mind the distinction of Book v, between δόξα and ἐπιστήμη, and the ascent from one to the other. This is treated, very much more satisfactorily, in the pure allegory of the cave; here an attempt is made to represent it in the diagram, where

---

[1] To call the line diagram a simile, as Murphy and Joseph, for example, do, is misleading. Nothing is being compared to a line; its use is purely that of a diagram.

[2] See, for example, Ross, pp. 46 f.; Joseph, *Knowledge*, ch. iv.

[3] 509 D 4, D 8.   [4] 510 A 9.

it is in noticeable conflict with the symbolic imagery. Thus the construction of the line is due to several, ill-fitted forces. As symbol, shadow and object (in the visible world) suggest image and reality (in the metaphysical 'world'); as allegory, the four stages of the cave are prefigured in the four sections of a line. It is unfortunate that there are four sections in each case, thus leading Plato to believe that he could combine his two visions in one illustration. Thereby both are confused and blurred.

There is little more to be said about the line passage as symbol: as we were led to expect, it is an embroidery of the sun image, and could indeed have been included there. The associations of shadow and object are in place with the associations of light and darkness; we feel instinctively that they are part of the same unconscious psychological nexus.

We are not, however, as yet in a position to understand the line diagram as allegory. In the first place of course, it is inherently unsuitable as an allegorical equivalent for the fabric of concepts which it is intended to represent. It is at once too explicit and too uninformative. In allegory, we are accustomed to be given a parable in human terms of an intellectual myth. In this sense, *Pilgrim's Progress* may be accepted as archetypal allegory. Thus a diagram, which is as much a concept as metaphysical reality, tells us too little about the concepts which it is intended to illuminate. On the other hand, it tells us too much; by itself it means nothing and must be explained, as it is here by Socrates, in terms of explicit reference to the concepts and processes which it is supposed to illustrate. All the information which is contained in these pages might have been presented to us with equal clarity without reference to the diagram.

If we can sum up what has so far been suggested about the line diagram, we may be able to pass on to the cave and consider that, before venturing anything about the 'contents' of the four sections of the line. We have seen, first of all, that the illusion of continuity given by the line itself is misleading; that there is no essential connection between the shadow/object contrast of sections (A) and (B), and the contrast of method and aim implied in sections (C) and (D). The effect of continuity is caused by assimilation to the cave allegory, and by the fact that the metaphysical and epistemo-logical distinctions suggested by the original symbol have them-selves entered, as it were autonomously, into the diagram.

The allegory of the cave is an experience[1] to which the state of humanity with regard to enlightenment and its opposite is to be compared. The whole parable is to be fitted to what has been said previously;[2] endless discussion has been engaged over the meaning of this remark. From what follows, it seems clear that τὰ ἔμπροσθεν λεγόμενα refers to the whole of the sun-line passage considered as a unity, as indeed it was originally declared to be. Thus we shall not be surprised to find something of the same confusion that beset the earlier imagery in our present allegory. But the atmosphere of coherence is, at any rate on the surface, more convincing. At a first inspection, there is a straightforward 'plot', with four main stages: the habitual, chained state of the prisoners (514A 2–515C 3); the prisoner turned round and able to see the fire and the objects carried past (515C 4–E 5); the painful first arrival in the outer world and the process of habituation (515E 6–516B 3); the final ability to look at the sun, and the understanding of its func-tion in the universe (516B 4–C 2). It may be objected that the distinction between the stages of the world outside the cave is by no means as clear-cut as that in the cave; but that should not surprise us, if we remember that in the line diagram also the dis-tinction in the upper section was not of the same order as that in the lower. Moreover, while the line was a static analysis of stages, the cave emphasizes the aspect of process (where stages on the way are less easily distinguished), though both are, in part at least, con-cerned with the same subject. Interpreters have produced widely different schematizations of this allegory: they range from Mr Richard Robinson's eight stages to Mr N. R. Murphy's three.[3] But it seems beyond coincidence that, while there are clearly four divisions of the line, and, apparently at least, four stages in the cave

---

[1] πάθος (514A 1) seems an odd word for this allegory; it may almost mean 'incident' or 'story' (see Liddell and Scott, s.v.), but the connection with feeling is presumably intended.

[2] τὰ ἔμπροσθεν λεγόμενα, VII, 517A 8 ff.

[3] Robinson, *op. cit.* p. 194; Murphy, *op. cit.* pp. 160 ff.

allegory, these should not be in some degree parallel. The sort of interpretation mentioned earlier depends on a perverse logic that deduces from detail a view that contradicts one's immediate overall impression. Mr Murphy, for example, while admitting that allegory is 'not a logical form of statement',[1] suggests that we 'can infer from [the propositions laid down in the 'Line'] according to the ordinary form of a syllogism in "Barbara"'.[2] By means of this inference, he is able to believe that, in regarding only images at first in the outer world, the released prisoner is reverting to εἰκασία, and in seeing finally the solids of the upper world, returns finally to πίστις. This sort of conclusion is so wildly improbable that we may be pardoned for suspecting the method that arrives at it. Definitive schematization of the cave allegory is a Procrustes' bed so painful in its effects that we will be wise to restrict ourselves to more conventional furniture.

If, then, we consider the cave as it presents itself to us (that is to say, as allegory), some things are at once evident. The imagery is clearly dictated by the symbolic use of the sun earlier, thus making more obvious the psychological unity of the whole passage. Here, however, while the sun, within the allegory, still clearly symbolizes the Form of the Good, with the same attendant associations which we found earlier, its position in the visible world is in turn symbolized by the fire within the cave.[3] This results in something of the same distortion that was evident earlier: the ὁρατόν/δοξαστόν substitution reappears, and for much the same reason. But in general the cave is far clearer. It is an allegory of consciousness, since in Plato's view the attainment of ἐπιστήμη is a process of becoming conscious of the real world, to understand which is the mind's real task.[4] The principal question, of course, which remains

---

[1] Murphy, *op. cit.* p. 162 n. 1. Murphy also admits that the cave *is* allegory (*op. cit.* p. 162).

[2] Murphy, *op. cit.* pp. 160f.

[3] 517B 1 ff. Note τὴν...δι' ὄψεως φαινομένην ἕδραν. The appearance of δοξαστόν is marked by περὶ τῶν τοῦ δικαίου σκιῶν (517D 8f.).

[4] The theme of consciousness is suggested by the ὕπαρ/ὄναρ image of 520C 6ff. The cave, as a symbol of the unconscious, occurs frequently elsewhere; cf. Yeats' poem *The Gyres*, and Vivienne Koch, *W. B. Yeats: The Tragic Phase*, pp. 102f.

to be answered is: what are the stages of this process to the mind which passes through them? The general discussion of this question would take us far out of the bounds of this study, but we must at least consider it from the standpoint of ethics. We may observe in passing that the whole of this passage stems from Plato's attempt to describe that attainment of ethical certainty which is the duty of the φύλακες. This fact deserves our most careful attention, since it follows that the ethical implications of this chain of images must have been well to the fore in his mind. Yet strangely, it is not a subject that has been much discussed.[1] With the assistance of Professor Cornford's article (referred to below) and the text of Plato itself, we must attempt an ethical interpretation of the line and cave passages.

The lower division of the line diagram contained, in section (A), images such as reflections, and in section (B), the sources or causes of these images, i.e. the objects of the physical world. In the cave, the chained prisoners are gazing at shadows moving on the wall opposite them, while the first stage on the way of release is being turned round and watching instead the objects which have been casting the shadows. The two stages are clearly the same in both cases, but the realization of this does not remove all difficulties. We have already observed that the contrast between these two states of mind, as expressed by the symbol, is a direct legacy from the sun symbolism, and that it has no inherent connection with the division of the upper line. This may make what is sometimes called the 'illustration' theory of this lower division seem more convincing.[2] And up to a point we may accept it, if instead of illustration we refer to 'symbol'. We have already seen that the shadow/object contrast is not a constructed illustration, but, beginning from the opposite end, a symbol 'ayant l'expansion des choses infinies', in Baudelaire's phrase, or as Goethe puts it in an aphorism: 'in a true symbol the particular represents the universal, not as dream or shadow, but as a living, instantaneous revelation of the

---

[1] The most obvious reference is to Cornford in *Mind*, n.s. XLI (1932), pp. 37 ff. and 173 ff. Much of the detail in his exposition is doubtful, but in general it is an extremely valuable contribution to this neglected subject.

[2] See, for example, A. S. Ferguson in *Classical Quarterly*, XV (1921), pp. 143 ff.

unfathomable'.[1] However, we cannot follow Professor Ferguson in his belief that εἰκασία and πίστις 'are not stages of apprehension, prior to διάνοια and νοῦς'. He is able to hold this view because he does not believe that cave and line are parallel; if on the other hand we accept that this is the case, we must agree that four consecutive stages are really visualized by Plato.[2] What then are the two lowest of them?

I must approach this question by a digression. It has long been recognized that the ascent of ἔρως in the speech of Diotima to Socrates is in some way parallel to the ascent of the mind in *Republic* VI and VII.[3] The parallel cannot be rendered systematically, but there is an obvious connection. The first stages of the ascent in the *Symposium* are: first, falling in love with some particular beautiful person and, secondly, recognizing the unity of physical beauty and falling in love with all physical beauty. This suggests a way in which, from an ethical standpoint, the line and the cave may image the same process. On this interpretation, εἰκασία will be the state of mind which is, strictly speaking, incapable of morality, only of instinctive goodness or evil, since it treats each separate instance of an action or choice without relation to any other, asking such questions as 'should I pay Jones the 1s. 6d. I owe him?' and represents a quite unconscious reaction to 'moral' problems. πίστις, then, will be a morality which co-ordinates actions in the physical world, and is able to ask questions such as 'Is it right to pay one's debts?' but without reference to any absolute standard transcending the mass of instances. It may be asked in what way the first stage, of εἰκασία, is acceptance of images (εἰκόνες) of the objects treated as real by πίστις. We must of course be cautious in applying the image of shadow and object, since it is in important respects alien to its context; but in any case it would be according to Plato's usage to describe the individual example of an action as an εἰκών of the general case.[4]

---

[1] *Collected Works*, Jubiläums-Ausgabe, vol. XXXVIII, p. 266 (Stuttgart and Berlin, n.d.).   [2] Cf. Ross, *op. cit.* pp. 47f.

[3] *Symp.* 210A 4ff. For the parallel between *Symposium* and *Republic*, see, for example, Cornford, *The Unwritten Philosophy*, pp. 75ff.

[4] In much the same way as Plotinus (*Enn.* III, 8, 4) describes practical activity as the 'shadow' of contemplation (σκιὰν θεωρίας καὶ λόγου).

From this point of view, paying one's debts to a person *p* at a time *t* in a situation *s* is an image of the general case, paying one's debts: perhaps it is only we, with our Aristotelian attitude to abstraction, who would feel that the truth is the other way about.

It is suggested then that εἰκασία and πίστις represent two moral attitudes restricted to the world of phenomena. Neither ventures beyond the specification of acts, but πίστις recognizes, as εἰκασία does not, the essential connection between acts of the same type. If other views seem equally valid, this is because Plato is less interested in the lower stages, which he dismisses together as δόξα, than in the articulation of διάνοια and νόησις.

Bearing this in mind, we may find it easier to discover a way to an understanding of this latter question somewhat less fraught with conflicting opinions. It is clear, in the first place, that both states of mind recognize the existence of absolute, transcendent moral standards. But διάνοια is to be distinguished by two features: its use of the concrete example, the object of πίστις, and its lack of interest or ability to relate its discoveries to an unhypothetical first principle. With regard to the latter, Cornford is clearly right in saying of the thinker who has reached a definition of some particular moral Form (the Forms, of course, are the standards with which διάνοια and νόησις deal) that

> he has as yet only one piece of knowledge. He must mount further to the supreme Idea in the moral field, and define the nature of the Good. Only then will the full significance of the truth discovered be seen in its relation to the rest of truth. If he stops short, his definitions of Justice and other Ideas, though correct, will be analogous to a mathematical hypothesis that is true but awaits deduction from the first principle. But if he can reach the Good, he will 'acquire *nous*' (νοῦν ἔχειν, 534 B), that illuminated vision of the whole field that can only be had from the summit.[1]

From this point of view, διάνοια may reach an understanding of any number of unrelated moral Forms, but cannot achieve complete ethical certainty until these Forms are seen in relation both to one another, and to the origin of them all, the Good. This is,

---

[1] *Mind*, n.s., XLI (1932), p. 183.

for instance, the situation reached in Book IV of the *Republic*, when four ἀρεταί have been defined, but not so related; it accounts for the reference to the 'longer road'.[1] But there is another deficiency in διάνοια. It was suggested earlier that the definitions of ἀρεταί were rather of the nature of illustrations;[2] this was because these definitions were couched rather more in empirical terms (i.e. the terms of the physical world) than the pure realization of a Form would warrant. That is to say, διάνοια grasps a Form only by considering it in the light of the phenomenal world, in its reference to the types of action or choice arrived at by πίστις, or to the empirical 'psychology' of the tripartite soul. In neither respect can διάνοια penetrate to the essence of the Form, which must remain unrevealed except to the superior insight of νόησις. Thus ethical διάνοια, like mathematics, is still subject to the flaws for which it is criticized in the explanation of the line diagram.

There remains νόησις. Adequate understanding of what is involved in this Plato probably believed to be beyond those who have not themselves reached it. We can describe it only in terms ultimately as irrelevant as those in which the definitions of Book IV are set out. As Glaucon says, it is a vast undertaking.[3] When it is reached, the articulation of all the moral Forms and their derivation from the Good is passed through and understood. All is related, all is given its true perspective; certainty rests at last on comprehension of the whole of moral reality. The ideal society now stands on the foundation of certainty tested and assured. But the mechanics of the process are, at the heart of the matter, beside the point. Plato's whole theory of moral knowledge, sophisticated and complex as it seems, is as simple, to the philosopher who has passed through it, as Socratic ἐπιστήμη. To us it appears a συχνὸν ἔργον, but that is because we have reached only the stage of knowing how it is to be done, not that of knowing what it is like.

There is one more task to be faced, before this chapter can be considered complete. The complex purposes of our passage were earlier divided into the philosophical and the formal. Something must now be said about the latter. The images of the sun, line and cave represent the culmination of effort in the *Republic*, both

---

[1] IV, 435D 3; VI, 504B 1 ff.   [2] See above, p. 152.   [3] VI, 511C 3 ff.

philosophically and formally. We should now, if ever, be in a position to mark out the structure of the dialogue, difficult though we have agreed such an undertaking to be. In this, we are assisted by the consideration of the cave allegory, in particular, in the foregoing pages. The point that I want to suggest is that this passage is, in effect, a poetic summary of the 'plot' of the *Republic*, as it was of its philosophy. The *Republic* is a myth of experience. By this, I mean that it is a poetic attempt to meet the challenge of experience; it is not, of course, myth in M. Frutiger's sense, and it may be that to call it myth in any sense is to destroy the meaning of the word.[1] But better regard it as myth than see in it a document in the history of political theory; if the *Republic* errs, it is on the side of the intractability of poetry, not the aridity of political logic. That it has to do with experience, however, is undeniable. The eternal Adam, innocence, is abandoned early; the city of swine, with their morality of innocence, is agreed by all to be an impossibility. There is evidence of this in the equivocal attitude which seems to be taken towards it; we cannot tell whether Socrates and Glaucon regret or rejoice at its abandonment. But it is never possible to adopt a straightforward valuation of the inconceivable. The *Republic* grants that the world we live in is the world of experience, and irrevocably so, but it seeks to meet experience as well as it may be met. Its construction is the construction of a defence against the onslaught of experience.

Parallel with the construction goes the 'plot'. If the philosophical discussion of Book I is naïve, the naïvety of εἰκασία is already behind us, for the *Republic* begins to trace the ascent of the mind from the second stage of the line diagram; the prisoners' heads are already turned round. Book I represents the state of πίστις: it nowhere passes beyond the phenomenal world, and its attempt, doomed of course to failure, is to understand justice wholly in terms of specified acts and choices. It fails, and in Book II we enter the sphere of διάνοια.[2] This section culminates

---

[1] Frutiger, *op. cit.* p. 100.

[2] The major break, in the line diagram, between δοξαστόν and νοητόν, is perhaps hinted at, when Book II begins, by Socrates' remark that he thought the conversation had ended: II, 357A 1.

in the definitions of Book IV, and we have already seen enough to realize that they should not be accepted, as they sometimes are, as Plato's final word on these four ἀρεταί. We are intended to feel that, like διάνοια, these definitions do not reach the heart of the matter, as we are intended to feel at the end of Book I that only the very surface has been touched. All along, Plato characteristically reinforces his explicit teaching by the emotional assistance of our feeling of disappointment, as each section, with its aim of completeness, falls short of what we had expected.

Much of Book V is in the nature of an interlude, or rather a prelude to the climax of Books VI and VII. As we have seen, the construction of these two books depends upon the distinction of Book V between δόξα and ἐπιστήμη. In the images which this chapter has discussed, and particularly in the latter part of Book VII, we have suggested the achievement of νόησις. It is not, like πίστις and διάνοια, rendered in action also, by those taking part in the discussion. That would be impossible, but we are told all that can be described, in terms however inadequate. Exposition, even in symbol and allegory, cannot go further; the rest is with the efforts of the human mind.

Sun, line and cave, then, act as a poetic restatement of what the *Republic* has expressed in its conversation. They present to us, in its most concentrated form, the theme both of its teaching and of its 'story': indeed these are one. As Cornford said, we can understand both only from the summit.

CHAPTER XIII

THE 'REPUBLIC':
THE DISINTEGRATION OF THE ΨΥΧΗ

IF Books VI and VII are the summit of the *Republic*, the way, from now on, leads down; the rest of the dialogue is a chronicle of decline. In the main, it is not very much to our purpose, but indirectly, since it displays the gradual abandonment of all that Plato values, it throws light on what he has tried to achieve in the *Republic*. Book VIII opens by recapitulating the pretence that the whole subject-matter of the last two chapters in this study was a digression from the real purpose.[1] It refers back to the beginning of Book V, where Socrates was about to describe the four parallel vicious forms of human being and society, when the interruption of Adeimantus forced him to fill out the detail of his account of goodness, and so led him on to the 'digression' of Books V–VII— a digression on a par with that other so-called 'philosophical digression' in the *Seventh Letter*;[2] that is to say, a digression containing what is ultimately the most valuable matter in the whole work. This curious structural device is, in part of course, one of many similar attempts to disguise the formal flow of the conversation,[3] but it has, in addition, the effect of putting Books V–VII on another plane, as indeed they are, and of underlining the break between διάνοια and νόησις that, it was earlier suggested, falls at the end of Book IV.[4]

This, however, does not explain the most striking point about *Republic* VIII–X: why, following immediately on the most concentrated and powerful attempt at construction that he had so far undertaken, does Plato now portray the other side of the medal, the progressive defeat and decline of the human spirit? Plato seems to feel the embarrassment of this question, and answers it, as he

---

[1] VIII, 543 C 4 ff.   [2] *Ep.* VII, 342 A 7–344 D 2.
[3] See above, pp. 154f.   [4] Above, pp. 180f.

says, 'in high-flown language' (τραγικῶς): 'Hard it may be for a society so constituted to be shaken; yet decay is the universal fate of all things in this world of change, nor will even a framework such as we have built last for all time: it must suffer dissolution.'[1] Here a feeling that lies behind much of the *Republic* comes out into the open, a sense of the ineradicable process of decay, of a distance from the ideal too far to be traversed: it is this that makes up the note of sadness. Hope has never been very certain, and now another key is established. The word 'necessity' (ἀνάγκη) and its derivatives become central. A detailed discussion of the implications of ἀνάγκη, and its effect on Plato's ethics, will be kept to the next chapter; but we may note here its appearances in the *Republic*. In general, what there is in common to all these contexts is a bond of feeling, which varies in its outward appearance from a hint of despair to an explicit statement. In Book IX, for example, Socrates divides pleasures into necessary, artificial and harmful. The philosopher, however, will call all pleasures other than the pleasure of understanding 'necessary in the true sense, since he would have no use for them, necessity apart'.[2] Yet, though we can distinguish in theory between necessary and artificial pleasures, even such of the latter as are actually harmful (παράνομοι) are to be found in every human being; though they can be held in check by law and the other, better pleasures, with the aid of reason, in some men they will gain the upper hand.[3] This note of pessimism later gains in strength: a first hint of the fatalistic attitude of some passages in the *Laws* is found in Book x. In advising against grief, Plato suggests that 'nothing human is of great import'.[4] A little later, life, as in the *Laws*, is compared to a game: '... and we should make our moves in this game of life with an eye to what the fall of the dice allows, letting reason choose the best course it can'.[5] With

---

[1] χαλεπὸν μὲν κινηθῆναι πόλιν οὕτω συστᾶσαν· ἀλλ' ἐπεὶ γενομένῳ παντὶ φθορά ἐστιν, οὐδ' ἡ τοιαύτη σύστασις τὸν ἅπαντα μενεῖ χρόνον, ἀλλὰ λυθήσεται (546A 1 ff.).
[2] τῷ ὄντι ἀναγκαίας, ὡς οὐδὲν τῶν ἄλλων δεόμενον, εἰ μὴ ἀνάγκη ἦν (IX, 581E 3 f.). [3] 571B 4 ff.
[4] οὔτε τι τῶν ἀνθρωπίνων ἄξιον ὂν μεγάλης σπουδῆς (x, 604B 12 f.).
[5] ...καὶ ὥσπερ ἐν πτώσει κύβων πρὸς τὰ πεπτωκότα τίθεσθαι τὰ αὑτοῦ πράγματα, ὅπῃ ὁ λόγος αἱρεῖ βέλτιστ' ἂν ἔχειν (604C 5 ff.).

the myth of Er, ἀνάγκη holds the centre of the stage; the spindle past which the soul must go is the Spindle of Necessity, 'and it turned upon the knees of Necessity'.[1] The fates too, are daughters of Necessity, and when the final choice is made, the προφήτης announces to the assembled souls that each is now to choose the life 'which necessity will make his lifelong companion' (ᾧ συνέσται ἐξ ἀνάγκης). Here again we are reminded of the *Karma* doctrine of the *Laws*.[2] From the moment of choice, even the moral character of a man's soul is irrevocably determined.[3] And we may note that the last landmark on the journey to the Plain of Lethe is the Throne of Ἀνάγκη.[4]

Thus, during the course of Books VIII–X, the concept of ἀνάγκη, and its emotional concomitant, despair, grow from a mere tint, a suspicion of darkness in a bright whole, to colour the entire work, so that, when finished, it is remembered as informed by sadness. This is the impulse that drives on the catalogue of defeat. The process begins when the φύλακες 'beget children at an ill-fated moment'; it will appear first as a tension between the elements of society (or, similarly, within the individual character, between the εἴδη ψυχῆς), a disruption of the original functional unity. This tension is temporarily allayed by a compromise, which lasts until the process is carried a stage further. Here, I shall argue that it is the decline of the human personality, the defeat and enslavement of the individual ψυχή, that is foremost in Plato's intention.[5] As in the construction of the ideal society, the degeneration of society acts as an enlarging mirror, to reflect on a scale where the process is easily recognizable the same events as they take place in the human individual. The introduction of society was, we remember, in the first place illustrative, 'the same inscription...set up else-

---

[1] 617B 4. On this passage, see Proclus, *In Tim.* vol. III, p. 274.

[2] 617E 2f.; *Laws*, X, 904B 8ff. (above p. 100). On the *Republic* passage, see Onians, *Origins of European Thought*, ch. VIII, especially pp. 403f., and pp. 306ff.

[3] X, 618B 2ff.

[4] 620E 6ff. Other instructive references to ἀνάγκη are, for example, VI, 489D 10ff., 493C 4ff., VIII, 565C 1ff. (and Adam's note), 566A 2ff., 567C 1ff.

[5] Moreau, I believe, is right in saying (*Construction*, p. 210): 'L'enquête sociologique, dans la *République*, sert de support à une dialectique de l'activité.' On the primary significance of Plato's account of the *individual*, see also A. E. Taylor's remarks in *Mind*, n.s. XLVIII (1939), pp. 37f.

where in larger letters against a larger background'.[1] For the understanding of the Republic as an ethical dialogue, it is the consideration of Plato's account of the individual that is of primary importance. This is peculiarly the case here, because, while Plato's view of degenerate society is to some extent influenced by his observation of existing societies (e.g. Sparta and Athens), his view of the ψυχή is less affected by approximation to individual characters.

The man typical of timocracy (τιμοκρατικὸς ἀνήρ), the first degenerate type, is notable chiefly for his self-assertiveness, the result of the supremacy of τὸ θυμοειδές within him.[2] This in turn results from a reaction against the lack of practical effect which a man of intelligence has in a society which makes no use of him. His character, then, owes its origin directly to the inability of the elements in human nature to fulfil their natural function: the drive towards self-assertion (τὸ θυμοειδές), when it cannot fall into place by assisting the mind to achieve its proper aim, becomes distorted and overdeveloped. Thus society certainly plays an important part in the disintegration of the ψυχή, since, in the last resort, it is society that prevents the proper coalition of the εἴδη ψυχῆς:[3] it is clear enough that at this period Plato regards ἀρετή as an ideal only to be attained through society, but it is not clear that he has yet abandoned the individual as the unit of ἀρετή, the potential ἀγαθόν, as seems to be the case in the Laws. From this point of view, the distinction between the two dialogues seems to be that in the Republic, society, though as setting and as illustration it plays an altogether greater part than in the early dialogues, has not yet usurped the position of the individual as the entity which is striving towards ἀρετή: in the Laws this usurpation is already accomplished. The ideal society, in the Republic, is perhaps the necessary condition of the man who has achieved his true stature as a man (the ἀγαθὸς ἀνήρ), but the latter is not yet without significance: in the myth of Er, it is the individual who must choose (αἰτία ἑλομένου),[4] not, as we must feel in the Laws, society.

[1] II, 368D 4f.   [2] VIII, 548E 4ff.
[3] Cf. VI, 487B ff.   [4] X, 617E 4.

In the character of the τιμοκρατικὸς ἀνήρ, 'control has been given to the intermediate element in the soul which craves status and drives a man to self-assertion'.[1] But because such a character is without the guidance of a 'thoughtful and cultivated mind' (λόγου...μουσικῇ κεκραμένου),[2] the lowest element also is without a natural function. So that, stealthily, avarice, the outward sign of τὸ ἐπιθυμητικόν, is at work; below the surface as yet, but in the character of the ὀλιγαρχικός, it becomes overt and indeed paramount. 'Is it not the case that wealth and the demands of man's true nature (ἀρετή) are opposed to one another like weights at opposite ends of a balance; that as one rises, the other falls?'[3] As money now becomes increasingly the aim of life, ἀρετή fades from consideration. In the search for wealth, only the 'necessary' pleasures are indulged, but because reason and education are absent, the other appetites (κηφηνώδεις ἐπιθυμίαι)[4] will begin to make themselves felt. As the ties that unify the ψυχή are relaxed, so gradually the equilibrium of the personality becomes more unstable: as this equilibrium is, at each stage, tentatively achieved, the forces which will cause its overthrow at once appear, so that the practical ability of the individual to act as a unity grows increasingly more problematical. Of the ὀλιγαρχικός, Plato says: 'Such a man cannot be without internal cleavages: he will no longer *be* one person, but a sort of dual character.'[5]

The process continues, through the δημοκρατικός (in whom the unnecessary desires have the controlling power) to the τύραννος, until the actively pernicious ἐπιθυμίαι, the desires that present themselves only in sleep, have swept all else out of the ψυχή, and prevented each of the three εἴδη from fulfilling its function.[6] These passions rise from an unconsciousness below even the level of unconsciousness of the average ἀπαίδευτος: in the τυραννικὸς ἀνήρ, the true nature of the ψυχή is completely inverted: 'In his waking life, he behaves as we said men do in the world of dreams.'[7]

---

[1] τὴν ἀρχὴν παρέδωκε τῷ μέσῳ τε καὶ φιλονίκῳ καὶ θυμοειδεῖ (VIII, 550 B 5 f.).
[2] 549 B 6 (Cornford's translation).
[3] 550 E 6 ff.   [4] 554 B 7.
[5] οὐκ ἄρ' ἂν εἴη ἀστασίαστος ὁ τοιοῦτος ἐν ἑαυτῷ, οὐδὲ εἷς ἀλλὰ διπλοῦς τις (554 D 9 f.).
[6] IX, 571 C 3 ff.   [7] 576 B 4 f.

To Plato, the state of such a soul is enslavement to the worst in human nature; recalling his earlier theory of βούλησις, he says: 'If one judges by the demands of the whole personality, the soul of the dictator, itself dictated to, will least of all achieve its purpose.'[1]

We have thus come as far as we may from the ideal individual matched with an ideal society; we have reached the spectacle of a man dictated to by passions that he cannot control, and in a perpetual state of war not only with his fellow men, but even with himself. We are reminded of Socrates' declaration at the very beginning of the *Republic*,[2] that injustice can only bring about an internal disruption so great as to make action impossible. Eight books later, the same conclusion has again been reached, after a more thorough and perceptive analysis of the ψυχή. We are now, therefore, in a position to see what light this complete negation of all Plato's values throws on those values themselves.

There is every reason to suppose that Plato would have agreed with Aristotle's view that human happiness is to be found in the actualization of (specifically) human potentialities. But the ψυχῆς ἐνεργείᾳ envisaged by Plato would be somewhat different. The characteristics of human life, to Plato, are to be found in the fact that it takes place within the dimensions of good and evil. Therefore, the potentiality which the human being is called upon to make actual is the potentiality for ἀρετή. In doing this, the ψυχή is alone capable of functioning naturally, as a unit of behaviour and intention. This is the sense in which the definition of δικαιοσύνη in Book IV was intended: in its outward aspect, ἀρετή can be considered as a harmony of the forces within man, 'which are like three notes in a chord, arranged in a descending scale'.[3] It is also the sense in which unity is declared to be the ultimate value for a legislator,[4] not an enforced unity, contrary to the true nature of the ψυχή, but a unity arising out of the proper operation of each εἶδος. Cornford has shown, in his Samuel Dill Memorial Lecture on *Plato's Commonwealth*,[5] how much Plato was concerned at all

---

[1] καὶ ἡ τυραννουμένη ἄρα ψυχὴ ἥκιστα ποιήσει ἃ ἂν βουληθῇ, ὡς περὶ ὅλης εἰπεῖν ψυχῆς (577E 1 f.).
[2] I, 350D ff.   [3] IV, 443D 5 ff.   [4] V, 462A 9 ff.
[5] Reprinted in his *Unwritten Philosophy*, pp. 47–67.

periods with the drifting apart of the various aspects of the human personality. The problem is put at its simplest in the *Gorgias*, or in the autobiographical sections of the *Seventh Letter*, where the cleavage is between contemplative philosophy and political activity. In the *Republic* the break-up is more complex, because the human personality itself is recognized as more involved. Similarly the task of resolving this cleavage is more difficult. We have seen, in the previous chapters, something of the task as Plato conceived it; what we are now trying to understand is the psychological aspect of the same process.[1]

A point which Cornford (*loc. cit.*) notices is that the amount of emotional energy available to the ψυχή is spoken of as though it were limited: 'the amount of energy directed into one channel,' he observes, 'is withdrawn from the others'. This metaphor of a stream diverted into a new channel is used in Book VI.[2] The psychological 'economy' envisaged by Plato is thus intended to be the one which makes the best use of such energy. But this is not the whole story: if an obstacle appears that prevents the stream of energy in any one of these channels from flowing freely, then the original coherence is broken up. This is the process which Plato has been describing in Books VIII and IX.

The unity of the ψυχή, which enables a man to act with complete success as a human being, is present, Plato believes, only in the philosopher, and in him only when his social environment allows him to live wholly in accordance with his purpose (βούλησις). Thus, as soon as the framework of society begins to crumble, the φιλόσοφος tends to become a recluse, with that ineffectiveness which Socrates admits in Book VI, and with which Callicles taunts him in the *Gorgias*. When this happens, the force of self-assertion, which had hitherto been an integral part of the success of the whole personality, becomes alienated and is established as a (disruptive) force in its own right.[3] From this point on, the process continues of its own momentum, until it reaches its logical conclusion in the character of the τυραννικὸς ἀνήρ. From this point of view, integration of the personality is the aim of the whole construction of the *Republic*. Here it may perhaps be helpful to point to an

[1] See Cornford, *op. cit.* pp. 69ff.   [2] VI, 485 D 6ff.   [3] VIII, 549 C 2ff.

analogy between Plato's conception of the ψυχή and Freud's theory of the *libido* and the neurosis. Cornford has written that 'the standpoints of Plato and Freud seem to be diametrically opposed'.[1] But the difference seems to be a difference largely in the historical theory of origins, not a disagreement about valuation. According to Freudian analysis, obsessions and neuroses develop when the normal functioning of psychic forces is in some way impeded; and sublimation, though in a sense 'artificial', is as much a value to Freud as the psychological integration of the philosopher is to Plato.[2] The similarities are not merely superficial; we are entitled to regard the psycho-analytical theory of the neurosis as a helpful analogy for Plato's view of the disintegration of the ψυχή, in much the same way as we used earlier Christian 'faith' as an analogy for Socratic ἐπιστήμη: this, provided of course that we realize that it is not valid to argue from one to the other. If it be objected that neuroses and psychoses do not make up, as do the δημο-κρατικοί of Plato's account, the greater part of the contents of the human world, we may remember that Freud found evidence of essentially similar mental states and processes in most human beings.[3]

Plato ends his account of decadence with a summary of the nature and value of its opposite, true justice. The principle of government is not, as Thrasymachus thought, slavery to the detriment of the subject, but integration under the guidance of the 'divine' element in man (τὸ θεῖον); infinitely preferable, 'since it is better for all of us to be governed by that element which is divine and possesses true understanding, and best if that element can be found as an integral part of our own souls; if that cannot be, then it must activate us from without, so that we may all, under one guidance, be united and of a like character'.[4] The value that the man of understanding (ὁ νοῦν ἔχων) will always have in mind is the concord of the soul (ἡ ἐν τῇ ψυχῇ συμφωνία).[5] At the end, it

---

[1] Cornford, *op. cit.* p. 78.   [2] See Freud, *Introductory Lectures*, pp. 17f.

[3] Freud, *Psychopathology of Everyday Life*, *passim*.

[4] ὡς ἄμεινον ὂν παντὶ ὑπὸ θείου καὶ φρονίμου ἄρχεσθαι, μάλιστα μὲν οἰκεῖον ἔχοντος ἐν αὐτῷ, εἰ δὲ μή, ἔξωθεν ἐφεστῶτος, ἵνα εἰς δύναμιν πάντες ὅμοιοι ὦμεν καὶ φίλοι, τῷ αὐτῷ κυβερνώμενοι (IX, 590D 3 ff.).

[5] 591 C 1 ff.: a use of συμφωνία which comes close to the *Laws*.

seems, he will owe his allegiance to a society not in the physical world: for it is at last admitted (under the growing compulsion of ἀνάγκη) that the ideal society of the *Republic* nowhere exists on earth: 'But perhaps there is a pattern laid up in the heavens for the man who is willing to observe and then to build his life upon what he has seen. But it makes no difference to such a man whether such a pattern anywhere exists or ever will: it remains the only society whose life he can live; there is no other.'[1]

In Book x there is little to concern us, until we reach the myth of Er. In a long work such as the *Republic*, with its many threads and many purposes, it is difficult to maintain sight of the constant objectives: the myth brings us back to the focal point where, it was earlier suggested, the effort of the dialogue was principally exerted;[2] the point at which the philosophical conversation extends (or was intended by Plato to extend) into the practical life of those who read it. That point is the moment of choice. By placing it in the 'Orphic' context of the life-after-death, Plato arrests the life of humanity to uncover the momentous importance of choice. Such a theme, the urgency of choice and its consequences, has been central from first to last in Plato's writings. Here, in the myth, it is given poetic form; the urgency heightened, the consequences brought together out of the extent of time.

The souls that gather to make the choice of lives have already been rewarded or punished in an after-life for their behaviour in a previous existence:[3] they are aware, then, as we perhaps are not, of what the choice implies. They are not to act in ignorance, but while they still have memory of what they have undergone. The encampment of souls is compared to a gathering of pilgrims at a festival.[4] On the way to the place of choice, they come to the Spindle of 'Ανάγκη and are in sight of the whole ordered system of the universe. The speech of the προφήτης insists on their individual responsibility, above all for their moral character; for ἀρετή is

---

[1] ἀλλ' ἐν οὐρανῷ ἴσως παράδειγμα ἀνάκειται τῷ βουλομένῳ ὁρᾶν καὶ ὁρῶντι ἑαυτὸν κατοικίζειν. διαφέρει δὲ οὐδὲν εἴτε που ἔστιν εἴτε ἔσται· τὰ γὰρ ταύτης μόνης ἂν πράξειεν, ἄλλης δὲ οὐδεμιᾶς (592B 2ff.). For the meaning of ἐν οὐρανῷ, compare Cornford's caveat (translation of the *Republic*, p. 312 n.) with Adam (vol. II, pp. 369f.).

[2] See above, p. 142.   [3] 614D 5ff.   [4] 614E 3.

subject to no master (ἀρετὴ δὲ ἀδέσποτον).[1] The lots are scattered and the lives laid out before the souls. 'At that moment, it seems, my dear Glaucon, everything is at stake.' Only one knowledge can help us, that which gives the power 'to distinguish the lives of good and evil, and always and everywhere to choose the best that is open to us'.[2] The one necessity in life is, therefore, the understanding of good and evil, and the relation of all other things to that standard. 'For we have seen that, in death and life alike, this is the most momentous choice of all.' Awareness of good and evil is a belief (δόξα) which must be maintained steel-hard against the allurements of wealth and power. It must be an awareness of the whole being, for when the choice is made, the most disastrous is that of one who had previously been rewarded for his life, 'since he had achieved ἀρετή, but by mere habituation without the pursuit of understanding'.[3] Mere habituation, though it may succeed by chance, when faced with a deliberate choice is incapable of supporting the individual. Many of those who had come from the rewards of heaven fell into this trap, since they were not disciplined by suffering (ἅτε πόνων ἀγυμνάστους). Most souls exchanged lives in their choice, because they had not passed beyond habit (συνήθεια).[4]

'And so it was, Glaucon, that the story was saved from destruction; and now it may save us, if only we will follow its guidance.'[5] At the end of the *Republic*, Socrates has answered the plea of Glaucon and Adeimantus in Book II, and provided, so far as he could, the arguments and considerations to support them in their choice of the best, the just life. If they will listen, he concludes, they will pursue with every means justice with the help of understanding, 'so that we may achieve peace within ourselves and peace with the gods, both in our time in this world and afterwards when, like victors in the games collecting their prizes, we receive the prize for justice; thus both in this world and in that thousand-year journey I have described, we shall fare well'.[6]

---

[1] 617E 3.   [2] 618B 6ff.
[3] ἔθει ἄνευ φιλοσοφίας ἀρετῆς μετειληφότα (619C 7f.). The use of ἔθος here in a derogatory sense strikes a very different note from the *Laws*.
[4] 620A 2.   [5] 621B 8f.   [6] 621C 6ff.

CHAPTER XIV

THE 'TIMAEUS':
THE CONCEPT OF ἈΝΆΓΚΗ

'I would mention that there are impossibilities
in this world.'   KEATS

IN the last chapter we noticed the appearance of ἀνάγκη in the
Republic. It was only possible there to observe its effects, or to
be more accurate, the emotional atmosphere which was found
with it, the beginnings of despair and pessimism: in the present
chapter we shall consider this atmosphere too more fully, but
before we can do that, we must examine the term ἀνάγκη by itself,
in order to determine the connotations which the word has elsewhere, which will in turn enable us to define it more accurately
in Plato's writings. This is the more necessary because there are
signs that misconceptions about the meaning of ἀνάγκη are still
prevalent.

Friedrich Solmsen, in his book *Plato's Theology* (1942), describes
'Necessity' in the *Timaeus* in terms strongly reminiscent of a
description of mechanism or classical physics. He speaks of 'laws'
of Necessity,[1] and uses words such as 'determine' in phrases like
'the chain of "necessary" causes which determine the physical
processes'. Necessity is even compared to order (τάξις), since 'the
processes in the Universe' are caused by the geometrical structure
of the atoms of the four elements, which in turn owe their order
to the imposition of regularity on the primeval chaos. This attitude
creates a number of problems: what are we to make, for example,
of Aristotle's (and Plato's) association of ἀνάγκη with chance
(τύχη)?[2] These difficulties are avoided if we accept the suggestions

---

[1] Solmsen, *op. cit.* pp. 106, 107. Cf. 'empirical causality' (p. 107).

[2] Aristotle, *Physics* B, 8. Cf. *An. Post.* B, 11 (94B 27ff.). Cf. Plato, *Laws* X,
889C 1f. (κατὰ τύχην ἐξ ἀνάγκης) and compare *Tim.* 46E 1ff., where causes
(αἰτίαι) which produce motion ἐξ ἀνάγκης are equated with those ὅσαι
μονωθεῖσαι φρονήσεως τὸ τυχὸν ἄτακτον ἑκάστοτε ἐξεργάζονται.

192

of Mr D. M. Balme on the subject of ἀνάγκη and mechanism.[1]
Mr Balme points out that the Greeks of Aristotle's age did not
assume the truth of Newton's First Law of Motion; at its simplest,
they did not believe that a body continues to move unless something stops it. In Aristotle's case, this difference 'forbade him to
conceive of a mechanist theory in the nineteenth-century sense.
It enabled him to hold, what must seem self-contradictory to us,
that all events have definable causes without there being a universal
nexus of causes and effects... and it compelled him to believe that
nature could not be orderly unless guided by a purposive force.'[2]
It is clear enough, as we shall see, that the concept is connected
with the pre-existence of the materials on which the creative
forces must work. ἀνάγκη is the limited possibility of those
materials. 'Physis must use materials in order to create. It follows
that Physis is limited by the possibilities in the materials and can
only produce from them what their interactions are capable of.'
However, 'Ananke does not govern sequences... Ananke is the
general name for the workings of the material when they are
distinguished from the purposeful movements initiated by Physis'.[3]
This serves to explain why it is that 'the phenomena which
Aristotle ascribes solely to ἀνάγκη are always accidental attributes,
συμβεβηκότα'.

If these considerations preclude the idea that Aristotle intended
a rigid scientific mechanism by his references to ἀνάγκη, they
apply a fortiori to his predecessors. In the case of Plato, the arguments have been fully considered by Cornford, to whom we may
now turn.[4] Mr Balme distinguishes Plato's use of ἀνάγκη (in the
Timaeus) from Aristotle's: 'where Plato distinguished Ananke
and Nous as separate factors each with its own properties, Aristotle
cannot allow that any properties are due to anything but Form:

---

[1] Classical Quarterly, XXXIII (1939), pp. 129 ff. (I) and XXXV (1941), pp. 23 ff.
(II).
[2] Loc. cit. (II), p. 23. Cf. Cornford, Plato's Cosmology, pp. 163, 169. On the
Greek view of motion and inertia, see Butterfield, Origins of Modern Science,
pp. 3 ff. Cf. M. Meldrum in J.H.S. LXX (1950), p. 66, n 10.
[3] Loc. cit. (I), p. 130. Cf. ibid. p. 134: 'the future will be determined eventually; but there is no causal nexus between then and now.'
[4] Plato's Cosmology, pp. 159 ff.

and as such they must be purposeful'.[1] Cornford would seem to agree with this distinction. In his account of Plato's view, he writes: 'the body of the universe...contains motions and *active powers* which are not instituted by the divine Reason and are perpetually producing undesirable effects'.[2] Aristotle's view need no longer concern us, but with Plato's the rest of this chapter will be concerned.

An example of the workings of ἀνάγκη which Cornford considers deals with the function of bone.[3] Bone was designed to protect the brain and marrow from injury; it had, therefore, to be hard. But an unavoidable (yet accidental) concomitant of hardness is brittleness. This is undesirable: thus the useful quality hardness, which is indispensable for the function of bone, happens to involve brittleness (an undesirable quality) as a necessary concomitant (Cornford compares, from another context in the *Timaeus*,[4] συνέβαινεν ἐξ ἀνάγκης). ἀνάγκη, then, is a general word for those unavoidable but fortuitous undesirable characteristics of the material which the craftsman–creator (δημιουργός) must work upon. Behind this, of course, lies the thought that the δημιουργός is not omnipotent, but must come to terms with his material: this is an assumption which Cornford has shown that it was natural for Plato to make.[5] He refers to Professor G. C. Field's view that purpose and omnipotence, as generally conceived, are incompatible; purpose is seen in struggle with material, choosing this rather than that in order to achieve its ends.[6] And purpose, it cannot be doubted, is fundamental in Plato's view of the δημιουργός and his task.

This discussion of the nature of ἀνάγκη has been brief, because Cornford and others have already produced very full accounts. The distinction between Reason and Necessity is one of the *Timaeus*' most characteristic contributions to Plato's thought: Cornford (*op. cit.* p. 35) calls it 'the central utterance of the whole

---

[1] *Loc. cit.* (I), p. 136.
[2] Cornford, *op. cit.* p. 176 (my italics)
[3] *Tim.* 73 E 1 ff.
[4] 77 A 1 f.
[5] *Plato's Cosmology*, pp. 35 ff. For the unconscious associations lying behind the concept of ἀνάγκη, see Onians, *Origins*, pp. 332 ff.
[6] Field, *Studies*, pp. 122 ff.

dialogue', finding it summarized in the phrase: 'reason governing necessity by persuading her to direct the greater part of things in this world towards what is best'.[1] The connection, however, between this and Plato's ethics is perhaps not yet clear. Cornford, in an Epilogue to his commentary, draws a moral from the whole work which has implications for Plato's ethical beliefs. Plato is concerned 'with the enthronement of wisdom and justice in human society.... There lies, beyond and beneath this problem, the antithesis of cosmos and chaos, alike in the constitution of the world and within the confines of the individual soul.' In the *Critias*, 'the city of uncompromised ideals...in the death-grapple with the lawless violence of Atlantis, goes down in a general destruction of mankind. The unwritten *Hermocrates*, we conjectured, would have described the rebirth of civilized society and the institution of a State in which the ideal would condescend to compromise with the given facts of man's nature. So humanity might find peace at last. And the way to peace...lies through reconcilement of the rational and the irrational, of Zeus and Fate, of Reason and Necessity, not by force but by persuasion.'[2] This stirs a memory. We have already considered a society in which 'persuasion' figured largely, the ethical society of the *Laws*. The suggestion, then, must present itself that what Plato abandoned in not writing the *Hermocrates*, he undertook in the *Laws*: that the society in which the ideal compromises with fact is the society of Magnesia. The way to peace, for Plato, led to the *Laws*, and the *Timaeus* opens that way. We may perhaps feel uneasy that the 'supreme place' in Plato's achievement should, in the end, seem to be given to the *Laws*; it has a ring less congenial than the conclusion of the *Oresteia*, to which Cornford compares it. Yet in both, it is true, 'Zeus and Destiny are reconciled'; the disaster of unreconciled opposition gives way to the peace of compromise. Thus the importance of the *Timaeus*, in ethics as in metaphysics and cosmology, is that the movement of compromise is here

---

[1] νοῦ δὲ ἀνάγκης ἄρχοντος τῷ πείθειν αὐτὴν τῶν γιγνομένων τὰ πλεῖστα ἐπὶ τὸ βέλτιστον ἄγειν (48 A 2 f.). We are reminded of Aristotle's dictum that nature is only regular ὡς ἐπὶ τὸ πολύ (*Metaphys.* E, 1027 a 8 ff.).
[2] Cornford, *op. cit.* pp. 363 f.

begun. Since the *Timaeus* is concerned with cosmology, the implications of the interactions between Reason and Necessity are not so obvious in their bearing on ethics. These are the implications which this chapter is to investigate.

Reference was made in an earlier chapter to the passage towards the beginning of the *Timaeus*, where the correlation of δόξα with phenomena, and ἐπιστήμη with the Forms is mentioned.[1] It is introduced in explanation of Timaeus' belief that only a 'likely story' (εἰκὼς μῦθος) is possible where the physical world is involved. This unreal (ὄντως δὲ οὐδέποτε ὄν) world of change and destruction can be grasped only by an opinion fettered to unreasoning sensation (δόξῃ μετ' αἰσθήσεως ἀλόγου δοξαστόν). There are echoes (in the phrase 'as reality is to becoming, so is truth to belief') of *Republic* VI.[2] Here, as there, it is clearly implied that about the physical world and its contents (both sensible, i.e. objects, and non-sensible, i.e. actions),[3] no higher degree of certainty can be achieved than δόξα. At a point later in the dialogue, this distinction is reiterated.[4] In this case, the separate existence of the Forms is in fact deduced from the (agreed) difference between δόξα and ἐπιστήμη. Moral certainty, then, in the physical world, cannot go beyond δόξα: the theory of Forms is actually allowed to rest on this foundation, so sure had Plato become of its truth. This is the first hint of despair and pessimism in the *Timaeus*, as it was in the *Republic*: a few pages later it is confirmed. After some passages on the δημιουργός and the body of the world, which themselves contain hints of Plato's pessimistic (or should we say 'realistic'?) state of mind,[5] the description of the World-soul and its human likeness opens.

Soul is an intermediate entity between the true existence of a Form and the becoming of the phenomenal world. As Proclus comments: 'Soul is an entity midway between the real (in the true sense of the word) and the ebb and flow of change: it is com-

---

[1] 27D 5 ff. See above, p. 163.   [2] *Rep.* VI, 511E.
[3] See Hardie, *Study in Plato*, p. 31.
[4] *Tim.* 51D 3 ff. Cf. 37B 3 ff, 52A 1 ff.
[5] Note, for example, κατὰ δύναμιν (30A 3), of the δημιουργός and his attempt to produce a likeness of himself; κατὰ φύσιν (30B 6).

pounded of things similarly intermediate.'¹ The *Phaedo* also visualized the soul as an intermediate, and saw in the fact a hope for immortality; soul there is 'most closely akin to all that is divine, immortal and intelligible, to all that possesses absolute unity of form and suffers no dissolution, but remains everlastingly unchanged'.² In the *Timaeus*, the emphasis falls on the other side of the picture. Proclus again gives a just impression in saying: 'Since the existence of soul is intermediate in [metaphysical] status, it also fills the no-man's-land between reason and the irrational; in its highest aspect, it is companion to reason, but in its lowest, it totters and leans towards [irrational] sensation.'³ If the soul is capable, by means of the divine in it, of assimilation to the real world of Forms, it is also welded to earth by its lower forces. In describing the creation of the human soul, Plato dwells on the inescapability of sensation and emotion.⁴ Archer-Hind has noted the recurrence of ἀνάγκη here, and again when the soul, or rather its mortal aspect, is actually fashioned by the created gods.⁵ The fate of the individual soul turns on its ability or inability to master these ἀναγκαῖα παθήματα; its task is described as 'drawing into the train of uniformity (συνεπισπώμενος) the welter of fire, water, air and earth, which is turbulent and unreasoning (θορυβώδη καὶ ἄλογον ὄντα)'. Thus the soul also is the battleground of Reason and Necessity, and responsibility for the outcome of the struggle lies not with the δημιουργός, but with the individual.⁶

It is, moreover, during the description of the human soul, as Cornford points out,⁷ that the 'errant cause' begins to come into view, as we approach 'what happens of Necessity'. 'The language', Cornford says, 'hints at a certain analogy between the task of the human Reason and the task of the Demiurge himself, who "took

---

¹ ψυχή ἐστιν οὐσία μέση τῆς ὄντως οὔσης οὐσίας καὶ γενέσεως, ἐκ τῶν μέσων συγκραθεῖσα γενῶν (*In Timaeum*, vol. III, p. 254; ed. Diehl).

² τῷ...θείῳ καὶ ἀθανάτῳ καὶ νοητῷ καὶ μονοειδεῖ καὶ ἀδιαλύτῳ καὶ ἀεὶ ὡσαύτως κατὰ ταὐτὰ ἔχοντι ἑαυτῷ ὁμοιότατον (*Phaedo*, 80 B 1 ff.).

³ ἐπεὶ γὰρ μέσης ἐστὶν οὐσίας ἡ ψυχή, καὶ τὸ μεταξὺ συμπληροῖ νοῦ καὶ ἀλογίας· τῷ μὲν γὰρ ἀκροτάτῳ ἑαυτῆς νῷ σύνεστι, τῷ δὲ ἐσχάτῳ νεύει πρὸς τὴν αἴσθησιν (Proclus, vol. I, p. 251).

⁴ 42 A 3 ff.

⁵ Archer-Hind, edition of the *Timaeus*, p. 143. The later passage is 69 C 5 ff.

⁶ 42 D 3 f.   ⁷ Cornford, *op. cit.* p. 147.

over all that was visible, not at rest but in discordant and unordered motion, and brought it from disorder into order"' (30 A 3 ff.). The entrance of the soul into time is described with great power: for the moment, the revolution of the Same, the faculty of reason, is halted by the flood of sensation, the incursion of ἀνάγκη. The shock is so great that it can only be compared to a man suddenly standing on his head, reversing the direction of right and left.[1] When the soul first comes into existence, sensations (παθήματα) deprive it of reason (νοῦς). Here is Plato's primal opposition, the opposition of the Phaedo earlier, but there is a revealing difference of emphasis; here it is made to seem insurmountable; reason and sensation are not merely opposed, they are irrevocably locked together; the soul is bound into the body.[2]

A few pages later, it becomes impossible to avoid mention any longer of 'what happens because necessity demands it so'.[3] 'This world of change exists by virtue of a compromise: it is born of the balanced opposition of necessity and reason.'[4] The cosmos has come into existence through the victory of reasonable persuasion (πειθοῦς ἔμφρονος) over Necessity: it is only a victory 'for the most part' (that is the burden of the Timaeus), but without even such a victory, no cosmos at all would be possible. The δημιουργός has created the cosmos by introducing Reason into the primal chaos. This chaos is described by Cornford as follows: 'Chaos is, in some sense, an abstraction—a picture of some part of the cosmos, as it exists at all times, with the works of Reason left out (ὥσπερ εἰκὸς ἔχειν ἅπαν ὅταν ἀπῇ τινος θεός).[5]...Now if you abstract Reason and its works from the universe, what is left will be irrational Soul, a cause of wandering motions, and an unordered element of the bodily, itself moving without plan or measure.'[6]

---

[1] 43 E 4 ff.   [2] 44 B 1. Cf. Arist. Protrepticus fr. 60 (Rose).
[3] τὰ δι' ἀνάγκης γιγνόμενα (47 E 3 ff.).
[4] μεμειγμένη γὰρ οὖν ἡ τοῦδε τοῦ κόσμου γένεσις ἐξ ἀνάγκης τε καὶ νοῦ συστάσεως ἐγεννήθη. σύστασις, the combination of different factors, is a favourite word with the later Plato. It first occurs in the Symposium (188 A 1) or in the Republic (VIII, 546 A 3), but is most frequent in the Timaeus and Laws. It perhaps reflects the growing preoccupation with analysis of factors in opposition, which we are now meeting in Plato.
[5] 53 B 3 f.   [6] Cornford, op. cit. p. 203.

We may be more than a little chary about accepting his suggestion concerning 'irrational Soul',[1] but in general Cornford's account is convincing. The 'wet-nurse of the world of change' (τιθήνη γενέσεως) is a factor, separable by intelligent analysis, not empirical observation, in the cosmic, and therefore the human, situation. This is stressed again later, when the mortal aspect of soul (ἄλλο...εἶδος ἐν αὐτῷ ψυχῆς...τὸ θνητόν)[2] is created. It contains 'terrible, yet inescapable emotions' (δεινὰ καὶ ἀναγκαῖα παθήματα), pleasure and pain, temerity and fear, passion hard to allay (δυσπαραμύθητον), and hope that is all too easily tempted. These, in the microcosm of man, are analogous to the πλανωμένη αἰτία in the cosmos, and they too can be reduced to order only 'for the most part': 'As necessity demanded, the creator gods made the fabric of the mortal aspect [i.e. of the soul] by compounding these elements with irrational sensation and desire that shrinks from no venture.'[3] The creator gods would have wished to keep this mortal aspect of soul separate from the divine, but they could accomplish their aim only 'so far as they were not absolutely bound by ἀνάγκη'.

If the force of ἀνάγκη is the final arbiter of possibility in the universe, the parallelism which Cornford adduced between its function there, and in the human individual, must have considerable repercussions in human conduct and morality. The sort of question which we are bound to ask ourselves is: if the δημιουργός can only 'persuade ἀνάγκη to guide the greater part of things in this world towards what is best', can the human reason ever attain perfection in the moral sphere? And the answer is bound to be that it cannot; the implications of Plato's view of ἀνάγκη are fatal to an idealist morality, such as Socrates was able to hold. The faculty of νοῦς (and even νοῦς, we must remember, is restricted to 'a small fraction of humanity': 51 E 6) has only limited powers of persuasion over ἀνάγκη, and its moral capacity is confined by the bonds which tie it to αἴσθησις. All this is implied in the Timaeus. It is perhaps not stated, but we shall expect to find signs of pessimism in what the dialogue has to say about the human personality.

[1] See G. Vlastos in Class. Quart. XXXIII (1939), pp. 77 ff., and, most recently, H. Cherniss in Proc. Amer. Phil. Soc. XCVIII (1954), pp. 26 ff.   [2] 69 C 7 f.   [3] 69 D 4 ff.

Such indications are not hard to detect. We have already noted references to the damaging powers of emotion in the soul. The stress on such δεινά παθήματα seems to be more insistent here than in the *Republic*. The tripartite psychology of that dialogue is fitted (perhaps a little uneasily)[1] into the discourse of Timaeus. The physiological location of the three εἴδη is connected with their moral function. The neck, for instance, prevents too close an association between the immortal soul (located in the head) and the instinct of self-assertion (θυμός), which is found in the heart; yet, in order that θυμός might be 'within hearing of reason's arguments',[2] it could not be put further apart from the head. Its partnership with νοῦς seems to be, at the least, uneasy. The vehicle of passion, τὸ ἐπιθυμητικόν, is like a Fury, cowed but only just held under in desperate struggle. 'The lower mortal part, the appetitive', Cornford writes, 'is tethered like a stalled beast' to the stomach, which is compared to a manger.[3] It is a 'savage creature, yet its maintenance side by side with the rest was inevitable, if any mortal race was ever to come into existence'.[4] The design of the creator is to crush its tumult and clamour (θόρυβος καὶ βοή) to the smallest possible. The description is tinged with an extreme disgust, greater even than that which appears in the three-bodied beast of the *Republic*; and the effort to hold it under results in some desperate measures, notably the construction of the intestine to slow down the cycle of physical desire (ἐπιθυμία) and its fulfilment, without which expedient humanity would be 'beyond the controlling voice of what is most divine in us'.[5]

But the efforts of the δημιουργός to make humanity perfect are doomed to failure, or to a mere partial success. Consequently there appear some features in the account of the human personality given in the *Timaeus*, which have puzzled commentators by their pessimism. Towards the end of the dialogue, disease becomes the subject of discussion, and disease in the soul is said to be due to

---

[1] See J. B. Skemp, *Plato's Statesman*, p. 239.
[2] τοῦ λόγου κατήκοος (70 A 2 ff.).
[3] Cornford, *op. cit.* p. 286.
[4] θρέμμα ἄγριον, τρέφειν δὲ συνημμένον ἀναγκαῖον, εἴπερ τι μέλλοι ποτὲ θνητὸν ἔσεσθαι γένος (70E 4 f.).
[5] 73 A 7 f.

bodily condition.[1] Professor Hackforth has sought to show that
this passage (which he rightly connects with others in the *Sophist*
and *Laws*)[2] is the result of a reaction from the (comparative)
idealism of the *Republic*.[3] Without making too much of the
importance of this passage in Plato's ethical theory, we may rather
see in it a reflection of his current concern with the influence of
opposed forces on one another. The physical processes, in particular those of sex, are pictured as creating disorder (ἄνοια) in
the soul; as Cornford remarks, '"Folly" (ἄνοια) means any state
in which the divine reason (νοῦς) is not exercising due control
over the rest of the soul.' For the greater part of a man's life, he is
maddened (ἐμμανής) by the intense pleasures and pains which are
an unavoidable (ἀναγκαῖον) concomitant of the functioning of
his body. Thus ἄνοια is merely one more of those undesirable
consequences which 'come about by Necessity'. Given such
physical conditions, the ψυχή incurs a predisposition towards un-
chosen evil, which can only be met by careful training: in such a
case the blame for moral failure must rest with the society. The
responsibility of the individual begins, however, with the possibility of self-education (ἐπιτηδευμάτων μαθημάτων τε).[4] Reason,
here also, must seek to persuade Necessity, and try to bring soul
and body into proportion, for the ἄνοια just described is the result
of a disproportion between physical and spiritual processes, whereby the former are enabled to control the latter. The note of proportion (συμμετρία) is one characteristic of Plato's later works:
the word itself, and its cognates, seem to be confined to the
dialogues of the last period.[5] It is indicative of the newly felt need
to 'strike a balance' between forces in opposition, part in fact of
the *ambiance* of compromise.

   Our present section of the *Timaeus* ends with an exhortation:
by care of the ψυχή, and in particular of its divine and rational part,
the human individual can grasp immortality as far as his nature

---

[1] 86B 1 ff. Or possibly, 'may be due' (since not *all* ἄνοια is due to bodily
condition): see Hackforth in *Classical Quarterly*, XL (1946), p. 119, and Cornford, *op. cit.* p. 346.
[2] *Soph.* 227D 13 ff.; *Laws* IX, 863 B ff. (on which see above, pp. 126ff.).
[3] Hackforth, *loc. cit.* pp. 118 ff.   [4] 87B 6ff.
[5] See Ast, *Lex. Plat.* s.vv.

allows (καθ' ὅσον... μετασχεῖν ἀνθρωπίνῃ φύσει ἀθανασίας ἐνδέ-χεται) and attain the best life which the gods offer to man (τοῦ προτεθέντος ἀνθρώποις ὑπὸ θεῶν ἀρίστου βίου).[1] This is as near to optimism as the *Timaeus* comes: yet even here hope is held in check by the impossibilities of this world.

The *Timaeus*, then, is seen to be a landmark on the 'way to peace', the peace, that is, of compromise. We have to consider how far along that way it lies. It has long been accepted that the *Timaeus* is very late, perhaps the last of Plato's works (with its unfinished companion-piece, the *Critias*) before the *Laws*. Sir David Ross, for example, believes it to have been written before the *Philebus*, but places it after Plato's third visit to Sicily in 360 B.C.[2] Recently, however, discussion has been reopened: Mr G. E. L. Owen[3] suggests that it is relatively early in the last group of dialogues, even as early as the *Parmenides*. According to this view, which Professor Skemp seems, in part at least, to accept, the *Timaeus* would antedate the two dialogues which form the subject-matter of the rest of this study. There seems no *prima facie* reason why this should not be so: we have already noted elements which the *Timaeus* has in common with the *Republic*. It would be unwise, however, to stress the point: whatever its date, the *Timaeus* develops tendencies found in the *Republic* and has certain features which recur in the *Politicus*. The question which must interest us most is how early can one place the overall pessimism which the *Timaeus* displays? In a recent book, the American scholar David Grene traces the despair of the last years back as far as the *Parmenides*.[4] He sees in that dialogue, and in the rather distant, impersonal view which it gives of Socrates, a surrender to 'the full tide which is sweeping from Plato every-thing and everybody singular into the world of quality, not action; rhythm, not fact; unending pattern, rather than single beauty'. He points out that in the *Parmenides* is found already the

---

[1] 90A 2ff.   [2] Ross, *op. cit.* pp. 9f.

[3] Mr Owen's views are quoted by Professor Skemp, *op. cit.* pp. 237ff. (They have now been published in an article in the *Classical Quarterly*, n.s., III (1953), pp. 79ff. Mr Owen seems to me to have established his case beyond a reasonable doubt.)

[4] David Grene, *Man in his Pride*, pp. 179ff.

striking tendency of Plato's last dialogues to exalt the wisdom of the old.[1] We may add to this the emphasis which the *Parmenides* lays on the difficulties involved in the theory of Forms,[2] and the general air of puzzlement which pervades the earlier part of the dialogue. It is not hard to connect this with the more articulate despair of the *Timaeus*. From these hints, one may perhaps reasonably infer that pessimism is the distinguishing mark (even more, perhaps, than the change of style first noted by Campbell and Lutoslawski) of the whole group of 'late' dialogues. The *Timaeus* would stand as prelude to this group, in making explicit the source of pessimism, the ever incomplete victory of Reason over Necessity.

[1] Grene, *op. cit.* p. 178.
[2] See, for example, *Parm.* 131 E 6f., 133 A 8f., 134E 9ff.

CHAPTER XV

THE ETHICAL OUTLOOK OF
THE 'POLITICUS'

THE considerations adduced in Professor Skemp's appendix to his translation of the dialogue (and referred to in
the last chapter), would bring the *Politicus* into close relation with the *Timaeus*. We cannot, of course, be certain in our
dating of Plato's works, but the connection between the *Politicus*
and the *Timaeus* is clear enough even in the absence of any new
theory about their respective dates. Professor Cornford, who
follows the traditional dating of the *Timaeus*,[1] elucidates the relation between Reason and Necessity in that dialogue by reference
to the myth in the *Politicus*.[2] In doing so, he follows ancient
precedent, in the comments of Proclus and Simplicius.[3] The
evident connection of theme and outlook perhaps serves to corroborate the attempt to bring the dates of the two dialogues closer
together, but exists independently of it.

In the *Politicus*, the interplay between the values of form and
content, between, that is, dialectical (in Plato's sense) and ethical
(or political) motives, is complex. The *Politicus* has this, among
many other characteristics, in common with other dialogues of
Plato's last years, notably the *Sophist* and *Parmenides*. There seems
no need to enter into the controversy about its 'real purpose',
which is reflected in Professor Skemp's introduction.[4] Even to
draw a sharp distinction between form and content, and still more
to subordinate one to the other, is an ingenuous and misleading
simplification. We may accept the fact that the *Politicus* contains
something of significance both for Plato's dialectic and for his

---

[1] Cornford, *Plato's Cosmology*, p. 1.
[2] Cornford, *op. cit.* pp. 206ff.
[3] Proclus, *In Tim.* vol. III, p. 273; Simplicius, *In Phys.* 1122, 3. Cf. Plutarch,
De Animae Procreatione, 1015A. These passages are discussed more fully below.
[4] Skemp, *op. cit.* pp. 18, 66ff.

ethics. I shall be concerned here only with the latter significance, but that is not to deny the existence of the former.

Yet if its interest in the method of Division shows the *Politicus* to be a genuine dialogue of the so-called 'critical' period, it occupies within that final group a somewhat ambiguous position, akin in some respects to the *Philebus*. For side by side with the discussions typical of the last years, we find a peculiarly Socratic atmosphere. The respondent to the Eleatic Stranger is Young Socrates, not entirely a mask, though little more than a figure of naïve idealism. Moreover, the hall-marks of Socratic ethics, the words ἐπιστήμη and τέχνη, occur more frequently here, in spite of the impression given by Ast's *Lexicon*, than in any other dialogue of comparable length outside the early period. At the outset it is agreed that the πολιτικός of the title is 'a man of ἐπιστήμη'; moreover, his possession of an inward understanding is made more important than his ability to manipulate political power. He is 'a man of royal stature, if only because of the art he possesses',[1] even though he is only an adviser of one in power. A little later, we find, perhaps to our surprise, a latter-day declaration of the importance of 'agreement' (ὁμολογία):[2] Campbell indeed rightly compares the important passage in the *Gorgias*. Throughout, the powers of the πολιτικός, and in particular his position above law, are explained by reference to his possession of ἐπιστήμη (or τέχνη: the words are used interchangeably), even though it is admitted that we have as yet no clear idea of the true nature of his ἐπιστήμη.[3] There are several direct reminiscences of earlier, 'Socratic' dialogues. The introduction, for example, of an ἐπιστήμη of values, towards the end of the dialogue, to enable us to discover, not how, but when or whether to use subordinate τέχναι, cannot fail to remind us of a similar passage in the *Euthydemus* (290 B ff.), as M. Diès and Professor Skemp have remarked.[4] In

---

[1] κατά γε τὴν τέχνην αὐτὴν βασιλικός (*Polit.* 259 B 4 ff.).

[2] 260 B 6 ff. Cf. 277 A 1 ff.; *Gorg.* 472 B 6 ff. Campbell, ed. of the *Polit.* p. 12; see above, pp. 18 ff.

[3] *Polit.* 292 C 2 f. For references to ἐπιστήμη/τέχνη (not in Ast), see, for example, 284 C 2, 292 B 6 f., 293 C 6 ff., 294 A 7 f., 295 E 4 ff., 296 E 4 ff., 297 A 5 ff., 301 C 8 ff., 304 B 1 ff.

[4] Diès, *Politique* (Budé ed.), p. lix; Skemp, *op. cit.* pp. 44; 220 n. 1.

all this, we can recognize the Socratic note; yet it is impossible to regard the *Politicus* as anything but a work of Plato's old age. The pessimism of the *Timaeus*, though not present here so conspicuously, underlies all that Plato says about conduct and the πολιτικὴ τέχνη.

In the divisions of the early part of the dialogue (258 B 2–268 D 5), there is little to concern us. We have seen already that· the πολιτικός is ἐπιστήμων τις. His τέχνη, we are then told, is more nearly 'intellectual' (γνωστική) than it is 'manual or generally practical':[1] here perhaps we have a first faint indication of weariness; for the mind, even the whole personality of the true ruler, seems in danger of being divorced from action. But the balance is redressed soon after, since the βασιλικὴ τέχνη is classed with architecture and building (ἀρχιτεκτονική), and distinguished from pure calculation. Its position in the world of action is consolidated by inclusion under the class of 'skills in leadership' (ἐπιτακτικαὶ τέχναι).[2] But the definition of βασιλικὴ τέχνη which now emerges, as 'the art of shepherding hornless non-interbreeding wingless land-animals' is sufficiently unhelpful and productive of a sense of anti-climax for us to realize that Plato, as so often, is using our sense of disappointment to underline the difficulty both of applying the method of Division and of grasping adequately the nature of πολιτικὴ τέχνη itself. The rise to a new level of seriousness, as so often, is marked by the myth.

Consideration of the *Politicus* myth must once again involve the question of Plato's method and intention in the creation of myths. Protesting against the assimilation of the present myth to the *Timaeus*, Professor Skemp presses too far, I think, the detail of Plato's mythical imagery.[3] He seems to disregard what Proclus[4] calls Plato's 'riddling in mythical terms' (μυθικὰ αἰνίγματα), and his freedom in the manipulation of symbols. Professor Skemp asks (*loc. cit.*): 'How can contrary *rotations* be co-existent?' Such a question argues an absence of surrender to the imagery itself; Proclus, from his standpoint, was able to allow that Plato had separated in the myth (for the purposes of his image) forces

---

[1] 259 C 10f.   [2] 260 A 9ff.
[3] Skemp, *op. cit.* p. 89 and n. 1.   [4] Proclus, *In Tim.* vol. I, p. 289.

which were, in the world, in simultaneous existence.¹ Towards understanding the picture of life under Kronos, we need do no more, for example, than allow it to *suggest* to us a reversal of all our current values and the modes of our existence, according to the pattern of the Greek mind; to be more literal is to misunderstand Plato's intention.

The imagery of the myth involves the alternation of two forces which control the cosmos. In one period the universe is under the direction of the δημιουργός; in the other, released from his guidance, it turns back on its divine revolution and rotates in the opposite sense. The reversal is 'an unavoidable aspect of its nature',² and the universe turns back, 'because it is a living creature, and because it owed its capacity to understand (φρόνησις) to him who constructed it in the beginning'.³ This must surely mean that its φρόνησις is due solely to its creator and begins to ebb away as he removes his guidance: its ability to move under its *own* guidance (or lack of guidance) is implied in its being a living thing.⁴ This is in accordance with the rest of what we are told about the reversal. It comes about 'of necessity' (ἐξ ἀνάγκης), because sameness does not belong to 'the nature of material body' (σώματος φύσις); thus the reversal is connected with 'the corporeal' (τὸ σωματοειδές) from the start. Proclus, indeed, goes so far as to identify the πόντος ἀνομοιότητος, into which the universe is in danger of sinking, with matter (ἡ ἀληθῶς ὕλη).⁵ In part at least, this is a Neo-Platonic, even Gnostic, interpolation, but it does not seem so far removed from what Plato says in the myth. After the reversal, the universe gradually forgets the teaching (διδαχή) of its creator:

¹ Proclus, *op. cit.* vol. III, p. 273, especially ἀεὶ τοῦ κόσμου τὴν συναμφοτέραν ἔχοντος, τοῦ δὲ μύθου χωρίσαντος ἀπὸ τῆς δευτέρας τὴν προτέραν. Cf. vol. I, p. 389 and Frutiger, *Mythes de Platon*, p. 191.

² ἐξ ἀνάγκης ἔμφυτον (269D 2f.).

³ ζῷον ὂν καὶ φρόνησιν εἰληχὸς ἐκ τοῦ συναρμόσαντος αὐτὸ κατ' ἀρχάς (269D 1f.).

⁴ I cannot agree with what appears to be the view of Campbell, Diès and Skemp (Campbell, p. 46; Diès, p. 21; Skemp, p. 145) that it is *owing to* its possession of φρόνησις that the cosmos is able to revolve in a sense contrary to the guidance of the δημιουργός. All the associations of φρόνησις in Plato would be against this.

⁵ Proclus, *op. cit.* vol. I, p. 179.

responsibility for this is once again laid upon 'the corporeal element in the compound'.[1] The material element in the cosmos goes back to the primeval ἀταξία, the effects of which become more and more pronounced as time passes after the reversal. This cosmic ἀταξία produces everything 'that is intractable and evil in the cosmos', and in a remarkable phrase, is said to 'engender' these evils 'in turn in the living creatures within it' (Professor Skemp's translation: p. 152).[2]

The reversal, as we saw, was ἀναγκαῖον: it had to happen (ἔδει γίγνεσθαι),[3] and 'destiny and its own inborn urge' (εἱμαρμένη τε καὶ σύμφυτος ἐπιθυμία) seized control of the universe. There is emphasis throughout on the fact that the change is due to nature (φύσις):[4] the reversal is an integral part of the nature of the universe, so that when revolving in the opposite sense, it can be said to be αὐτοκράτωρ τῆς αὑτοῦ πορείας.[5] The cosmos, with its ineradicable tendency towards evil, controls at times both itself and all within it: human beings then live their lives 'in the very image of the course that the universe as a whole pursues'.[6] But however inevitable the rotation away from the divine, it is still 'the slightest possible deviation from its true motion'.[7] This brings the feeling of the *Politicus* myth even closer to the *Timaeus*; in both we have the idea that the falling away from the ideal is as slight as possible, and yet beyond doubt ineradicable. More markedly than in the *Timaeus*, the theory is here given poetic treatment. The imagery rises out of the emotional background; the cosmos is here a ship,[8] abandoned by its captain and in danger of foundering in the 'infinite sea of unsameness, because of the confusion which has struck it'.[9] But it is only the quality of the feeling that is different; the philosophical theory which gives rise to it is the same. 'Both

---

[1] τὸ σωματοειδὲς τῆς συγκράσεως (273 B 4).
[2] 273 B 7ff.   [3] 272D 7.
[4] Cf. the use of ἔμφυτος, σύμφυτος, etc.
[5] 274A 5. Cf. δι' ἑαυτοῦ: 270A 5.   [6] 274D 6f.
[7] σμικροτάτη τῆς αὑτοῦ κινήσεως παράλλαξις (269E 4).
[8] On the ship simile, see Skemp, *op. cit.* p. 96 and n. The image recurs at *Critias* 109 C 1 ff.
[9] There is a striking resemblance between this part of the *Politicus* myth and the New Testament story of Christ asleep on the ship.

myths', as Cornford says, 'present a picture of the universe as it would be if the works of reason were abstracted' (*Plato's Cosmology*, p. 207). The details perhaps of the two accounts cannot be assimilated to one another, though Cornford takes the parallel to its very limits, but in outline the theories of the two dialogues are remarkably close.

We will expect, then, that in other ways too, the similarity between the *Politicus* and *Timaeus* will be evident in the rest of the dialogue. We have seen already that, in its insistence on the need for τέχνη, the *Politicus* recalls the early works; there are as many hints of what is to come, in the *Philebus* and *Laws*. Almost at once after the myth, comes an explicit statement of the *humanity* of the governor of our world (οἱ ἐνθάδε νῦν ὄντες πολιτικοί):[1] he is not a god, but a man 'like his subjects', with a similar education and upbringing. A foretaste, evidently, of the rulers of the *Laws*, who also are scaled down to the dimensions of their subjects and limited by the same bounds of humanity. There are many other characteristics of Plato's last years prefigured in the *Politicus*; in particular, his renewed interest in Pythagoreanism, and through it an approximation to the ethical vocabulary of Aristotle.[2] Pythagoreanism, as Cornford and Taylor have observed, is behind much of the *Timaeus*; in the *Politicus*, it is represented chiefly by the passage (283 B–287 B) on the 'technique of calculation' (μετρητικὴ τέχνη). Here we observe a new devotion to τὸ μέτριον, an absolute, not a relative mean;[3] the very existence of τέχναι is repeatedly declared to depend on acceptance (or awareness) of τὸ μέτριον.[4] In particular, existence of an absolute mean is held to be vital to 'men of practical intelligence' (οἱ περὶ τὰς πράξεις ἐπιστήμονες); even the ultimate verification of truly accurate knowledge rests upon the mean.[5] This clearly has much in common with the *Nicomachean Ethics*; we have only to observe such Aristotelian collections of 'mean terms' as τὸ μέτριον καὶ τὸ

---

[1] 275 B 8 ff.
[2] See J. E. Raven, *Pythagoreans and Eleatics*, pp. 180 ff.
[3] 283 E 8 ff.   [4] 284 A 5 ff., D 4 ff.
[5] On this, see Campbell's note, *op. cit.* pp. 105 f. He is clearly wrong, however, in supposing that Plato's mean is relative.

πρέπον καὶ τὸν καιρὸν καὶ τὸ δέον.[1] The gulf (if at this period we can call it a gulf) between Plato and Aristotle is here at its narrowest. There is a further link with Plato's earlier writings in the passage (277 A–279 A) dealing with 'illustrations' (or 'symbols': παρα-δείγματα). Professor Skemp insists that the παράδειγμα is 'not a visible object "illustrating" a Form. It is a simpler Form...which helps us to understand a more complex Form.'[2] In a sense he is perhaps right, but the connection with visible examples remains. Weaving is chosen as a παράδειγμα of Government, not merely because it is simpler, but because it admits of visible, concrete illustration. Thus the passage reminds us of the account of διάνοια in Republic VI, whose dependence on the sensible illustration was a characterizing trait. The use of examples is, as Plato points out, an essential part of the way in which the human mind works at its lower levels; it is part of 'our situation with regard to ἐπιστήμη'.[3] We are as men whose knowledge is like the 'knowledge' one may have of objects in a dream; if we wake up, we find that we know nothing.[4] With the Republic in mind, we may compare our present passage with another later in the Politicus, which deals with 'certain sensible likenesses'.[5] This latter is in fact connected with the παράδειγμα of weaving, thus corroborating the bond between παράδειγμα and the visible illustration. Likenesses, the Stranger says, exist in the sensible world only in the case of those 'real existents' (ὄντα) which are already easy to understand; the most important class of existents have no such εἴδωλα. Therefore, these ἀσώματα can only be described by reason (λόγῳ), which in turn demands prolonged training (μελέτη) of the sort which the Politicus conversation is designed to illustrate. This is a clear reminiscence of what is said in the Republic about the upper section of the line diagram. The dialectic of the later dialogues is not, perhaps, as far removed from that of the Republic as would at

---

[1] 284E 6f. On the connection with the Philebus and Aristotle, see Skemp, op. cit. pp. 78ff. On μετρητικὴ τέχνη, Raven, op. cit. pp. 186f.

[2] Skemp, op. cit. p. 81.

[3] τὸ περὶ τῆς ἐπιστήμης πάθος ἐν ἡμῖν (277D 7).

[4] D 2ff. The ὄναρ/ὕπαρ contrast reminds us of Rep. VII, 520C 6ff., as also does the use of the word πάθος. See above, pp. 174 n. 1, 175 n. 4.

[5] αἰσθηταί τινες ὁμοιότητες (285D 9ff.).

times appear. The feeling which places 'unfettered mind' above induction from examples is still present; in discussing a suggested definition of the πολιτικός, the Stranger remarks: 'Where it is a question of expounding some living thing to those who are capable of understanding, the proper means is not drawing or any art of the hand, but word of mouth, the discourse of reason.'[1] Here χειρουργία, presumably, is more closely linked to αἴσθησις and consequently less valuable.

But more important than those passages which provide links with what has gone before, are those which place the *Politicus* in the later development of Plato's thought about ethics; those, in fact, which sketch in the history of his thinking between the *Republic* and the *Laws*, by throwing light, not merely on the mood, but on the content of his mind at this period. There are several such passages, dealing in particular with law and the relation of the πολιτικός to it, and with Plato's new theory of psychological types. Professor Skemp, I think, is in danger of overstressing the difference of attitude to law between the *Politicus* and *Laws*.[2] In as far as a difference of emphasis covers a difference of outlook and feeling, he is so far right; but what is particularly striking about the *Politicus* is the degree to which the theories of the *Laws* have been anticipated. The *Politicus* approaches the question of law (292 B–303 D) from the prior question of the legal position of the true πολιτικός. The emphasis here falls very strongly on 'true': as elsewhere, Plato is at pains to distinguish the true statesman (ὁ μετὰ τέχνης νομοθέτης)[3] from his idle rivals. An essential part of the distinction has always been the insistence on the fewness of those who possess real τέχνη: ὀρθότης and rarity have always been connected. In this dialogue, the Stranger says: 'The true title to rule, if it is to *be* true, must be sought in one or two men, or at the most a very few.'[4] The real criterion of the

---

[1] γραφῆς δὲ καὶ συμπάσης χειρουργίας λέξει καὶ λόγῳ δηλοῦν πᾶν 3ῷον μᾶλλον πρέπει τοῖς δυναμένοις ἕπεσθαι (277C 3 ff.). On this passage, see Diès (Budé ed.), p. 34 n. 1.

[2] Skemp, *op. cit.* pp. 48 ff., 55, 196 n.

[3] 295 E 7 f.

[4] τὴν μὲν ὀρθὴν ἀρχὴν περὶ ἕνα τινὰ καὶ δύο καὶ παντάπασιν ὀλίγους δεῖ ζητεῖν, ὅταν ὀρθὴ γίγνηται (293 A 3 f.).

πολιτικός is that he should act in everything 'with the good as his aim' (ἐπ' ἀγαθῷ): the true πολιτικοί 'preserve their charges from disaster',[1] and they remain true only 'so long as they use their capacity for justice, to the limit of their powers, in preservation and improvement'.[2] This emphasis on rarity, on the possession of ἐπιστήμη and τέχνη, is designed to explain the standing of the true βασιλικός above law; it provides a guarantee of his meriting such a pre-eminent (and in another man pre-eminently dangerous) position, and of his using his supreme authority for the best ends. As in the *Laws*, Plato visualizes a law such that, by its own limitations, it demands the existence of some element in society that goes beyond it. For law, like the written work (another of Plato's *bêtes noires*, and for the same reason), is incapable of meeting the needs of the personal; it issues only one injunction, and is incapable of distinguishing individual characters or circumstances. The ideal, therefore, is 'not that the laws should hold undisputed sway, but rather the man of royal stature who possesses true understanding (φρόνησις)'.[3] Law is a mirror of the immutable, but in regulating human life, it must necessarily come up against the perennial mutability of human affairs (τὸ μηδέποτε μηδὲν ὡς ἔπος εἰπεῖν ἡσυχίαν ἄγειν τῶν ἀνθρωπίνων). Nothing so unqualified (ἁπλοῦν) as law can ever satisfactorily meet the inconstancy of existence in the physical world.[4] Legislation is a general rule aimed at the benefit of the average subject, because individual treatment is too large a task;[5] consequently the βασιλεύς must stand above (or at least outside) law, in the need for tempering the universal rule in the light of experience.[6] Thus, when the 'skilled legislator' (μετὰ τέχνης νομοθέτης) is said to have an inalienable right to revise laws, it is clear that his right rests on the same foundation as the right of making and protecting laws in the *Laws*; i.e. he goes beyond law, because he sees further (as the doctor sees further than the written prescription), in his capacity as τεχνικός.[7] It is from this point of view that the true πολιτικός is judged to rise above

---

[1] Cf. *Rep.* I, 341 c ff.   [2] 293 b 6 ff.
[3] οὐ τοὺς νόμους...ἰσχύειν ἀλλ' ἄνδρα τὸν μετὰ φρονήσεως βασιλικόν (294 A 7 f.).   [4] 294 A 6 ff. Cf. Pseudo-Demosthenes, *In Aristogeit.* I, 15 f.
[5] 294 E 8 ff.   [6] 295 B 10 ff.   [7] 295 E 4 ff.

the consent of the governed. His claim rests solely on his possessing to a yet greater degree the quality which gives value to law, that it attempts the execution of what is objectively beneficial (σύμφορον). All other considerations, such as consent, legality, wealth, are irrelevant.[1] Thus the power of the πολιτικός rests solely upon the authority of truth, as it is declared to do in the *Laws*; government will be true (ὀρθή) government, only if the governors employ 'the force of their skill to overrule that of law'.[2] The substance of the theory is finally summarized in the Stranger's words:[3] 'Whatever they do, rulers wise in the true sense cannot fail,[4] so long as they preserve one important condition: they must use their intelligence and skill to distribute the maximum of justice to those in their society; they must be capable of preserving them from disaster and leading them as far as possible along the road from evil to good.'

It is this that Plato has in mind, when he declares that 'constitutions' other than the one true constitution under the guidance of the true πολιτικός, fall short of the ideal.[5] They depend *solely* on a code of laws, without any element which can rise above law and direct it in accordance with real values. Thus, the account of law which the *Politicus* gives, is not, as Professor Skemp suggests, at variance with the later account in the *Laws*; in substance, if not in emphasis, the two accounts agree. At times perhaps there is a suspicion of strain: the effect of 'legalism', Plato says, is to prevent original discoveries or unconventional inquiry beyond the laws.[6] The reference, as the context shows, is to Socrates; it includes an echo of the famous οὐ βιωτὸς ἀνθρώπῳ of the *Apology*.[7] We may feel that the Nocturnal Council of the *Laws* proves, ironically enough, Plato's point. But the *Politicus*, within the same theory, stresses the need for vision, and part of the pessimism of the

---

[1] 296D 6ff.
[2] τὴν τῆς τέχνης ῥώμην τῶν νόμων...κρείττω (296E 4ff.).
[3] καὶ πάντα ποιοῦσι τοῖς ἔμφροσιν ἄρχουσιν οὐκ ἔστιν ἁμάρτημα, μέχριπερ ἂν ἓν μέγα φυλάττωσι, τὸ μετὰ νοῦ καὶ τέχνης δικαιότατον ἀεὶ διανέμοντες τοῖς ἐν τῇ πόλει σῴζειν τε αὐτοὺς οἵοί τε ὦσιν καὶ ἀμείνους ἐκ χειρόνων ἀποτελεῖν κατὰ τὸ δυνατόν (297A 5ff.).
[4] Cf. *Euthyd.* 280A 6ff.   [5] 297D 4ff.   [6] 299B 2ff.
[7] Skemp, *op. cit.* p. 208 n. *Apol.* 38A 5f.

dialogue stems from Plato's despair of ever finding 'the man to rule as a true man, with ἐπιστήμη'.[1] Yet he was never surer of the need for society to be founded upon inward vision, upon ἐπιστήμη and τέχνη. The 'bastard' constitutions give rise to a host of evils, 'because the foundation on which they rest makes them carry out their task, not with ἐπιστήμη, but through the written enactment and the sowing of habit'.[2] It is their ignorance of those principles which are ultimately most important, that causes their own collapse;[3] worse perhaps, in the Socratic-Platonic view, is their unfounded belief that they have actually plumbed the truth of social conduct. The folly of their state is so great that Plato is filled with wonder at the immense inherent strength and resistance to defeat that human society seems to display. The gap between these pseudo-constitutions and the guidance of the true πολιτικός is like the gulf between gods and men.[4] Yet, at the end, the function of the βασιλεύς in the *Politicus*, as it is that of the νομοφύλακες in the *Laws*, is to surpass law in the attainment of truth; his place in society is that of the protector.

With the close of the passage on law and the πολιτικός, we soon reach our final subject, Plato's new theory of psychological types. It is one of the most striking differences which an interest in empirical observation has brought about, between the outlook of Socrates and that of Plato's last years. It is not surprising, then, that it is introduced in the *Politicus* (306 A to the end) with some hesitation. A clash between the 'aspects of ἀρετή' (ἀρετῆς μέρη) will be a gift for the sceptically minded to attack, suggests the Stranger.[5] In consequence the argument, and the considerations involved, are set out at some length. The cleavage is compared to a family quarrel;[6] it arises between the active, masculine virtues of self-assertion (e.g. ἀνδρεία) and the more passive, feminine virtues of restraint (e.g. σωφροσύνη).[7] A difference of value is explicitly denied,[8] yet the conflict of qualities appears to be carried up into the realm of Forms,[9] for the Forms of ἀνδρεία and σωφρο-

---

[1] 301 C 8 ff.   [2] 301 E 6 ff.   [3] 302 A 5 ff.
[4] 303 B 3 ff.   [5] 306 A 8 ff.   [6] 306 C 5.
[7] The comparison with the sexes is made at *Laws*, VII, 802 E. See above, pp. 114 f.   [8] 308 C 1 ff.   [9] 307 C 2 ff.

σύνη are said to be incompatible in a phrase which recalls the incompatibility of Rest and Motion in the *Sophist* (254D ff.).[1] This metaphysical cleavage between Form and Form is mirrored in the radical opposition of the two types of human character, active and passive. This latter part of the argument is reinforced by reference to observation, in particular to the events of contemporary history.[2] The observation of character is acute, but what makes the theory important for us is the evidence which it provides of Plato's latter-day empiricism, and in the significance which this theory of psychological types has in Plato's later thought. The theory is not entirely new; in the *Republic*, it was suggested that gentleness and self-assertion were contraries,[3] but they were there contraries which might somehow come to co-exist in the same person. Plato now appears to feel this impossible;[4] a sense of inevitable conflict runs through his account of the composition of society. And this sense of conflict seems to have been confirmed, for the theory, as we have seen, reappears in the *Laws*.

It is at this point that the πολιτικός reappears, and the παρά-δειγμα of weaving reveals its significance. The opposed types of character form the warp and woof of the fabric, which it is the function of the πολιτικός to form. With this final passage, we come very close indeed to the *Laws*. The bond which must bind society together into its essential unity, is the bond of 'true conviction' (ἀληθὴς δόξα) about what is good and valuable.[5] Such a universal view of values, δόξα, yet 'founded on absolute truth and settled as an unshakable conviction', is the divine element in society.[6] As in the *Laws*, this bond (δέσμος) is forged by the πολιτικὸς καὶ ὁ ἀγαθὸς νομοθέτης; it holds together the opposed psychological types which Plato finds in society. Those of both types who cannot be welded into the unity of society (309E 2f., E 7f.) are to be ejected, for the aim of the weaving is to make 'life a communal unity'.[7] The echoes of the *Laws* are numerous and all too clear; the divine bond of ὀρθὴ δόξα, a

---

[1] On this, see Skemp, *op. cit.* p. 223 n 1.   [2] See Skemp, *op. cit.* p. 66.
[3] *Rep.* II, 375C 6ff. Cf. III, 410C 8ff., and *Phaedrus*, 271Dff.
[4] But see 311A 4f.   [5] *Polit.* 309C 5ff.
[6] 310A 1ff.   [7] κοινόν...τὸν βίον (311B 9f.).

conviction shared by both types of character, underlies, in both dialogues, all the purely human bonds that the πολιτικός may seek to create. With society as conceived in the *Politicus*, we have already covered most of the ground that separates the *Republic* from the *Laws*. This is a society, as Plato envisages it, which will attain moral goodness and happiness by virtue of its internal organization and direction. In the *Politicus*, he expresses this faith as follows: '...and to fall nothing short of the limit to which society can achieve happiness'.[1] 'Society' (πόλει) is the word to note.

[1] ...καὶ καθ' ὅσον εὐδαίμονι προσήκει γίγνεσθαι πόλει τούτου μηδαμῇ μηδὲν ἐλλείπουσα (311 C 5 f.).

CHAPTER XVI

THE DIALECTICAL TENSION IN
THE 'PHILEBUS'

IN the introduction to his Budé edition of the *Philebus* M. Diès claims to see, between it and the *Politicus*, a considerable measure of difference: 'quand on passe du *Politique* au *Philèbe*', he says, 'on a l'impression de rentrer brusquement dans le cadre normal des dialogues platoniciens...'.[1] This seems to me largely to overstate the matter; the *Philebus* shares with the *Politicus* that strange uneasy contrast between a subject-matter which is broadly speaking Socratic and the dialectical method typical of the 'critical' period. While allowing that the work of M. Diès and Professor Hackforth[2] has done much to throw light on many of the apparent eccentricities of form and structure in the *Philebus*, one must recognize, I think, that these surface tensions and distortions go to the very root of the dialogue. These strains, which are so typical of all the critical dialogues and constitute a bond of feeling which links them together, are perhaps only resolved in the *Laws* with the imminence of death; and even there, one feels, the resolution, being a resolution born of weariness, is more apparent than real. Discussion of the *Philebus* in the present chapter will be somewhat restricted; almost half the dialogue is devoted to a detailed examination of the status of pleasure (31 A–55 C),[3] a subject which concerns us only in so far as Plato's interest in it reflects his attempt to come to terms with reality. We have here to consider the characteristic atmosphere of the dialogue and its contribution to our understanding of Plato's moral outlook.

Early in the conversation, Protarchus remarks: 'Still, though I dare say the ideal for a man of sense is to know everything, I imagine the second-best course is to know himself for what he

[1] Diès, *op. cit.* p. vii.
[2] R. Hackforth, *Plato's Examination of Pleasure.*
[3] On the proportions of the *Philebus*, see Diès, *op. cit.* pp. ix f.

is.[1] This may provide us with a starting-point for the consideration of Plato's general outlook at the time of writing the *Philebus*. For the disjunction in Protarchus' remark is at least negative evidence of Plato's development. It is clear enough that, for Socrates, 'knowing all' and 'knowing oneself for what one is' were, in some sense, one and the same.[2] It is no longer in itself surprising that Plato, at this period, should allow a character to subordinate one to the other; it is merely one more indication that Plato has moved away from the Socratic position. There are many such indications in the *Philebus*. At a rational level we observe once again the insistence on practical considerations, on accepting what is *there*, before one. For example, the ontological classification into four εἴδη (23 B ff.) is to include 'everything that *now* exists in the universe'.[3] As Professor Hackforth comments, 'the point of the word "now" may be to indicate that it is the actual world of our experience that is to be analysed'.[4] We find indeed most of the indications of pessimistic 'realism' that have come to our notice in other dialogues; insistence on the impossibility of knowing particulars,[5] coupled with an equal insistence on the rarity of true understanding;[6] above all, perhaps, the use of the word ἀνθρώπινος (human; as contrasted with θεῖος, divine) as a key-word in the dialogue.[7] θεῖος, in the *Philebus*, is almost equivalent to the impossible. Perhaps the single most striking example which occurs in the *Philebus* of this pessimistic falling-back upon the practicable is the passage (57E ff.) concerning dialectic. Dialectic, though admitted to the first place in the hierarchy of ἐπιστῆμαι, has hanging over it, as Professor Hackforth notes,[8] an aura of the impracticable, which is paralleled by an equally notable allowance

---

[1] ἀλλὰ καλὸν μὲν τὸ σύμπαντα γιγνώσκειν τῷ σώφρονι, δεύτερος δ' εἶναι πλοῦς δοκεῖ μὴ λανθάνειν αὐτὸν αὐτόν (*Phil.* 19C 1 ff.).
[2] This seems to emerge, for example, from the *Charmides*.
[3] πάντα τὰ νῦν ὄντα ἐν τῷ παντί (23 C 4).
[4] Hackforth, *op. cit.* p. 37.
[5] 17E 3 ff.: cf. 58E 4 ff.
[6] See, for example, 52B 7f. and compare the implied restriction at 11b 9ff.
[7] See Hackforth, *op. cit.* p. 82; for an example, 62A 7 ff. and compare 33b 6f.
[8] Hackforth, *op. cit.* pp. 113f.

of practical value, if no other, to rhetoric. Plato now disclaims all intention of discovering which art is 'the most significant and noble, that which helps us most',[1] but makes Socrates assert that he is simply in pursuit of that art which, to the greatest degree, gives its attention to 'precision, accuracy and a maximum of truth'. He goes so far even as to grant to rhetoric 'supremacy, where the practical needs of humanity are concerned' (πρὸς χρείαν τοῖς ἀνθρώποις κρατεῖν); but Socrates and his friends are to give no heed to 'any differences between ἐπιστῆμαι in point of practical value' (τινας ὠφελίας ἐπιστημῶν). This in itself is sufficiently striking, especially when we find it in a work subtitled, and rightly, 'an ethical dialogue' (ἠθικός): moreover, in its context it represents a curious, and indicative, ambivalence of feeling. It has been suggested that the *Philebus* gives evidence of a pessimistic falling-back upon the practicable; we cannot deny that this is so, yet at this point we find Plato defiantly casting practice to the winds, and giving aggressive allegiance to an admittedly impractical contemplation. This is the first sign of that atmosphere of tension and ambivalence which is peculiar to the *Philebus*. We have, of course, to remember the dangers of taking individual and isolated statements as definitive of the whole;[2] we can find, indeed, passages of an absolutely contradictory character within the *Philebus* itself to set against the present one. But to admit contradiction is not necessarily to understand it; our immediate task is to discover something of the roots of the conflict.

We shall be doing no more than justice to the intimate connection between form and content, if we notice here those formal peculiarities which the *Philebus* exhibits, and which led one nineteenth-century commentator to 'assume the *Philebus* to have arisen from a boldly executed junction of two originally separate dialogues'.[3] The contortions of the argument, its tendency to go back on itself, its curious lack of proportion (doubly curious in a work

---

[1] ἡ μεγίστη καὶ ἀρίστη καὶ πλεῖστα ὠφελοῦσα ἡμᾶς (58 B 9 ff.). The following quotations occur in the same speech.

[2] If we are to do justice to Plato, we must take statements such as this as definitive of *something*; they cannot be disregarded or explained away. But the *whole* cannot be so easily grasped.

[3] E. Poste, edition of the *Philebus*, p. 105.

which lays so much stress on συμμετρία)—all these are evidence of a conflict within Plato's own mind. The suggested theme, to discover the good for man, is in fact pursued to its end, but the surface unity is belied both by obvious contradiction and by formal distortion. A close investigation indeed reveals a fundamental dialectical tension within the *Philebus*, a tension between two opposed concepts, those of purity (καθαρότης) and mixture (μεῖξις). The tension is complex, because Plato's attitude remains ambivalent throughout. In the realm of practice, in the contest for selection as the good life for man, μεῖξις is found superior; but at another level, Plato's value judgment gives first place to καθαρότης. The reason for this is perhaps not difficult to discover, but we must first verify our impression of tension by reference to the dialogue.

When we consider that the victory in the contest for selection as the good life for man goes to the 'mixed life' in which pleasure and intelligence are both, to some extent, involved, it seems only plausible to suggest that the root concept of the *Philebus* is that of μεῖξις, σύγκρασις and the like. Neither of the pure lives is found to be adequate (ἱκανόν) for any human being.[1] The Good is found to reside (οἰκεῖν)[2] in the mixed life alone. M. Diès has shown[3] that the four ontological εἴδη also are intimately bound up with the idea of the mixed life, and with 'the mixed existence of this world of change' (μεικτὴ καὶ γεγενημένη οὐσία): their introduction is necessary simply to explain the structure of μεῖξις both as it concerns us in human life, and more generally in existence in the physical world. It is, of course, true that μεῖξις only attains value in so far as it exhibits measure and proportion (μετριότης, συμμετρία).[4] But even here we notice that measure and proportion can only be exhibited in a *combination of elements*; purity, as such, can exhibit neither. Thus if the final hierarchy of values gives first and second place to measure and proportion respectively,[5] we must remember that μεῖξις is implied in both, since both are

---

[1] 21ε 3f.; cf. 60c 6ff. (a recapitulation of the same statement).
[2] 61β 4ff.
[3] Diès, *op. cit.* pp. xcv ff.
[4] 64D 9ff.   [5] 66A 4ff.

'conditions or formal causes'[1] of the mixed life and of its value. The Good, then, or at least the Good for man, resides in a composite whole, characterized by possession of measure, proportion and reality.[2] This last (ἀλήθεια) is a puzzling inclusion, various explanations of which have been proposed.[3] We may agree with Professor Hackforth that this considerable concern with reality as an essential prerequisite of anything that comes into existence is another reflection of Plato's interest in practicability. Perhaps, as Professor Hackforth supposes, it is a 'quasi-humorous expression [of] a passing doubt', but even humour has roots.

This, however, is by the way. We have seen enough now to assert once again that in Plato's view at the time of writing the *Philebus*, the fundamental value in human existence is (correct) mixture. This would be in harmony with the concept of a partnership, however uneasy, between Reason and Necessity in the *Timaeus*, and the metaphor of weaving in the *Politicus*. At this point, however, we come upon the essential ambivalence in Plato's outlook. For a large part of the *Philebus*, after the lives of 'pure' pleasure and 'pure' intelligence have been rejected, is devoted to attaining, as a paramount consideration in the ingredients of the mixture, a maximum of 'purity'. No doubt this is purity in a somewhat different sense; the word now means, not 'without an admixture of the opposite quality' (i.e. pleasure or intelligence respectively), but 'without an admixture of falsity or unreality'. But the difference can be overstressed; the two senses blend and become confused, and indeed admixture of an opposite quality, especially in the case of pleasure, is a prime source of unreality.[4] Moreover, it is impossible not to be aware that at times purity becomes an autonomous value. The discussion of Dialectic (57 Eff.) closes with an assertion of this sort. Socrates declares 'that we find fixity, truth, purity and what we have called perfect clarity (εἰλικρινές), either in those things that are always, unchanged, unaltered and free of all admixture (ἀμεικτότατα), or in what is most

---

[1] R. G. Bury, ed. of the *Philebus*, p. 209.
[2] 64A 7ff.
[3] See, for example, Hackforth, *op. cit.* pp. 132ff.; Diès, *op. cit.* pp. lxxxiif.
[4] See, for example, 52D 3ff. and Hackforth, *op. cit.* pp. 102f.

akin to them; everything else must be called inferior and of secondary importance'.[1] There is in fact no need to multiply instances of the use of the term 'purity' as a term of approval; it is clear that whatever Plato may explicitly say about μεῖξις and human life, he is still very much drawn towards the concept of 'purity'.[2]

I have said that the reason for this ambivalence is not difficult to find. Professor Hackforth has already remarked on the 'associations of religious and moral purity' of the words καθαρός and καθαρότης.[3] To this we may add their obvious sexual connotations. From this one fact alone it is possible to hazard the suggestion that Plato's allegiance to καθαρότης is an emotional and irrational sympathy. Such a suggestion is perhaps a little dangerous, because difficult to support; but there is one passage in the dialogue which shows clearly that Plato's emotions, as well as his faculty of reason, are engaged over this point. In the closing pages, Protarchus makes the following speech: 'There is a curious thing about pleasure: whenever we see anyone experiencing pleasure—and, I might add, the greater the pleasure, the more true this is—we feel an element of the ridiculous in the situation, even a sense of extreme repugnance; we ourselves feel ashamed and do our best to make pleasure invisible, to hide it, and to give over such things to the realm of night, feeling that daylight should not find it exposed.'[4] Less than a page later, Socrates admits that his opposition to Philebus was due to the fact that he 'felt distaste' for the hedonist position.[5] It is clear enough that this feeling of repugnance to pleasure belongs to the same nexus of emotional responses as Plato's inclination towards καθαρότης as a value, and its corollary, a revulsion from μεῖξις. At an emotional level, for whatever reason, Plato is committed to the support of anti-hedonism, in all

[1] 59 c 2 ff. (Professor Hackforth's translation).
[2] Further examples are 51 D 7, 55 C 7, 62 C 1 f., 66 C 4 ff., etc.
[3] Hackforth, op. cit. p. 82.
[4] ἡδονὰς δέ γέ που, καὶ ταῦτα σχεδὸν τὰς μεγίστας, ὅταν ἴδωμεν ἡδόμενον ὀντινοῦν, ἢ τὸ γελοῖον ἐπ' αὐταῖς ἢ τὸ πάντων αἴσχιστον ἑπόμενον ὁρῶντες αὐτοί τε αἰσχυνόμεθα καὶ ἀφανίζοντες κρύπτομεν ὅτι μάλιστα, νυκτὶ πάντα τὰ τοιαῦτα διδόντες, ὡς φῶς οὐ δέον ὁρᾶν αὐτά (65 Ε 9 ff.).
[5] 66 E 2 (δυσχεραίνειν).

forms. But this whole body of response runs counter to what we have called Plato's sense of reality, which in a general way has provided the key-mood of his later years. The clash of these forces becomes explicit at times during the conversation in the *Philebus*. When finally pleasures and, in less detail, forms of ἐπιστήμη have been valued in terms of their possession of καθαρότης, the ingredients of the mixed life are selected from them. In the case of knowledge, in spite of an agreed difference in value, all forms are eventually admitted to the mixture. For Socrates and Protarchus agree on the complete impracticability of knowing only about the 'divine circle', etc. (i.e. the Forms), without any grasp of 'the circles with which human beings have to deal'.[1] It is therefore impossible to avoid throwing in (ἐμβάλλειν) the less pure forms of knowledge, 'if we are going to be able to find the way home when we want to'.[2] Socrates, 'like a porter jostled by a crowd', is forced to let open the doors, and every sort of knowledge pours in. The proposed method of obtaining the mixture (in accordance with purity) has in the end broken down.[3] The image of the porter and the crowd is revealing; it suggests a sense of external pressure, a feeling of being forced from without to abandon a deeply rooted position. Professor Hackforth is, of course, right in saying that 'it would be foolish to suppose that Plato is now for the first time struck by the thought that you cannot build a house by the light of pure mathematics and nothing else',[4] but the point is somehow missed in this caveat. The importance of this passage, for us, is that, if not for the first time, still more markedly than previously we can observe Plato allowing his sense of reality to override his settled conviction of the value and comparative status of δόξα and ἐπιστήμη. His sense of reality forces upon him awareness of the inextricable and everpresent μεῖξις of opposites both in human life, its emotions and values, and in the physical world

---

[1] οἱ ἀνθρώπινοι κύκλοι (62 A 7 ff.).
[2] εἰ μέλλει τις ἡμῶν καὶ τὴν ὁδὸν ἑκάστοτε ἐξευρήσειν οἴκαδε. This image reminds us of the 'road to Larissa' illustration in the *Meno* (97 A ff.). The divorce between knowledge and opinion, which was there a problem, is here at its widest; it seems to be accepted as a *fait accompli* and is perhaps the source of the pessimism of the *Philebus*: see above, pp. 138 f., 162 f.
[3] 62D 8 ff.   [4] Hackforth, *op. cit.* p. 127.

in general.¹ And acceptance of the conditions of human life implies, to some degree at least, abandonment of his scheme of values. It is easy enough to see how Plato might have externalized this compulsion into a sense of pressure from without, such as the image of the porter forced from the doorway suggests.

But it is also clear that Plato has not completely accepted the necessity of acquiescing in human limitation and the reality principle. The whole ambivalence of the *Philebus* prevents us from supposing so. The effect of the dialectical tension is a strain, which at times produces extreme examples both of the acceptance of, and of the flight from reality. The whole pessimism of the *Philebus* and the inclusion, perforce, of *all* forms of knowledge in the Good for man, are examples of the former. And there are at least two passages which seem to illustrate the flight from reality. Socrates remarks that to prefer anything to the good life, which is a completely satisfying object of choice, could only be the result of ignorance or of 'some sort of unhappy necessity'.² This strange phrase seems, as Bury suggests, to refer to the incursion of divine temptation or infatuation (ἄτη);³ but whatever identification is to be made, admission of ἀνάγκη οὐκ εὐδαίμων as an explanation of human conduct clearly falls outside the bounds of rational explanation. Equally Plato seems to explain behaviour of which he approves by invoking irrational intervention; in a curious passage, Socrates suggests that the expectation of pleasant satisfaction which a man who is 'dear to god' (θεοφιλής) experiences will be *for that reason* 'truer', i.e. more likely to be fulfilled.⁴ It is true that such examples merely make overt an observable tendency towards the irrational in Plato, but it is significant that it *becomes* overt in the *Philebus* and other late dialogues, in a context of tension and strain between the drives of reason and emotion. As we have observed

---

¹ See, for example, 50C 10ff., where this feeling is well to the fore.
² τινος ἀνάγκης οὐκ εὐδαίμονος (22B 6ff.).
³ R. G. Bury, *op. cit.* p. 34. The word ἄτη itself occurs only twice in Plato, once personified as the goddess Ἄτη(*Symp.* 195D 2), and once in the quotation of a proverb, ἐγγύη, πάρα δ' ἄτη (*Charm.* 165A 3f.). On irrational explanation of human conduct in Plato, see, in general, E. R. Dodds, *The Greeks and the Irrational*, ch. VII *passim*.
⁴ 39B 10f.

Plato gradually accepting the reality principle as the dominating factor in his thinking about human conduct, the tension in his own mind has been growing; in the *Philebus* it has reached the surface, and become the keynote. In the *Laws*, perhaps, as we have seen, the reality principle is completely, if still reluctantly, accepted; but the flight from reality was there still evident, and the *Laws* is a work born of tiredness.

BIBLIOGRAPHY

(a) CLASSICAL AUTHORS

The works of Plato are quoted from the latest edition of Burnet's text in the Oxford Classical Texts series; references are to the page numbering of Stephanus and to the lines of Burnet's edition. References to Aristotle denote the pages, columns and lines of the Berlin edition. Hippocrates is quoted from the edition of Littré; Isocrates, Plutarch and Proclus from the relevant latest edition in the Teubner series.

Pindar and Bacchylides are cited from Bruno Snell's Teubner editions (Leipzig, 1953 and 1949 respectively); Sappho from that of E. Lobel (Oxford, 1925). The remaining lyric poets are quoted from Ernest Diehl's *Anthologia Lyrica Graeca* (Leipzig: authors included in fascicules 1–3, from the 3rd ed., 1949–52; the remainder, from the 2nd ed., 1923–4). Hesiod (*Works and Days*) is quoted from Rzach's Teubner text.

The following abbreviations have been used:

Dindorf-Maass= *Scholia Graeca in Homeri Iliadem*, edited by G. Dindorf and E. Maass. Oxford, 1875–88.

DK= Hermann Diels' *Die Fragmente der Vorsokratiker* (6th ed.), edited by Walther Kranz. Berlin, 1951–2.

Kaibel= *Comicorum Graecorum Fragmenta*, edited by G. Kaibel. Leipzig, 1899.

Nauck²= *Tragicorum Graecorum Fragmenta*, edited by A. Nauck, 2nd ed. Leipzig, 1926.

All other authors are quoted from the relevant latest edition in the Oxford Classical Text series.

(b) MODERN AUTHORS AND COMMENTARIES

ADAM, J. The '*Republic*' *of Plato*, 2 vols. Cambridge, 1926–9.

ALLAN, D. J. Edition of *Republic* I (2nd ed.). London: Methuen, 1953.

ARCHER-HIND, R. D. Edition of the *Timaeus* of Plato. London: Macmillan, 1888.

ARCHER-HIND, R. D. Edition of the *Phaedo* of Plato (2nd ed.). London: Macmillan, 1894.

AST, F. *Lexicon Platonicum* (2nd ed.). Berlin, 1908.

BALDRY, H. C. 'Plato's "Technical Terms"', in *Classical Quarterly*, XXXI (1937), pp. 141 ff.

BALME, D. M. 'Greek Science and Mechanism. I. Aristotle on Nature and Chance', in *Classical Quarterly*, XXXIII (1939), pp. 129 ff.

BALME, D. M. 'Greek Science and Mechanism. II. The Atomists', in *Classical Quarterly*, XXXV (1941), pp. 23 ff.

226

BIBLIOGRAPHY

BARFIELD, OWEN. *Poetic Diction* (2nd ed.). London: Faber, 1952.

BLUCK, R. S. *Plato's Life and Thought.* London: Routledge and Kegan Paul, 1949.

BRUNS, I. *Platos Gesetze vor und nach ihr Herausgabe durch Philippus von Opus.* Weimar, 1880.

BURNET, J. *Greek Philosophy: Thales to Plato.* London: Macmillan, 1914.

BURNET, J. 'The Socratic Doctrine of the Soul', in *Proc. Brit. Acad.* 1915–16, pp. 235 ff.

BURNET, J. Edition of the *Phaedo* of Plato. Oxford, 1937.

BURY, R. G. Edition of the *Philebus* of Plato. Cambridge, 1897.

BURY, R. G. Edition of the *Laws* of Plato, 2 vols. (Loeb series). London: Heinemann, 1926.

BURY, R. G. 'The Theory of Education in Plato's *Laws*', in *Revue des Études Grecques*, Vol. L (1937), pp. 304–20.

BUTTERFIELD, H. *The Origins of Modern Science.* London: Bell, 1949.

Cambridge Ancient History. Edited by J. B. BURY, S. A. COOK and F. E. ADCOCK. Cambridge, 1926–39.

CAMPBELL, L. Edition of the *Sophistes* and *Politicus* of Plato. Oxford, 1867.

CHERNISS, H. 'On Plato's *Republic* X, 597 B', in *American Journal of Philology*, LIII (1932), pp. 233 ff.

CHERNISS, H. 'The Philosophical Economy of the Theory of Ideas', in *American Journal of Philology*, LVII (1936), pp. 445 ff.

CHERNISS, H. *The Riddle of the Early Academy.* Berkeley: Univ. of California Press, 1945.

CORNFORD, F. M. *Before and After Socrates.* Cambridge, 1932.

CORNFORD, F. M. 'Mathematics and Dialectic in the *Republic*, VI–VII' (I and II), in *Mind*, n.s. XLI (1932), pp. 37 ff. and 173 ff.

CORNFORD, F. M. Translation of Plato's *Republic*. Oxford, 1941.

CORNFORD, F. M. *Plato's Cosmology.* London: Routledge and Kegan Paul, 1948.

CORNFORD, F. M. *The Unwritten Philosophy and other Essays.* Cambridge, 1950.

CORNFORD, F. M. *Principium Sapientiae.* Cambridge, 1952.

CORNFORD, F. M. Cambridge lectures on the *Charmides* of Plato (unpublished).

CORNFORD, F. M. *Socrates and Plato.* Lowell Lectures (unpublished).

CROISET, M., DIÈS, A., et al. *Platon, Œuvres Complètes* (Budé series). Paris: Belles Lettres, various dates.

DENNISTON, J. D. *Greek Prose Style.* Oxford, 1952.

DODDS, E. R. 'Plato and the Irrational', in *Journal of Hellenic Studies*, LXV (1945), pp. 16 ff.

DODDS, E. R. *The Greeks and the Irrational*, Sather Classical Lectures. Berkeley: Univ. of California Press, 1951.

ENGLAND, E. B. Edition of the *Laws* of Plato, 2 vols. Manchester, 1921.

FERGUSON, A. S. 'Plato's Simile of Light. I. The similes of the Sun and the Line', in *Classical Quarterly*, XV (1921), pp. 131 ff.

FESTUGIÈRE, A.-J. *Contemplation et vie contemplative selon Platon*, 2nd ed. Paris: Vrin, 1950.

FIELD, G. C. *Studies in Philosophy*. Univ. of Bristol Studies, III. Bristol, 1935.

FIELD, G. C. *Plato and his Contemporaries* (2nd ed.). London: Methuen, 1948.

FOSTER, M. B. *The Political Philosophies of Plato and Hegel*. Oxford, 1935.

FREUD, S. *Introductory Lectures on Psycho-analysis*, trans. by Joan Riviere. London: Allen and Unwin, 1922.

FREUD, S. *Psychopathology of Everyday Life*, 2nd ed., trans. by A. A. Brill. London: Benn, 1948.

FRUTIGER, P. *Les Mythes de Platon*. Paris: Alcan, 1930.

GIGON, O. *Sokrates: sein Bild in Dichtung und Geschichte*. Bern, 1947.

GOLDSCHMIDT, V. *Les Dialogues de Platon*. Paris: Presses Universitaires de France, 1947.

GRENE, D. *Man in his Pride: a Study in the Political Philosophy of Thucydides and Plato*. Chicago, 1950.

GRUBE, G. M. A. *Plato's Thought*. London: Methuen, 1935.

HACKFORTH, R. *Plato's Examination of Pleasure*. Cambridge, 1945.

HACKFORTH, R. 'Moral Evil and Ignorance in Plato's Ethics', in *Classical Quarterly*, XL (1946), pp. 118 ff.

HARDIE, W. F. R. *A Study in Plato*. Oxford, 1936.

HELLER, ERICH. *The Disinherited Mind*. Cambridge: Bowes and Bowes, 1952.

HIRSCHBERGER, J. *Die Phronesis in der Philosophie Platons vor dem Staate*. Philologus Supplementband, XXV, 1. Leipzig, 1932.

JAEGER, W. *Paideia: the Ideals of Greek Culture*, trans. by G. Highet. Oxford: Blackwell, 3 vols. 1939–45.

JAEGER, W. *Theology of the Early Greek Philosophers*. Gifford Lectures for 1936, trans. by E. S. Robinson. Oxford, 1947.

JONES, W. H. S. *Philosophy and Medicine in Ancient Greece*. Supplement to the *Bulletin of the History of Medicine*, 8. Baltimore: Johns Hopkins, 1946.

JOSEPH, H. W. B. *Essays in Ancient and Modern Philosophy*. Oxford, 1935.

JOSEPH, H. W. B. *Knowledge and the Good in Plato's 'Republic'*. Oxford Classical and Philosophical Monographs. Oxford, 1948.

KIERKEGAARD, SØREN. *Journals*, a selection ed. and trans. by A. Dru. London: Oxford University Press, 1938.

KOCH, VIVIENNE. *W. B. Yeats: the tragic Phase*. London: Routledge and Kegan Paul, 1951.

LEHRS, K. *De Aristarchi studiis Homericis* (3rd. ed.). Leipzig, 1882.

LODGE, R. C. *Plato's Theory of Ethics*. London: Routledge and Kegan Paul, 1950.

MAGUIRE, J. P. 'Plato's Theory of Natural Law', in *Yale Classical Studies*, X (1947), pp. 151 ff.

MASON, RONALD. *The Spirit above the Dust*. London: John Lehmann, 1951.

MOREAU, J. *La Construction de l'Idéalisme Platonicien*. Paris: Boivin, 1939.

MURPHY, N. R. *The Interpretation of Plato's 'Republic'*. Oxford, 1951.

BIBLIOGRAPHY

NACHMANSON, E. *Erotiani vocum hippocraticarum collectio.* Collectio scriptorum veterum Upsaliensis. Upsala, 1918.

NOVOTNÝ, F. *Platonis Epistulae.* Brno, 1930.

ONIANS, R. B. *The Origins of European Thought.* Cambridge, 1951.

OWEN, G. E. L. 'The Place of the *Timaeus* in Plato's Dialogues', in *Classical Quarterly*, n.s. III (1953), pp. 79 ff.

POSTE, E. Edition of the *Philebus* of Plato. Oxford, 1860.

RAVEN, J. E. *Pythagoreans and Eleatics.* Cambridge Classical Studies. Cambridge, 1948.

RAVEN, J. E. 'Sun, Divided Line, and Cave', in *Classical Quarterly*, n.s. III (1953), pp. 22 ff.

RITTER, C. *Platos Gesetze: Darstellung des Inhalts.* Leipzig, 1896.

RITTER, C. *The Essence of Plato's Philosophy*, trans. by A. Alles. London: Allen and Unwin, 1933.

ROBIN, L. *Platon* (Les Grands Philosophes) (2nd ed.). Paris: Alcan, 1938.

ROBINSON, RICHARD. *Plato's Earlier Dialectic* (2nd ed.). Oxford, 1953.

ROSS, SIR DAVID. Edition of Aristotle's *Metaphysics*, 2 vols. Oxford, 1924.

ROSS, SIR DAVID. *Plato's Theory of Ideas.* Oxford, 1951.

RYLE, GILBERT. *The Concept of Mind.* London: Hutchinson, 1949.

SCHAERER, RENÉ. 'Επιστήμη *et* τέχνη: *Étude sur les notions de connaissance et d'art d'Homère à Platon.* Mâcon, 1930.

SCHUHL, PIERRE-MAXIME. *La Fabulation Platonicienne.* Paris: Presses Universitaires de France, 1947.

SCHUHL, PIERRE-MAXIME. *Essai sur la formation de la pensée grecque* (2nd ed.). Paris: Presses Universitaires de France, 1949.

SIMETERRE, R. *La Théorie Socratique de la Vertu-Science selon les 'Mémorables' de Xénophon.* Paris: Téqui, 1938.

SKEMP, J. B. *Plato's Statesman.* London: Routledge and Kegan Paul, 1952.

SNELL, BRUNO. *Die Ausdrücke für den Begriff des Wissens in der vorplatonischen Philosophie.* Philologische Untersuchungen, 29. Berlin, 1924.

SNELL, BRUNO. *Die Entdeckung des Geistes* (2nd ed.). Hamburg, 1948. (Translated into English, with some additional matter, by T. G. Rosenmeyer as *The Discovery of the Mind.* Oxford: Blackwell, 1953.)

SOLMSEN, F. *Plato's Theology.* Cornell Studies in Classical Philology. Ithaca, N.Y.: Cornell Univ. Press, 1942.

STENZEL, J. *Platon der Erzieher.* Leipzig, 1928.

STENZEL, J. *Plato's Method of Dialectic.* Oxford, 1940. (*Studien zur Entwicklung der Platonischen Dialectik*, trans. and edited with an introduction by D. J. Allan.)

STEVENSON, CHARLES L. *Ethics and Language.* New Haven: Yale Univ. Press, 1950.

TARRANT, DOROTHY. 'Style and Thought in Plato's Dialogues', in *Classical Quarterly*, XLII (1948), pp. 28 ff.

TAYLOR, A. E. 'The Analysis of ἐπιστήμη in Plato's Seventh Epistle', in *Mind*, n.s. XXI (1912), pp. 347 ff.

229

BIBLIOGRAPHY

TAYLOR, A. E. *Plato: the Man and his Work* (3rd ed.). London: Methuen, 1929.

TAYLOR, A. E. *Socrates*. London: Peter Davies, 1932.

TAYLOR, A. E. Translation of the *Laws* of Plato. London: Dent, 1934.

TAYLOR, A. E. 'The Decline and Fall of the State in *Republic* VIII', in *Mind*, n.s. XLVIII (1939), pp. 23 ff.

THOMPSON, E. S. Edition of the *Meno* of Plato. London: Macmillan, 1937.

TUCKEY, T. G. *Plato's 'Charmides'*. Cambridge Classical Studies. Cambridge, 1951.

VLASTOS, GREGORY. 'The Disorderly Motion in the *Timaios*', in *Classical Quarterly*, XXXIII (1939), pp. 71 ff.

WITTGENSTEIN, LUDWIG. *Tractatus Logico-Philosophicus*. London: Routledge and Kegan Paul, 1922.

WALBANK, F. W. 'The Causes of Greek Decline', in *Journal of Hellenic Studies*, LXIV (1944), pp. 10 ff.

I. GENERAL INDEX

Note. This index is intended to be used in conjunction with the following Index of Greek Words. Some headings, therefore, will be found only under the appropriate Greek word: for example, references to Education will be found under παιδεία; to Virtue under ἀρετή, etc.

II. INDEX OF GREEK WORDS

NOTE. This is merely an outline index; it contains only those words which seemed important in the context of this book and is necessarily incomplete.

III. INDEX OF PLATO'S WRITINGS

V